Praise for *Clara's War*

"This vividly detailed and taut narrative is a fitting tribute to the bravery of victims and righteous gentiles alike."
—*Publishers Weekly*

"Lucidly told with deeply etched personality sketches."
—*Kirkus Reviews*

"A superlative memoir of survival. . . . Few wartime memoirs convey with such harrowing immediacy the evil of the Nazi genocide. . . . Her book is a model documentary."
—*Daily Telegraph* (London)

"Compelling."
—*Literary Review*

"I must say I approached this memoir warily, having read so many wartime histories/memoirs/novels, and feeling sated. I thought there probably wasn't much I didn't, alas, now know about all the horrors the Jews endured, especially Polish Jews. But that was the surprise of this one—I mean, to find it was not only a record of terrible deprivation but also a kind of unexpected nobility. It's the Becks' story that seems so incredible, their whole relationship with the Jewish families. So often it seemed hard to credit that this couple and their daughter would do what they did and yet, obviously, it must be true, written as it is by Clara. The twists and turns of the story are extraordinary, and it was so satisfying, at the end, to have the debt repaid and the Becks saved. Clara's taking her diaries to the officer to save [the Becks] by proving what they'd done at such risk is pure Hollywood. . . . The best writing is to do with the detailing of the day-to-day life in the bunker—straightforward, not shirking all the stuff to do with how they coped with refuse, etc., and evoking very vividly the heat and claustrophobia. It is a valuable addition to all the recollections of the agonies people went through in the war—so awful to realize that in several areas of the world they are being gone through again. The lessons of history ignored."

—Margaret Forster, author of
Keeping the World Away and *Lady's Maid*

"I hesitated to begin a book I knew would be full of tragedy, brutality, and fear. . . . But it is utterly compelling. At times, the tension is as high as in any thriller designed to stop your heart. . . . Is the world fundamentally mad? Is God mad? Read this book and tell me, if you can."

—John Clare, *Sun-Herald* (Australia)

"Kramer's book vividly recalls the tensions within her hidden community. . . . Of particular interest are revelations about the family who hid the Kramers, particularly how an anti-Semitic Polish householder demonstrated great courage in shielding Jews in his basement." —*Library Journal*

Clara's War

Clara's War

ONE GIRL'S STORY OF SURVIVAL

CLARA KRAMER

with Stephen Glantz

An Imprint of HarperCollins Publishers

HarperCollins books may be purchased for educational, business, or sales promotional use. For information, please write: Special Markets Department, HarperCollins Publishers, 10 East 53rd Street, New York, NY 10022.

The images of Clara's diary used on the endpapers and in the plate section are reproduced courtesy of the United States Holocaust Memorial Museum. The views or opinions expressed in this book, and the context in which the images are used, do not necessarily reflect the views or policy of, nor imply approval or endorsement by, the United States Holocaust Memorial Museum.

Originally published in Great Britain in 2008 by Ebury Press, an imprint of Ebury Publishing, a Random House Group Company.

A hardcover edition of this book was published in 2009 by Ecco, an imprint of HarperCollins Publishers.

FIRST ECCO PAPERBACK EDITION 2010

Library of Congress Cataloging-in-Publication Data is available upon request.

ISBN: 978-0-06-172861-7

12 13 14 OFF/ RRD 10 9 8 7 6 5 4 3

And you shall teach them diligently to your children, and you shall speak of them when you sit at home, and when you walk along the way, and when you lie down, and when you rise up.

Deuteronomy 6:4–9

*

For my parents,
who taught me compassion and decency;
for my little sister,
who showed me true bravery;
and to the Becks,
who saved my life and restored my
faith in mankind

CONTENTS

The Reizfeld family

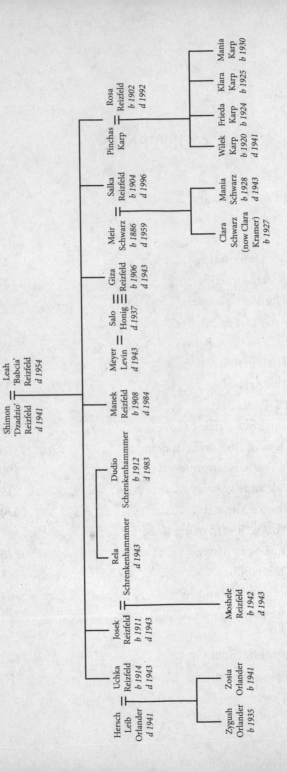

Shimon 'Dzadzio' Reizfeld d 1941 == Leah 'Babcia' Reizfeld d 1954

Hersch Leib Orlander d 1941 == Uchka Reizfeld b 1914 d 1943

Josek Reizfeld b 1911 d 1943 == Rela Schrenkenhammer d 1943

Dudio Schrenkenhammmer b 1912 d 1983

Manek Reizfeld b 1908 d 1984

Meyer Levin d 1943 == Salo Honig d 1937 === Giza Reizfeld b 1906 d 1943

Meir Schwarz b 1886 d 1959 == Salka Reizfeld b 1904 d 1996

Pinchas Karp == Rosa Reizfeld b 1902 d 1992

Zygush Orlander b 1935 — Zosia Orlander b 1941

Moshele Reizfeld b 1942 d 1943

Clara Schwarz (now Clara Kramer) b 1927 — Mania Schwarz b 1928 d 1943

Wilek Karp b 1920 d 1941 — Frieda Karp b 1924 d 1941 — Klara Karp b 1925 — Mania Karp b 1930

The house

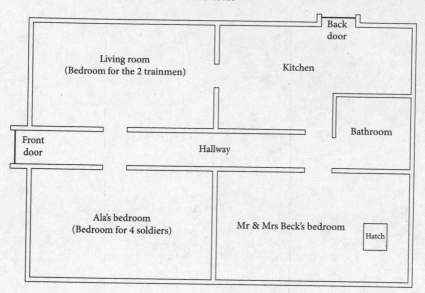

Living room
(Bedroom for the 2 trainmen)

Kitchen

Back door

Bathroom

Front door

Hallway

Ala's bedroom
(Bedroom for 4 soldiers)

Mr & Mrs Beck's bedroom

Hatch

Under the house

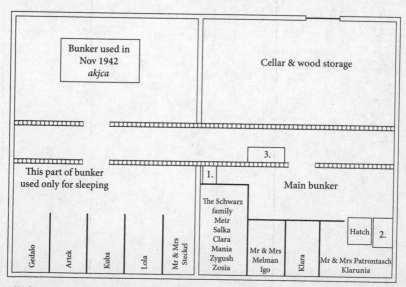

Bunker used in
Nov 1942
akjca

Cellar & wood storage

This part of bunker
used only for sleeping

Main bunker

Gedalo

Artek

Kuba

Lola

Mr & Mrs Steckel

The Schwarz
family
Meir
Salka
Clara
Mania
Zygush
Zosia

Mr & Mrs
Melman
Igo

Klara

Mr & Mrs Patrontasch
Klarunia

Hatch

1.

2.

3.

1. Hotplates

2. Table for storage & food

3. Toilet buckets

Not to scale

A NOTE TO THE READER

Writing this book was like walking out of my kitchen door in Elizabeth, New Jersey, and straight into my home in Zolkiew. Although the events in this book happened over 60 years ago, they have never left me. As with many survivors, I relive them in the present.

I am 81 years old, and I am one of the lucky ones. Ever since the day I left the bunker, I have done my best to live a worthy life. I have dedicated myself to the teaching of the Holocaust. The privilege of surviving comes with the responsibility of sharing the story of those who did not.

Everything in this book is as I lived and remember it, although I have taken the liberty of reconstructing dialogue to the best of my recollection. I have also used the spelling and names most familiar to me. During the 18 months I spent in the bunker I kept a diary which today is in the Holocaust Memorial Museum in Washington DC. There was little light and less paper and only one nub of a pencil to write with. I documented as much as I could in my diary, but although I often spoke about my life, the idea of writing it never occurred to me. Thank you to Stephen Glantz for encouraging me and for taking this journey with me back to Zolkiew. And thank you for capturing my life so beautifully on paper. I am so grateful that my great-great-grandchildren will be able to meet those of us who came before.

From my memory to theirs, and to yours.

Where the beginning of a chapter is in italics, it is an extract from my diary.

Clara Kramer

Clara's War

PROLOGUE

1 September 1939

My entire family was camped out on blankets and goose-down bedding in the apple orchard behind Aunt Uchka's little house. Out of all my aunts, Uchka was my favourite. Not even ten years older than me and not much taller, she was more like a best friend. Zygush, her three-year-old son, scampered about the orchard picking up fallen green apples. His father Hersch Leib was on his heels, but only managed to catch his shadow. After 20 minutes or more, Uchka finally intervened, handing her little baby Zosia to Babcia, my grandmother, and reaching out to capture the laughing boy as he ran by.

Zygush didn't understand that he shouldn't be laughing or running or having a good time. He would only be quietened with the traditional bribe of a cookie. For him it was just a night-time picnic like those we enjoyed on Paradise Hill. He didn't know that Poland had been invaded by the Nazis that morning while we had been sleeping. Poor Mr and Mrs Gorski's house, on the outskirts of town and surrounded only by ripening rye and wheat fields, had been bombed. There were still planes flying above us headed for Lvov just 35 kilometres away. Even though the noise of the engines was deafening, none of us said a word. In my 12 years of life, I could not think of another time my family had sat together in silence. But we were all petrified that the pilots might hear us and attack us instead. When my restless little sister Mania had run out from under the apple tree to get a better look, Mama hadn't dared raise her voice and had had to resort to feverish gestures to get her to sit back down.

I didn't know who had first come up with the idea that we should all sleep outside, but the idea had travelled faster than gossip up and down our streets. After what had happened to the Gorskis we were afraid to stay in our homes. We had rummaged the closets for our old feather beds, which Mama and Babcia decided could get filthy. After we had packed up some bread, fruit and cheese, the nine of us who all lived together in the same house had walked the kilometre to Uchka's. Our town seemed to have been spilt in two. One half, loaded with blankets and food, was making an exodus, while the other half stood staring, dazed, wondering if they should join us. As we passed near the Gorskis', I was filled with a morbid curiosity. I had never seen a bombed-out house before and wanted to go and look at it, but Mama wouldn't hear of it. She didn't want us separated. In typical fashion Mania had ignored her and already run ahead to Uchka's, while I was stuck walking at a snail's pace. Babcia and Dzadzio, my grandparents, who were portly and only walked distances in considerable pain, kept telling us not to worry about them and go on already. But Mama didn't want her parents to be alone if there was another bombing.

Mama was nicknamed Salka the Cossack because she went through life as if she were mounted on a horse, wielding a sword at any of life's problems. She could manage anything from her kitchen table. But no matter how much we talked and talked and talked, trying to make sense of the new reality, today was a day of questions without answers.

Across the fields and in all the pastures and farms

surrounding our small city of Zolkiew, dozens of other families were getting ready to sleep under the stars. Even though it was a warm September night, with the air fragrant with the scent of newly mown hay, no one could sleep. But eventually exhaustion had triumphed over fear and, in ones and twos, everyone but me had succumbed. I had never been a nervous and anxious girl; I was the quiet, studious daughter. But as I watched and listened for more planes to come, I felt I would never be able to sleep again.

In the distance I could make out the silhouettes of Zolkiew's baroque church spires with their pregnant onion tops and golden domes. Not a light was on, and my familiar town looked eerily deserted, almost haunted. It felt as if the war's shadow had physically darkened our town. Our family had been here in this corner of Galicia in south-eastern Poland for ever. I couldn't imagine living anywhere else. We had been rooted here longer than most of the white birch and the Russian pines that formed the islands of forest in the steppe. I had never heard Dzadzio and Babcia speak of another place in our family's history.

As long as I could remember, my family moved and lived in a pack. You couldn't turn around in our little stone house without bumping into somebody. Now, spread out under the apple trees, sleeping in piles, huddled together on the feather beds, using each other as pillows, we resembled a pack more than ever. The only one missing was Aunt Rosa, who lived in the thick forests of central Poland. When Aunt Rosa had got engaged to her husband Pinchas, Babcia had gone into mourning. Rosa was the prettiest of the sisters and Babcia had always said she could have had any man she wanted in town. It wasn't that Pinchas, a timber merchant, wasn't a catch any mother wouldn't brag about, it was because he lived on the other side of Poland in Josefow and she would have to leave Zolkiew.

Next to me, my little sister Mania, tan from the summer sun, slept. She was the first to drop off and was asleep even before the little ones. And asleep was the only time she was ever still. At ten she was faster than most of the boys her age and her thin arms and legs were as strong as the braided wire the peasants used to bale their hay. The skipping rope that she always wore round her neck like a necklace lay next to her. On the other side of Mania was my aunt Giza, Mama's second youngest sister. An amateur actress, she looked like the star of a silent movie. When Giza was on stage, playing some tragic figure, she would ring her sable eyes with kohl and paint her lips red. But real tragedy had struck Giza off the stage. She became a widow at 33. When she left to go to her husband's birth town of Vienna for *yahrzeit*, she ended up staying there for a year.

When Giza finally came back to Zolkiew and moved in with my grandparents on the other side of the house we shared, all Babcia wanted was for her to find another husband. But instead of having grandchildren, Giza had started an undergarment business. 'Of all the *fachoted*, crazy, ideas!' Babcia had said. 'You'll *fradrai dich den kop*, you'll give me a knock in the head! When the new dress doesn't fit, they'll blame you!' Babcia had been especially appalled and embarrassed when Giza had put a sign in our front window. The women didn't just come to buy a girdle. They sat. They had tea. They had pastry. They talked. Then they bought. Then they sat some more. Our house had become Giza's factory, showroom and café all in one. Zolkiew at the time had a large regiment of Polish cavalry stationed at the castle and soon our front room was filled with officers' wives. Once word got out that even the Polish nobility was wearing Giza's products under their gowns, she couldn't make them fast enough. Of course, despite the ranting, Babcia became Giza's best customer, closely followed by her sisters. And soon she was boasting that anyone who was anybody in Zolkiew wore a girdle by Gizela, which was Giza's given name, and much more sophisticated than the diminutive everyone called her by.

Spread out next to Babcia, Dzadzio was snoring loudly. Even though I knew my dzadzio was ancient, he seemed whole and hearty in my eyes. I adored him. When I got my report cards, I would run home to show them to Dzadzio first. He would pick me up on his lap and cluck his teeth and shake his head and say, 'Clarutchka, Clarutchka, what am I going to do with you? Zeros again?' I had never got anything less than an A in my life and I knew this was his way of praising me. Dzadzio still went to *minyan* every day, but the rest of the time he would sit in his big chair by the window and watch the world go by.

Dzadzio had passed on his part of the ownership of the oil-press business, which we shared with two neighbouring families, the Melmans and the Patrontasches, to my father. The men's wives, Fanka Melman and Sabina Patrontasch, were friends with Mama. They shared everything, including a house-keeper, Julia Beck, who was as good at cooking Jewish as Mama. Mama and Klara, Mr Patrontasch's widowed younger sister, had even nursed together as infants at the breast of Julia's mother, who was their common milk mammy and our grandparents' housekeeper. Klara and Julia had been raised together like sisters and were the best of friends.

Under the tree near Dzadzio were my uncles Manek and Josek, who also lived with us. I adored them both. Mama said that Josek, with his deep blue eyes and golden hair the colour of silk in lamplight, was the Don Juan of the family. Dzadzio followed Josek around like his conscience. Mr Patrontasch had a lovely 17-year-old sister, Pepka, whom Josek would talk to across the fence for hours at a time. In our little town, when a boy talked to a girl more than twice, their parents would run to get the *shadkhyn,* the matchmaker, and start working out the marriage contract. When Dzadzio, sitting at his habitual place by the window, couldn't take it any longer, he would walk out and drag Josek away, yelling at his son: 'Are you going to send that girl up the chimney or marry her?' He didn't want his son to send their neighbour's daughter's reputation up in smoke.

Manek was the complete opposite of Josek, an ardent Zionist who supported a little kibbutz that some of the young people in Zolkiew formed. Mania loved to follow him around and would go along with him to many of the meetings of the kibbutzim. She was at the kibbutz so often that somebody once asked her if she was going to be a kibbutznik when she grew up. She laughed at the absurdity of the question. 'Are you crazy? There's a whole wide world to explore!' It was Manek who had taught us how to dance. Whenever there was a wedding, Mama, her sisters, all the girls in Zolkiew were lucky to get a dance from Manek because we tried to keep him to ourselves.

Uchka's wedding had been beautiful. Since Uchka was the youngest of the Reizfeld sisters, the tradition was to throw a huge party. My grandparents didn't skimp. Rosa came with her husband Pinchas Karp and their four children, Wilek, Frieda, Klara and Mania. It was traditional for parents to name their children after departed parents and grandparents, which often resulted in duplicate names among cousins. In our family we had two Zygushes, two Wileks, two Gizas, and even a third Mania. But nobody in the family was ever confused and none of us children felt like we were wearing hand-me-down clothes. Like everything else in my life before the war, this made perfect sense.

Uchka and Hersch Leib looked like they were no older than 16 as they stood under the *chuppah.* Whenever there was a Jewish wedding, the poor of Zolkiew, or any town in Poland for that matter, knew they would be welcome. There was a long table on one side of hall reserved for anyone who wanted a good meal. Mama had hired a modern band from Lvov that played tangos and waltzes. I danced with all my uncles and cousins. But Mania and I monopolized Manek for most of the evening. We might have let him dance once or twice with the bride and his sisters. Before the end of the evening, Uchka's brothers and some of the other young men danced around the hall with Uchka in a wicker throne mounted on their shoulders. The newly married couple then left, way before the other guests. They weren't going on a trip, they were going home to spend their wedding night in Dzadzio and Babcia's room, where Mama and Papa and all the other sisters and their husbands had spent their first night together. My grandparents had a massive bed where we had all been born. Everyone from Mama to her brothers and sisters, Mania and me, and most recently Zygush and Zosia, had been born in that dark mahogany bed. Promptly nine months after the wedding, Zygush was born.

That had been only three years ago. Now, instead of getting ready for the coming school year and gossiping with my friends, we were getting ready for a war.

It had been brewing for a long time. We had been listening to the ranting speeches of Hitler on Dzadzio's radio for years now. Even though they could understand every word, Mama and Papa didn't believe anyone that extreme could rule for very long. They were convinced that the German people would rise up and overthrow him. But against their expectations, Hitler continued to gain power. Despite the mounting anti-Semitism all across Europe, my parents didn't believe that the tragedy of Nazi Germany would reach us in Zolkiew. Our town had a tradition of tolerance that dated back to Jan Sobieski, the legendary king of Poland, saviour of Europe, who had defeated the Turks in the Battle of Vienna. His family had made Zolkiew its official residence in the 16th century.

I was proud to be part of the Sobieski tradition and I liked to think that his Enlightenment ideals were still alive in our town. Zolkiew had dozens of political and religious organizations: Zionist, Hassidic, Orthodox, Communist, Bundist, Socialist and others. Jewish life in Zolkiew was *shtetl* life, a thick soup of schools, synagogues, charities, clubs and fraternal organizations. The customs and traditions nourished us but also gave us plenty of indigestion. Papa always said we were five thousand Jews with ten thousand opinions! We were always at war with each other over one thing or another, but our city was nevertheless something of an oasis in the anti-Semitic Eastern Europe.

For over a year now, since shortly after Germany had taken over Austria, our town had been filling up with refugees. There was barely a room or a flat that had not been taken. The Joint Committee for Welfare supported over 200 refugee families. There were two meals a day for more than 640 children. We did our share too. Every Wednesday at noon the Herzbergs, a very nice refugee couple from Vienna, came to our house for lunch. Over Mama's chicken soup served on the special china, the Herzbergs told us about the nightmare they had left behind. They told us how their synagogues were destroyed. How Jews were beaten in the streets and how shops and businesses were looted. They were very clear about what Hitler meant for Jews.

Last year, Uncle Manek had suggested for us all to emigrate to Palestine. He said that the world was on fire. When a large Ukrainian company wanted to buy the factory, Manek had begged Papa and Dzadzio to sell, saying that this was our chance, but they had refused. Dzadzio was so mad at Manek for wanting to sell his life's work that he had to live on our side of the house for a while. Manek never brought it up again. He didn't have to.

Not even a week ago, the Russians and Nazis had signed the Molotov-Ribbentrop non-aggression treaty. Papa had explained to me that it meant that Nazi Germany could now invade Poland and open an eastern front and the Russians would do nothing to stop them. The pact stunned all of Poland. No one could understand why Russia would relinquish their historical designs on our country. It was as if Stalin were handing Hitler Poland like a goose stuffed for the oven. After having been brutally occupied by the Tsar and the Russian Empire on and off for close to two hundred years, we had feared the Russians more than the Germans. But that was changing with Hitler. Most of Poland's defences were directed at the eastern border with Russia. We wouldn't have the time or the resources to defend our western border.

I must have fallen asleep at some point. When I woke the next morning it took a moment for me to remember why we were there. We gathered our blankets and made the long procession home, where we gathered around Dzadzio's radio hoping to hear of a Polish counter-attack. But all we heard was bad news. The Germans were advancing as fast as the tanks could travel. The mounted Polish cavalry was fighting bravely for every metre of Polish territory, but they were outmatched. Poland didn't have many tanks or aircraft, and most of the modern weapons we had produced had been sold to other countries.

Every day that followed seemed to bring nothing but more bad news. Every night we made the trip to the orchard and watched the Nazi aircraft fly overhead, filling the sky like locusts. Every morning we made the walk home to listen to the radio. On 4 September, the Nazi troops cut off Warsaw. On 5 September, they crossed the Vistula into eastern Poland. And on 6 September, Krakow surrendered. Rumours poured in with more refugees. The Nazis were advancing. In some Polish towns the *Volksdeutsche*, ethnic Germans, who had been sent to colonize Poland in the 17th and 18th centuries, were greeting the Germans with flags and flowers. So were many Poles and the Ukrainian Nationalists. There was no more opposition.

On 18 September 1939, the Nazis arrived in Zolkiew. But it was only the Wehrmacht and not a shot was fired. The German soldiers were polite as they wandered through the streets like tourists, climbing the wooden stairs of the castle walls, taking pictures of the churches, buying the inlaid birch boxes, lace tablecloths and napkins to send as gifts to wives, girlfriends and mothers. They showed off their weapons to curious boys and flirted with the girls. I only heard this second-hand from Manek, Josek and Papa. Mania and I were terrified and didn't dare venture beyond the sheltered backyards of our street.

Not one week later, we learned about a secret amendment that had been made to the original Molotov-Ribbentrop pact. Hitler would now control the western part of Poland and Stalin would keep the east. Zolkiew was less than 100 kilometres from the Russian border. All the Jewish families of Zolkiew got down on their hands and knees to thank God for his mercy.

Within days young Russian soldiers with cheeks like apricots from the Crimea marched into town to replace the Germans. For hundreds of years the Russians had dealt with dissidents by deporting them to the vast freezing extremities of their country where they would never be heard from again. The Tsar had deported so many Poles to Siberia that there were entire towns larger than Zolkiew there where only Polish was spoken. But if we kept to ourselves, and didn't aggravate or oppose the Soviets, they would leave us in peace. We felt we could tolerate life under the communists. We would surely have to practise our religion in private, and we might have to give up our business, but we would be spared the persecution of the Nazis.

Only Dzadzio cried like a prophet: 'You don't know who's coming here! You don't know!' He despised the Russians. He had hated the tsarists and now he hated the communists. He had been captured in 1914 when he was a soldier in the Polish army and had spent six years in a Russian concentration camp, four under the tsar and two under the communists. He had experienced Stalin's hell. Dzadzio knew that the Soviets were magicians, able to change the world with mere words. Invitations into threats. Plenty into hunger. Loyalty into fear. Smiles into lies. He never talked about what he went through in the Russian concentration camp. Not even to his wife. But Mama told me he still had nightmares. He would wake up screaming, covered in so much sweat that Babcia would have to change the sheets.

A few days after the Soviets arrived, Aunt Rosa, her husband and their four children showed up on our doorstep with just the clothes on their backs. Our family was reunited. Whatever happened to us, we would stay together as a pack. That was our hope.

Chapter 1

MY GRANDFATHER

From March 1940 to June 1941

For those of us not sent to Siberia, the Russians had brought Siberia to us. Every bit of fuel, everything that could burn, even tiny birds' nests, was sent to the front. I practically lived in my heavy grey Afghan coat lined with rabbit fur. That coat was my saviour. Thank heavens Aunt Uchka had married a furrier. Hersch Leib had had coats made for everyone in the family. We could have chosen anything, even a famous Zolkiew fur, so popular in Paris. But with the icy winds blowing off the steppes, nothing was warmer than Afghan lamb. So that is what my family wore.

Six months after the Soviets occupied Zolkiew we were still in the icy grip of our first occupied winter. The news on my grandparents' radio was just as chilling. We despaired when the United States announced its neutrality. And even though England and France had declared war on Germany, nothing had been done about the occupation of Poland. All France did was invade a lightly defended area of Germany. They made it all of 12 kilometres before turning back. We had been abandoned.

On most days after school, I would stop off at Uchka's on the way home. I looked forward to sugar cookies, tea, and playing with Zygush and Zosia – especially Zosia. I had given up dolls for books when I was six, but I couldn't get enough of her. Zosia liked to put her cheek next to yours and clutch your face when she was carried. I didn't want to be any other place on earth when she did this. According to Uchka, I was Zosia's little mother, her *mammeleh*.

One day, when I went to Aunt Uchka's, her house was empty. Before, I would have thought nothing of their absence, but now I immediately assumed the worst. I ran through the lanes in Uchka's neighbourhood back to my house, praying to find them there. It was like a snow-covered maze behind my family's oil-press factory. I cut through the alley behind the pink walls of the convent to my street. I rushed up the steps into the foyer that separated our flat from that of my grand-parents', stamping off as much snow as I could. Even with my fur hat still over my ears, my coat collar up and my scarf wrapped tightly round it, I could already hear the noise coming from the next room. Something had happened. Everybody was speaking all at once. No one noticed I had walked in the room. I was relieved to see Uchka sitting in the corner holding the children in her lap. It took me a while to realize that everyone was beaming.

Mama finally sighted me. She rushed towards me with her arms out. 'Who knew? Who knew?'

I asked, 'Who knew what?' I couldn't imagine what had put such smiles on their faces. But everyone actually looked happy, which surely meant that nobody had died or been deported. It finally hit Mama that I really didn't know what she was talking about.

'You mean the entire town hasn't heard yet? Clarutchka,' she said, every word ripe with pride, 'out of all the children in Zolkiew, not only was your little sister chosen to sing the lead aria in the spring concert, but she was the youngest! Can you imagine? Mania! The youngest! And a lead aria! Who knew?'

Never in a million years would I have thought I would be hearing Mama crow about this. Not now, not ever! Mania was always pulling rabbits out of the hat of her life. We didn't even know that she had been asked to audition! I was as giddy as the rest of them. Who could have known that my little stick of a sister could really sing? We sang at holidays. We sang our children's songs at school. But an aria? From a real opera? What a blessing to have such a talent in the family. We even temporarily forgot that the concert was to celebrate the superiority of the Soviet system. Even Dzadzio, Grandfather, who never had a kind word for the Russians, said, 'At least they got this right.' Apparently, the Russians knew something we didn't about my baby sister. On the other side of the room, Mania was sitting on the baby bed where she slept. I could tell what she was thinking just by the look on her face. She would rather be out sledding while there was still snow on the ground and was ruing that she had brought up the concert at all. But it was like all the other things she had to confess to. Better to get it over with. Sooner or later Mama would have got it out of her anyway. She couldn't see the glory in it. She had been told to sing, so she would sing.

For the next three months, all we got was humming. Humming while she jumped rope. Humming while she ran in and out of the house. Humming while my mama made her do the homework she hated. The one time Mama asked her to sing, Mania refused. She was as wilful as Mama, Babcia and Dzadzio. We would have to wait for the concert.

The entire town was temporarily distracted from the Russian occupation. While waiting on the long lines which stretched outside the colonnaded shops, mothers bragged about the Ukrainian and Russian folk songs their children would be singing. There wasn't a loaf of bread to be found, but the air practically buzzed with gossip. I knew they were secretly keeping score. Which song was longer? Whose child was singing the favourites? Who had a solo and who was in the chorus? What would the mothers wear?

It didn't matter that Zolkiew was a speck on the map of the world, or that our house was on a dirt road covered in dust in summer and mud or snow in winter, Mama and her sisters always dressed as though they lived in a capital city like Warsaw or Vienna. Aunt Giza was the only who had actually lived in Vienna, and then only for a year. Although Giza reigned queen of the undergarment, even Dzadzio recognized Mama as the true Coco Chanel of the family. Whenever he wore out the elbows in his only sweater, my mother Salka had to be the one to pick out a new one; no matter that it would only be a *mispucha* – a relative by marriage – of the same charcoal grey sweater he bought every five years. September would bring Yom Kippur, Rosh Hashanah and the catalogues that arrived by mail from Paris, Berlin and Vienna. We would sit at the big kitchen table, catalogues everywhere, armed with scissors. Mama would have me cut out the bodice from one, the material from another, the skirt from a third, the collar from a fourth, ribbons from a fifth and put them together. She and her tiny doll of a dress-maker, Mrs Hirschorn, were thick as thieves. The two of them plotted out the family wardrobes for weddings as if they were military campaigns. Whenever Mania and I would show up in a new dress at the social hall we would see our friends wearing copies within weeks. Mama never said one word about how this pleased her.

But that was before the Soviets. Silk, satin, taffeta, sequins, feathers and lace were all one-way tickets to Siberia. Rough, olive green uniform wool was the fabric of this season. The peasant look was more than fashion; it was a matter of survival. Some of Mama's friends had even started to wear clothes that had once belonged to their cleaning ladies. Mama's beautiful silk dresses were now locked up in the massive mahogany armoire that had outlasted most of the governments of Europe. But like any mother whose daughter was making her debut, Mama wanted to look as proud as she felt. So after many hours and too many cups of tea, the Reizfeld sisters had decided that it was 'kosher' to wear the prettiest of their *schmatas*, rags.

Mania and I didn't even have that much of a choice. Lead aria or not, Mania was stuck wearing the navy blue sailor suit that was our school uniform. As was I. As was every other girl in Zolkiew. To compensate, Mama ironed so much starch into the uniforms they could have walked to the concert on their own. Our hair got the same treatment. Mama washed and rewashed Mania's dark hair until I could almost see my face reflected in its shine. It was one thing to argue with Stalin. It was another to argue with Mama.

When the day of the concert finally arrived, our little house was like a teapot filled to the brim with boiling water. The door flew open. Little Zygush had arrived, with Zosia on his heels. Nobody had ever taught him to knock. A knock was an insult. A knock said someone wasn't talking to somebody else in the family. Uchka followed just in time to see her children jumping up on me, like they always did. But today was not about fun and games. Before I could even give them a kiss, Mama was yelling at me from across the room. 'What's going on? Do you need a written invitation? And take the *kinder* with you.' She was telling me I better get dressed and bring Zygush and Zosia with me. I had, however, been dressed for hours.

Little Zosia, with her blond curls, black eyes and sweet disposition, was no more trouble than a little doll you sat on your bed. But for Zygush, small and dark-haired like his father, I needed a chair, a whip, a cage and a leash. He was already climbing me like his favourite walnut tree in the yard.

Dzadzio, dressed in a black suit and white shirt, the uniform of the orthodox Jew that he wore every day of his life, was the only quiet person in the room. As proud as he was of my sister, he refused to go to the concert. He and Babcia would stay at home. I could see the regret in his eyes, but his heavy black shoes were planted into the Persian carpet and he wouldn't budge. Ever since he had been captured by the Russians in 1918, he had refused to breathe the same air they did. Mama knew enough not to argue about matters of principle with her father. She respected him and knew his deeds were truth.

Every few minutes, Mama would drop what she was doing to fuss over Mania. Her fingers straightened Mania's collar and lingered on her shoulders. I could read Mama's mind. Through a caress of her hand, she prayed to imbue Mania with every ounce of her will, if such a thing were possible. Because today, for the first time in her life, Mania would be on her own. Mania knew what was at stake. The show was to 'honour' the Russians' ability to turn us, the children of corrupt capitalists and religious fanatics, into proper little Stalins and Lenins. And if we were really good students, into spies, informers and party members. She knew her teachers had agonized over the choice of singers. She knew they would watch white-knuckled and teeth clenched. She knew it all. Even at 11 she knew. Nobody had to say a word.

Mania had to run a gauntlet of hugs, kisses and pinches on the cheek before she could leave. Mama had parked herself at the front door. She straightened Mania's dress one more time. She made sure Mania's French knot was secure. She puffed out the ends of the red bandanna around Mania's neck. 'Stay still already!' Mama moaned. Mania was a racehorse at the starting gate. She had to be at the opera early. 'Enough already! Stop being such a nudge!' Babcia took Mama's hands off Mania's shoulders and guided my sister on her way with a kiss.

I watched as Mania walked down the street. But the walking lasted only until she came to the orphanage for Jewish girls, just two doors down. With a look back, a smile and a wave, Mania sprinted off. On any other day, Mama would have run after her with a rag and a tin of shoe polish. Mama's mouth hung open, but the words died in her mouth with a sigh. Tonight she just stood there and watched her daughter run down the street and out of sight.

An hour later, about 25 of us trooped off to the opera house in the sweet spring evening. The Russians hadn't managed to take away the fragrance of the lilacs and send it to the front with everything else. If Mania and I had been alone, the walk would have taken no more than 12 minutes. But now we were a herd of cattle, shuffling along at a grazing pace. I looked back and watched Mama and her three sisters walking arm and arm, as was their custom. There were a half a dozen crossed conversations going on. My family couldn't walk and talk at the same time. We would walk a few steps, one of us would greet a friend and all 25 of us would stop. We managed just a quarter of a mile in a quarter of an hour.

As we reached the sports field, there was a sea of girls in their blue sailor suits and red scarves, the uniform of the Russian Girl scouting movement, of which every able-bodied girl in Zolkiew was a proud member, whether she liked it or not. It seemed the entire town was flowing like a river up the street and towards the doors. Everyone had had the same idea: to be there early to get the good seats.

Our opera house, the Eagle, had been freshly painted. Large banners announcing the concert had been draped from the frieze. I had never seen so many cars in one place. The street was filled with cars that had been waxed to an inch of their lives. Each one had its own detachment of soldiers to make sure little boys like Zygush didn't commit acts of sabotage by getting fingerprints all over the finish. The cars belonged to the commissars who had taken all the big houses on Railroad Street, just outside the castle walls and across the street from the park. The previous owners were dead or in Siberia. If I wasn't worried about his safety, I would have let Zygush get his fingerprints all over the cars.

Papa greeted friends who no longer could be trusted. Friends who informed on other friends. Jews who informed on other Jews and sent children to die in Siberia. There were even children who informed on their parents. My father shook their hands and laughed at their jokes as they discussed the glory of the evening. Papa said that snubbing such 'old' friends amounted to suicide. My dzadzio would have slapped their faces and told them to go to hell. Under the banner, I saw the political officers who roamed the hallways of our school from time to time, smoking cigarettes with their comrades. I knew even children couldn't escape having a file. When we sang 'The International', 'May Day Morning' and 'The Partisan Song' at school, I tried to pretend they were just songs. But I felt I was denying my religion in a way I didn't when we sang Christmas carols.

I saw all my friends from school with their families and wanted to run to my three best friends, Giza Landau, who was also my second cousin, Genya Astman and Klara Letzer, but Mama told me to hang on to Zygush and Zosia. Mama who always told me how smart I was could in the next breath treat me like I was an absolute child. The officers waved at us students and without a thought tossed their cigarettes on the stone steps that had been washed and swept and polished by a troop of peasant women

Outside, an army band played as we advanced through the crush, trying to stay together. Inside, another army band was playing. Zygush and Zosia were hypnotized by the chandeliers throwing off pools of dancing light. The best seats had already been cordoned off for the officers and officials and their families of the Russian army, the communist party and the dreaded NKVD – the People's Commissariat of Internal Affairs, which ran the Gulag for Stalin. We fought our way upstairs and found a row of seats in the balcony. Zygush had to touch every red velvet chair on the way. From where we were sitting, we had a direct view of the orchestra and the boxes. Some of the Russian wives were wearing lingerie. They couldn't even tell the difference between a nightgown and a dress. These poor women, many from beyond the Urals, many from villages without a phone or even a road, assumed the stylish silk garments, decorated with lace décolletage, could be worn on the streets of Paris, Budapest or Berlin. Here I was, in this balcony, literally looking down my nose at these women glowing with pride. I wish I could say my cheeks burned with shame. Communism had given these women better lives. Many of them were friendly. Many were kind. I went to school with their children. Yet we were so frightened of their husbands that not one soul in Zolkiew dared tell them they were wearing lingerie.

Before the music, we had to endure the speeches. The generals and the commissars pretended they meant them and we pretended we believed them. 'We must unite in our unanimous opposition to reactionaries.' 'Revolutions are the locomotives of history!' 'Gaiety is the most outstanding feature of the Soviet Union.' 'Give us your children for ten years and we will give you a true Bolshevik.'

Mama, Rosa, Uchka and Giza all had the same idiot smile painted on their faces. The entire balcony looked like a collection of frozen statues in a graveyard. Zosia was squirming and Zygush was nudging. Every few minutes Zygush poked me and asked when Mania was going to sing.

But the moment Mania walked on to the stage, they were still with awe. She looked so slim and fragile, just like a willow. She was just a fraction of the size of the singers who preceded her. Down the row, I could tell that Mama's asthma was acting up. She could hardly breathe from all the *kvelling* – bursting with pride times a hundred. And when my little tomboy of a sister opened her mouth, out came a voice so powerful and clear that chills ran up my spine. *The winds are howling. The trees are bending. My heart hurts. And the tears are falling by themselves.* I could practically hear myself wondering: 'This is my sister? Is this my sister?'

Just for a moment everything was perfect. Nobody wanted to be any place else or thinking about anything else. If only she could have kept on singing. I knew as long as her voice, clear as sunlight and imbued with pure emotion, filled this hall, we were safe. And even as I knew all this, I also knew that her song would end and the open hearts of our Soviet masters turn back to stone. How much I loved my sister in that moment.

The Soviets had no way of knowing that listening to my sister sing would only make us long for the life they were telling us to abandon. Our enemies, the Russian officers and party leaders, ruthless and sentimental, who killed and deported and tortured us, wept as children weep. The applause went on and on and on. Little Mania bowed as she was taught to bow and accepted red carnations from a Russian general. There was talk that night, lots of it, about the career our Mania would have when the war was over. But even as we spoke of the future, I knew the words were hollow. They were meant as a balm to ease the world we would face again tomorrow and the day after.

When Mania and I lay in bed that night, I told her with all my heart how proud we all were of her. I told her that she surprised us with how wonderful her voice was and that she was able to keep it a secret from us for so long. Even in the darkness, I could see her smiling. I wondered how many other secrets she kept, like the perfect acorns, flower petals and stones Mama always found in the pockets of her dresses.

Mania was so worn out from the frenzy of her day that she fell asleep before she could finish the 'night' in goodnight. But I was sad, on this night of Mania's triumph. This was my sister and in so many ways she was a stranger. I loved her so much, yet she was a mystery to me. I knew less about her than I did about the characters in the books I read. As much as I wanted to know, I didn't dare ask her what she had been feeling on stage that night. I know she would just shrug off the question.

Tomorrow Mania would wake up, reach for her skipping rope and run outside without another thought of the concert. A spring day would be waiting for her outside the door.

Just weeks after Mania's aria, the Soviets were no longer seducing us with concerts and the promise of a workers' paradise. They were now demanding more than mere obedience. They wanted our very minds. Their security apparatus of secret police (the NKVD), spies and informers made you afraid to look at your own reflection for fear of being reported. The terror of deportation was around every corner.

Friend after friend and their families had disappeared in the middle of the night. Either they were accused of having too much money, or of being Polish loyalists. Or they might be intellectuals, whose minds might dare question what the communists were doing in Zolkiew. Or they might have simply voiced their opposition to communism once 20 years ago in a café conversation. The reason didn't make any difference, the result was always the same. Families weren't just deported. They just ceased to exist; they had never existed. By the sundown following their disappearance, Russians were already sleeping in their beds and eating the food in their pantries. I recognized my classmates' clothes on the Russian daughters and saw Russian sons playing with the toys of their little brothers. My friend Sonia Maresky, from Silesia, was one of the first to be deported with a hundred other Jewish refugees from Austria and the west.

Mama had decided that if we were to be on the next cattle car to Siberia, at least we would be prepared. Every spare minute was spent sewing knapsacks from green canvas and filling them with woollen socks, underwear and food, and hiding rubles and gold coins in secret compartments. And when the knock would come, and it would surely come, maybe in the hour of our deepest sleep, waking us from a dream into a nightmare, our clan, all 17 of us living in our little stone house, parents, sisters, grandparents, aunts, uncles and cousins would march out with our brand new backpacks.

Despite the new threat, we adjusted to life under the communists. Only Dzadzio stayed the same. Even after eight months he hadn't learned to keep his hatred of the Soviets to himself. Mama kept as busy as possible, but she was so worried that my father could no longer reassure her that because of the oil press we wouldn't be deported.

My poor father was now working almost 24 hours a day. There were no peasants or anyone in the army that could run the factory so the commissars were forced to let him run it. But they gave him Vasiluk. He was a big lazy Ukranian with some Russian blood who had a thick drooping moustache and did nothing but sit around my father's office to spy on him. If Vasiluk felt industrious, he would read the newspaper.

Papa said rubles were worthless. So we used oil instead of money. If I looked out of the window, I could see long lines of people waiting for their ration of oil at the refinery next to the factory. In our kitchen we exchanged the oil from Papa's factory with the cheese, produce, milk and eggs brought by the peasants. We then exchanged these for flour, sugar, tea and other necessities at the store my friend Genya's father owned. At least we never lacked for food.

My grandfather was the first of us to be taken by the Russians. I was in the hospital recovering from appendicitis when an old car had sputtered up to our house with three men dressed in cheap suits and hats pulled over their eyes. As Mama told me how they had taken Dzadzio down the four front stone steps to the waiting car, the image I had of my grandfather seemed to shrink and crumple up like a folded paper doll. There was nothing I could do except weep.

Once I had learned about Dzadzio, more terrible news was to come. My grandfather wasn't the only one who had been arrested. The same night, the NKVD had carried out arrests in every city, town, village and *shtetl* in their newly occupied territory. They had taken into custody every former Polish army officer and government official, as well as dozens of teachers, politicians and intellectuals and businessmen.

A few days later, I found out from Mama (who was bribing prison guards for information) that Dzadzio's kidneys hadn't been withstanding prison conditions and he had been moved to the very hospital where I lay. One day Dzadzio was brought out into the garden, guarded by a couple of armed soldiers. Their crazy assignment was to make sure that this old man in a wheelchair, dressed in a hospital gown with his feet bare, didn't escape. When my grandfather saw me, his eyes were glassy with tears. All he could say was *gey avek, gey avek* – go away, go away. His gestured with his hand, over and over, for me to go back inside. I knew he was afraid of what the soldiers might do to me, but I couldn't stop. I walked over to him and we embraced. I could barely ask him how he was. That was all. There was nothing to say. Nothing to do.

Even though we weren't able to speak properly with each other, I was happy just to sit with my grandfather. Over the next couple of days I could tell that our time together had lifted his spirits too. One afternoon, we were sitting in the garden in silence when two NKVD officers walked over. My grandfather was to go with them. There was no violence in their voices, no malice. To them, he was merely a package with sad eyes. The nurse ran to get the doctor. Dzadzio was in no condition to leave the hospital. Dzadzio smiled at me not to worry. It was the saddest smile I had ever seen on a human being. Then his face went white, and his body started shaking. I screamed, but the guards and the NKVD did nothing, because I was nothing. They loaded my poor dzadzio, in desperate pain, his eyes filled with terror, into the back of a horse-drawn wagon. The doctor argued, but only for a moment and only with half a heart. I backed away, afraid and helpless. They had put my dzadzio on a bed of straw and I was thankful for that. For a long time, I just stood there. As if by the act of standing still, time would stop as well. I knew Mama would bribe the guard again for news. All I could do was to wait for Mama to come and tell me what happened.

Mama didn't visit for three long days. When she finally walked into the hospital chapel she looked as if she was in mourning. She had brought me some soup. As she poured the broth into a bowl, she started to talk. The day after Dzadzio had been carted away, a prison guard ran up to our house to tell Mama that her father and the other political prisoners were being marched down to the train tracks. Mama and Uchka had immediately grabbed some rolls to bring to him. They knew he would need food for the long train journey. When they reached the central plaza opposite the castle walls, they saw Dzadzio marching in a line, guarded by Soviet troops. Mama and Uchka threw him the rolls, even after the guards had yelled at them to stop. They were arrested and taken to the jail in the tower. She had just been released this morning. She looked at me with anger in her eyes. 'Can you imagine, Clarutchka – they didn't even let him pick up one roll.'

The knock came for the rest of my family while I was still in hospital. It happened in the middle of the night, but Papa had been across the street at the oil press working, as always. The agents had arrest warrants in the name of Meir Schwarz. Mama could barely get the words out. She didn't have to say any more, I understood. My father's family was so religious that they had considered it irrelevant to have their weddings recorded by the state. So even though we went by the name of Schwarz in our day-to-day life, all our official papers, including my birth certificate, bore the name of Gottlieb. My mother was able to show the NKVD these papers, proving that we weren't the family they were looking for. My mother's face filled with shame. The others hadn't been so lucky. The NKVD took my babcia, Uncle Manek, Aunt Rosa, her husband Pinchas and their four children. Uncle Josek and Aunt Giza had been able to hide in the cellar. They had since gone into hiding in Lvov.

Mama had gone to the train station because this time the Soviets had allowed family members and the Jewish Joint Distribution committee to pass out food, bedding and other supplies to the prisoners. Mama was able to talk to Rosa and the others. Nobody had told them where they were going, how long the journey would take or what would happen to them once they arrived. Mama told me she had had to say goodbye to Babcia as if it were for the last time. We didn't know if my poor grandmother would survive the journey, let alone what the Soviets would have in store for them at their destination. Rosa tried to console her younger sister, telling Mama that she had done the right thing to save herself. But those words were no comfort for the grief and guilt I saw in Mama's face.

It had come to this for our family. The unthinkable. That some of our family would survive, perhaps not at the expense of the others, but with the knowledge that we couldn't save them. I couldn't stop crying. All I wanted to do was go home with Mama. I didn't want to spend another night away from my family. I needed to be in my own bed, to sleep next to my sister and across the room from Mama and Papa. It was the only way I knew we could stay together.

Mama kept one more secret from me. It was there waiting for me on the back steps of our house when I returned home from hospital. Two children were playing in our yard. She introduced me to Stalina and Volodya Dupak. Stalina was four years old with white-blond hair and so very plump that the witch in Hansel and Gretel would have loved to pop her in the oven. Volodya was my age. I knew him from school. Volodya greeted us formally. He knew I had been in the hospital and inquired after my health.

Once inside, Mama whispered to me, 'The sheets from Babcia and Dzadzio's bed weren't even dry when they moved in.

The father is NKVD.' Her eyes added, 'God doesn't even know if he was the one responsible for deporting Dzadzio.'

I had tried to prepare myself for the emptiness of our home without my grandparents. Their presence, voices, and laughter, as well as the smell of Grandma's cooking were things I had lived with every day of my life. Even if they were gone, I had thought that I would at least be able to feel something of them. But now, the door between the two halves of the house, which had never been closed during the day, was shut tight. I shivered at the thought that the NKVD was sleeping in my grandparents' bed.

Despite everything, it was a relief to be home. When I met Mr Dupak, with his bland face and thinning blond hair, he had nothing but pleasant smiles for me. And all of us were equally pleasant to him. They were the ideal communist family. They had benefited from the Soviet expansion and were convinced that they were bringing a better life to Zolkiew. Mr Dupak would leave the house in the morning, only to return late at night. His wife kept to herself and our interaction with them was mostly through the kids. The only thing they knew of the war was that their father was powerful and that all the children in town were especially kind to them. Nevertheless we were cautious. Before, we had never given a thought to how loud our voices were. Now, we hardly spoke above a whisper.

In the middle of June 1940, a letter finally arrived from Aunt Rosa. We had been waiting for news for almost two months, but now Mama seemed afraid to open the envelope. The opening lines put the worst of our fears to rest. They had all survived the journey. They were in Kazakhstan, somewhere in the endless desert of Central Asia, much closer to China than to our home. Rosa wrote that there were hardly any signs of the war; the place was remote and timeless. There were still camel caravans that moved goods from one town market to another. We were all relieved. How protected she must feel by the thousands of kilometres that separated them from the war. She went on to explain that they had just been thrown off the train along with everyone else and been told to find jobs. But there were no jobs. Rosa described how they had been close to starving until Uncle Manek had managed to find a job with an oil-press factory in Aktyubinsk that desperately needed specialists. They moved to the strange city, ready to start a new life. She described how thankful she was that they were together. They had food and shelter and would survive as a family. If only the letter had stopped there.

Mama continued to read and I watched her face grow taut as she came to the following words. Rosa wrote that her son, Wilek, had also found work in a factory. She described how nervous he had been to start his job without suitable overalls. Rosa had promised to buy him a pair so that he would have the proper work clothes for the next day. But in the first hour of his first day on the job, Wilek's belt had got caught in the gears of a huge machine. He had been dragged into the machine's belly, swallowed as if by a beast. Rosa wrote that there hadn't been enough left of her son for a proper burial. He had been all of 20 years old. Since Rosa's family had come to live with us in 1939, I'd thought of Wilek as an older brother. He'd only ever been sweet and protective. Mama mourned for her older sister and her nephew. When she looked at Mania and me, I knew she couldn't help thanking God that it hadn't been one of her daughters.

As the summer moved into autumn, I couldn't count all the changes in our lives under this grey regime. The church bells didn't ring. The Eagle stopped showing Hollywood films. The

Polish patriots we had studied before the occupation were now criminals. People were afraid to go to the synagogues, so Papa had to sneak across the street to Mr Melman's house where they now held secret *minyan*. Papa was now an employee. The Russians had taken over the vegetable-oil business our family had owned for five generations. Nobody talked about anything in public. The nuns in the convent up the street all wore long skirts now instead of their brown habits. We had to wear uniforms to school. Any kosher meat still available was delivered in secret. All the newspapers except the communist ones were closed. Mama was buying up woollen socks and underwear like crazy. The bags under Papa's eyes were the darkest shade of purple I had ever seen. Mama closed the curtains before we had *shabbat* dinner.

I pretended to be a good young communist girl. I was afraid all the time. But the biggest change of all was in Mama. She practically disappeared from our lives. Almost every day she took the bus into Lvov and went to the office of every commissar, party member, every politician she could find, searching for news of Dzadzio. She would come home sometimes late at night, sometimes not for days, but always with the weight of defeat and exhaustion on her shoulders. They took Papa's money, made promises and then didn't even let Mama back in their offices. I knew she loved her father. I only wished Dzadzio, wherever he was, could see just how much.

I also knew that Papa and Mama were doing their best to protect us not only from physical harm, but also from worry. But their words were small comfort in the face of the Nazis' lack of opposition in Europe. Two years ago, it would never even have occurred to me to wonder about what war felt like. War was something in Tolstoy, not in my life. Nobody could have convinced me that despite the occasional pogrom, our little town with its five thousand Jews tucked away in Galicia wasn't the best of all possible worlds. For 700 years we had been batted back and forth between a half a dozen countries and empires that were like cats playing with a ball of yarn. We changed nationalities like, in better times, Mama had changed dresses. Before I had always held the bookish belief that everything would work out in the future because it always had in the past, but now I had become somebody different, with different thoughts and different hopes. Even the small things in which I used to take so much pleasure, like reading or going to school, didn't make the empty feeling in my stomach go away. Despite the spoonfuls of optimism my parents fed to my sister and me, my mind was spinning. How could I read a novel when Hans Frank, the Gauleiter (Governor General) of Poland, had declared, 'I ask nothing of the Jews except that they should disappear.' What had become of my grandfather? What was going to become of us? Surely our green knapsacks wouldn't be enough to save us? We were stuck between two massively powerful nations, both of which hated us. The Russians hated us because we didn't adhere to their communist principles, and the Nazis hated us because of our religion.

Before the war, when the grown-ups spoke in hushed whispers, it was usually about a present for one of us, or some gossip. I never really cared much about either. Now I needed to hear every word, even if it brought demons into my sleep. The anxiety of not knowing was worse. I collected news, facts, anything that I knew I could rely on to be true.

In the past year, France had been invaded, along with Holland, Luxembourg and Belgium. Italy and Japan joined Germany in forming the Axis Powers. Hungary, Romania and Slovakia had become German allies. And close to a million Jews had been sealed off in ghettos in Warsaw, Krakow and Lublin.

The Allies had yet to make a single attack on the Nazis, who preened with their invincibility. Every apartment, every room in town, was filling up by the day with refugees from the Nazis. The horror stories were passed like the plague. Even my parents' whispers couldn't keep them from me.

The only thing that kept me sane was going to school. The churches had large libraries, as did some of the schools. There were also private libraries. Almost every day I made the rounds. The former nuns and Mr Appel, the old Jewish man who ran the private libraries, expected me and saved books they thought I might like. This was the year of Victor Hugo and Charles Dickens; and of course the great Russian novelists, Tolstoy, Turgenev, Dostoevsky and Gogol. I picked books by their length and their weight. The longer and heavier the better. More and more, I tried to shut out the world with literature.

In the spring of 1941, almost a year to the day she was deported, I received a letter from my friend Sonia Maresky, in which she described the brutal and fierce cold, and the backbreaking work her family had to do in the coal mines. She wrote that the workers usually died within a year. The Jewish Community had got together to obtain permission to ship them matzos for Pesach. She ended the letter, 'When this war is over only the *korhany*, the mass graves, will bear witness that there once were a people here.'

In early May, Mama somehow finally found Commissar Wanda Vashilevski, who was very high up in the NKVD. That Mama even dared to contact the NKVD spoke of her desperation about her father. She told us that Commissar Vashilevski seemed like a decent woman. The commissar said to Mama: 'I'm sorry for you. I'm not going to lie. You should know that only the official who ordered his arrest can release your father. But I will try. Only if he gets back will you know if I have succeeded.'

We had had a little hope, but Papa had warned that we couldn't be certain if Vashilevski was honest or a thief.

In the middle of June, Professor Ratusinski knocked on our door. He was a good-natured teacher at the Gymnasium and a neighbor. He had just been released from the Brigitka prison in Lvov, where he had been brought after trying to escape the Soviets and go to Romania. He told us that the prisoners had been kept in cells in alphabetical order. Just a few cells down from him was my grandfather. Not only was Dzadzio alive, but he was only 35 kilometres away. We prayed and thanked God for his mercy. It was a miracle. Mama brought him inside and made him tell her every detail. Professor Ratusinski told us that Dzadzio had been brought to the prison from a concentration camp in the east. We learned he was thin but in decent health, and with any hope, he might soon be released. Mama embraced him like a long-lost brother and put money in every one of his pockets before he left. Comrade Vashilevski, with the big or greedy heart, had come through.

The next morning, Mama took the first bus to Lvov and went to thank her and to try to speed up his release from there. Comrade Vashilevski did some checking and told Mama that there had been a mix-up with some of the paperwork, but that everything was fine. It would only be a matter of a few more days. Even though our patience was a frayed thread, we knew we could stand a few more days. Mama spent the rest of the day getting ready for Dzadzio's homecoming, thankful to have something happy to prepare for, for a change. She cleaned the little apartment in our basement for him, washed and ironed his clothes, and bartered for a chicken for soup. I couldn't think of anything else besides Dzadzio's homecoming as I helped Mama with the chores. Mama knew that even after months in exile and prison, her father would be in a fury that the man who might have sent him away and deported his wife and daughter was living in his house. Mama was afraid of what he might do. Twenty years ago, her father had put aside the clothing of a Hassid and picked up a gun to fight the Russians. Only the fear of what the consequences would mean for us might temper his actions.

We awoke the next day to a big commotion next door. Footsteps raced across the floor. Doors were flying open and shut. From our window we could see the Dupaks frantically loading boxes and suitcases into a Soviet army truck and then their children into a car. Stalina and Volodya looked sad and frightened, framed in the open car window.

We looked on with a sense of relief as they emptied the house of all their belongings. Dzadzio would at least be spared one heartache and be able to move back into his house. Comrade Dupak kissed his wife and children and watched as the truck and the car drove off. He came to our door and told us he had sent his family east. Hitler had broken the Molotov-Ribbentrop pact and had invaded Russian-occupied Poland. Shortly after that, Dupak left the house.

In the span of a few seconds I had gone from fearing and despising the Russians for tearing our family apart to wanting them to stay. This could only spell disaster for us. This time it wouldn't just be the Wehrmacht marching into town for a few days. We knew in terrifying detail what to expect. Rosa and the other refugees who had fled east had witnessed it all. It would be the SS, deportations and ghettos. The border to Nazi-occupied Poland was less than 60 kilometres away. And the general state of alarm up and down the street as the Russians packed off their families confirmed that no shots would be fired in our defence. We were being abandoned. Papa considered following the retreat; he went to see if it would be possible to go with the Russians. He came back soon thereafter saying it would be impossible. He had seen Malka and Rosa, two Jewish girls married to Russian soldiers, being helped on to trucks by their husbands, only to have the Russians wives throw them off.

Papa was still talking when Uchka came running in the door in a panic. My uncle Hersch had been ordered to report to the plaza. The Russian army was going door to door, impressing every able-bodied man between the ages of 17 and 45. They would be going straight to the front. She was surprised that my father hadn't been taken as well. We didn't know why he hadn't. We did think it might have been Comrade Dupak's doing. Mama ordered us to stay inside the house. We couldn't go to the plaza to say goodbye. Uncle Hersch was hardly bigger than a rifle himself and had the same dark eyes and sweet disposition as his son, Zygush. It was hard for me to imagine a man like him fighting at all. Uchka told us later that they had marched through the gate near Paradise Hill, which had been named by King Sobieski because he thought it was the most beautiful place he had ever seen. I couldn't imagine what Uncle Hersch could have been feeling as he was forced to stare up at the place where we had picnicked almost every Saturday and where his son had run wild through the thickly shaded forest, all the while marching with the army that had imprisoned his father-in-law, but was fighting the Nazi enemy. It was too much to digest. Poor Uchka told us how sad and excited the children had been. At only two and four years old, Zygush and Zosia hadn't quite known what they were waving at or waving for, as their father, one of hundreds of stunned faces, walked towards oblivion. Uchka had tried to hide how frightened she had been, despite knowing that she was probably saying goodbye to her husband for the last time. It would have been so wonderful to be able to be proud of Hersch Leib, marching off to protect us and his country. But all we could think of was the Nazis, and what that meant for us.

The Russians had taken every car, every cart and every horse. Zolkiew was in chaos. Every day, more and more Russians left. They packed up everything they could take with them: sewing machines, scrap metal, lumber, bathtubs, grain, desks. It seemed the entire contents of our town were being passed in front of our window. Comrade Dupak showed up again with a muzzled German shepherd. He had come for his things. The Nazis were close to Lvov and he would be leaving. He told us he had enjoyed living next to us and hoped we would meet again after the war. He said *dasv'danya* earnestly and shook my father's hand.

Not long after he left, the streets were filled with panic and weeping. At first we thought the Nazis had arrived. But then we learned that before leaving, the NKVD had emptied the local jail. The political prisoners were shot and then attack dogs were let loose on them. The dogs were tearing the faces off the prisoners. I couldn't believe that Comrade Dupak had done such a thing. He was such a nondescript man with his thinning hair and pleasant smile. As soon as Mama heard the horrible news, she began to fear the worst for her father. She had been trying to find Wanda Vashilevski for days, only to learn that she had fled with the others.

There was no way to know now if Dzadzio had been released or if he was alive. We couldn't bear to think what could be happening to him. And there was no longer any way to get in touch with Josek and Giza, who had remained in Lvov the entire year. There was nothing for Mama to do but wait. She had confidence that her brother would try his best to find out what had happened to their father.

Two weeks later Josek came home with Giza, a new wife, Rela, and several of her relatives, including her brother Dudio. The grief in their faces told us what had happened to Grandpa, and also what our own fate would be.

Josek told us that Lvov had been in chaos as well. The army and the commissars had been throwing civilians off the trains and shooting them if they didn't move fast enough. Every car, truck and wagon had been appropriated for the Russian flight east. A day later the Nazis had arrived. One of the first things the SS did was to go through the streets recruiting Jews for work in the prisons. Josek had gone, hoping to find Dzadzio.

He told us that the smell of death on entering the prison had been overwhelming. There had been bodies in the corridors, in the cells, in the courtyard. Just as in Zolkiew, the last act of the NKVD before leaving had been to murder and disfigure all the political prisoners so that the approaching Nazis wouldn't be able to identify them. They were protecting their own necks, but they let the real criminals, the murderers, the rapists, the thieves, all go.

We knew what was coming next. After the NKVD had shot the prisoners, they let the dogs loose. The beards of the Orthodox had been shaved when they were first imprisoned, so we couldn't even bury another Jew in my dzadzio's place. Josek and the others carried the bodies outside to the courtyard where families wandered among the corpses trying to find their loved ones. There were over 3,000 corpses. Many were children. Some were pregnant women with the bellies and breasts cut open. There were nuns and priests. Josek and the other Jews dug mass graves in the Ukrainian cemetery. They threw the bodies in and covered them with lime before they filled in the graves. But the burials were going too slowly for the Nazis. They ordered Josek and the others to simply cover the bodies with lime as they lay in the cellar and to brick up the doors and windows. Perhaps Dzadzio's remains were in a mass grave. Perhaps they were in the cellar of Brigitka prison. We would never know.

Only a few days later, the Ukrainian Nationalists with the encouragement of the Nazis murdered 4,000 Jews in Lvov. The Ukrainian Nationalists thought that all of Galicia belonged to them. They felt that the Poles and the Jews were invaders of their homeland. Stalin had starved millions of Ukrainians to death and so the Nationalists celebrated the Russian retreat and welcomed the Nazis as their saviours and allies. Josek, Rela and the others were lucky to get out with their lives and to reach Zolkiew safely.

Our grief was beyond any words. It brought with it the gathering sense that our lives were out of our hands. It felt like a storm pulling together, the sky growing increasingly dark. It didn't seem like anything in this world would make sense any more. Later we found out that all the old-time officers like Dzadzio who had been taken east and put in a concentration camp had been released and reunited with their families. The Soviets had decided they were too old and sick to give them any trouble. If Mama hadn't moved heaven and earth and spent so much money trying to save her father, he might now be safely in Kazakhstan with his wife and family.

Chapter 2

A PLACE TO HIDE

From July 1941 to November 1942

There is terror and panic in our city. The Jews are building bunkers of all kinds: underground, double walls, anywhere they can find a spot to hide. Others are looking for help from the gentiles. Others are crying in despair about the loss of their loved ones… There are rumours they are being poisoned with gas. Others say they are being electrocuted, burned or shot with guns. One thing is for sure, there is no return from there.

*

I was beginning to count the dead.

Wilek. Dzadzio. The sons of Mr Malinovski, who lived directly across the street from Mr Melman and a few doors down from us, had shared the same fate as Dzadzio. I knew this was just the beginning. The Nazis would be in Zolkiew any day, any hour.

We didn't leave the house any more, except for Papa, who continued to go to the factory. The peasants were trying to bring in as much grain as possible before the Nazis came. Papa knew every zloty might save our lives and so he worked the press around the clock. Nobody had to forbid us to go out in the streets. Even Mania stayed indoors on these glorious summer days, staring out of the window. I couldn't concentrate on my books. Nobody was in the mood for talking. Mama cooked. We made our beds. It was all we could manage. We knew we were facing some inevitable catastrophe, yet we couldn't do anything but wait. The moments were painfully endless. It felt like in a dream when you were are trying to escape some unseen horror, but as you start to run the ground swallows your legs and all your screams are silent. We were all restless. At night, I could sense Mania up next to me and hear Mama and Papa tossing and turning across the room.

Early in the morning of 5 July 1941, we were woken from our pathetic sleep by motorcycles roaring down our street. They were soon followed by trucks and then by soldiers marching past our window as if we were marshals in a parade. It was the Wehrmacht again. Papa went out and reported that, like in 1939, they were roaming around town, snapping pictures of the castle and churches like tourists. They were handing out candy to the children and cigarettes to the men, assuring the anxious townspeople that we had nothing to worry about. But still we didn't venture out of our door. Two days later, Papa rushed over from the factory to tell us that the Gestapo and the SS were arriving. He had heard that our Grand Rabbi, revered over all of Eastern Europe for his piety and knowledge, was planning to wait for them with the members of the Kahala, the Zolkiew Jewish Council, at the entrance of the town only a kilometre away from our house. They were prepared to beg and bargain for our lives. We waited for the results of this meeting, but were not optimistic. We didn't have to wait long before we heard shooting. The sound of the machine-gun fire was no louder than champagne corks. Even the ensuing wailing and crying was faint. But they were as loud as they needed to be to inform us that our nightmare had arrived.

We heard that the Grand Rabbi had hardly got a word out before the SS officer shot him. The accompanying members of the Kahala were arrested, including the father of Giza Landau. The SS officer then drove to the synagogue and ordered his men to strip it of every bit of gold and silver and anything that was valuable. A crowd of Jews gathered in the streets and watched in horror as the crowns on the Torah handles, the Torah covers embroidered with golden thread, the candelabras and the inlay on the pillars were packed into trucks. The many Hassid and Orthodox tore their clothing in mourning at the desecration. They knew they should have been hiding, but they couldn't help themselves. When there was nothing left to steal, the SS ran through the sanctuary pouring petrol on the benches, railings, prayer books, Torahs, the tallith, anything that would burn. The walls inside and out were also drenched with petrol. When the fire was lit with dozens of torches and the SS machine-gunned the huge windows to feed the flames with more oxygen, the Sobieski Schul erupted. It was a spectacle as the flames raced up the walls and shot out of the windows. Once everything made of wood and paper had burned, the flames on the walls died out. The paint had been seared off, but the building stood. The SS officer became furious and ordered his men to throw the lamenting Jews on the embers to feed the fire, as if the heat of burning Jewish flesh would be enough to turn brick to ash. A Wehrmacht officer driving by in his Mercedes reacted in stunned horror. He ordered his men to pull the Jews from the flames. The SS officer was outranked, so a few Jews were saved for who knows how long. As soon as the Wehrmacht left, the SS tried to burn the synagogue down a second time, but the walls still held firm.

In another time, the fact that the *schul* was still standing would have been termed a miracle. But it couldn't have felt more different for me. Since the beginning of the war in 1939, I had been secretly expecting a miracle. I dared tell no one. Not my parents. Not Mania. Not even one of my friends. I was so deeply and devotedly religious that I had been expecting something truly biblical. The killing of the Grand Rabbi and the burning of our synagogue had destroyed any hope I had that God would save us. I felt that the very Being I worshipped had abandoned us. It was now just the four of us – Mama, Papa, Mania and me – against the Third Reich.

Even before a representative came to our house to ask for a contribution, the news that the SS were asking for a ransom for the lives of the Kahala members had spread. When Mama told me how many kilograms of gold and silver they wanted, I couldn't believe there was that much money in the entire world. Mama donated our silver *chanukeah,* her wedding band, silver trays and candlesticks. The ransom was carted in wheelbarrows to the SS headquarters. They had taken over the town hall, which was in Sobieski's castle. Their offices looked out on the fountain of Madonna and the two big churches. But the piety of those buildings had no effect on the SS. The men were released and informed they were to run the Judenrat, which was responsible for all Jewish affairs. But their most important responsibility was making sure that all the SS orders were carried out to the letter.

The Nazis postered the town with the racial laws printed in the Gothic script that had become a weapon of hate. But we had already known them by heart well before the Nazis arrived. We weren't allowed to go to school or the park. We had a curfew. We weren't allowed to walk on the pavement, but had to walk in the street. My father, like every Jewish business owner in town, had his business confiscated by the Nazis. We had to wear the white armband with the blue Jewish star above the right elbow. Any offence was punishable by death. The day the order for the armbands came down, none of us could leave the house until my mother had embroidered them. It took Mama over two hours to do one armband. I was furious as I watched my proud mother as compelled to fabricate the emblems of our humiliation, as well those of Giza, Josek and poor Uchka, who couldn't sew a stitch. How would she explain them to Zygush and Zosia?

My dear friend, Helena Freymann, was killed one day as she walked out of her door and down the street. A Pole, someone whom she smiled at whenever she saw him and who had known her family for years, pointed her out to a soldier who was not even SS. He simply took out his pistol and shot her as if he were lighting a cigarette. She had forgotten her armband. This happened right down the block from our house one day after the edict came down. In this way we learned that the Pole or Ukrainian who might turn us in would not be a stranger. They would know us. Their children would be our classmates, their fathers would know our fathers, and their grandfathers would have known our grandfathers. I suppose, in the end, it made no difference if you were betrayed by a friend or an enemy. It really only meant that your heart might break a little more in the moment before you felt the bullet.

It was almost impossible to keep up with all the orders and edicts that came from the Nazi command headquarters. All the men were ordered to report to the town plaza for an examination by a doctor. Able-bodied men were designated A; those capable of light work were designated B; those who were sick, old, weak or crippled were designated C. Mama told Papa that many of our friends were paying off the Ukrainian doctors to get the C designation. She suggested my father do the same. His response was, 'For the Nazis, believe me, I don't want to be a cripple.' He didn't know then that this would save all our lives.

*

We had become a race of recluses, depressed by the news from the Nazi papers and radio stations as much as by what we were facing in our beloved little town. During the summer of 1941, the Nazis had taken Kiev, Karkhov, Minsk and all of the Crimea, with little opposition from the Soviets. From our living-room window, hidden behind the curtains, I watched young Jewish boys my age and younger as they struggled down the street, pushing carts and wheelbarrows filled with crushed stones. Papa came home and told us that they had been smashed into tiny pieces from the grave markers in the Jewish cemetery to pave the roads for German tanks. Some of the gravestones were over 300 years old. They even took the very first gravestone. The land had been given to the Jews by Sobieski. It was the most sacred responsibility of the Jewish faith to find hallowed ground in which to bury our dead. It came before building schools or a *mikvah* or even a synagogue. Dozens of our family members were buried there. Mama couldn't stop crying.

We knew there would be no more letters from Rosa and Babcia, but at least we knew what had happened to them. Uchka knew there would be no letter from her husband. The children asked about their father all the time. 'When is he coming home? Why isn't there a letter?' Zygush was old enough to pester Uchka. What was sadder was when he stopped.

Just as Papa was getting ready to leave the house on the appointed day and hour for those men whose name began with 'S', a soldier came to the house ordering him to come to the town hall. We were terrified. I don't think I took a breath until he came home. He had been told that he would carry on running the oil-press, at no salary of course. It wasn't an offer but an order. As soon as he had told us, Papa ran across the street to the factory, where the workers shook his hand. They told him they were lost without him and couldn't run the damn machines.

They were terrified that the SS would think they were incompetent and shoot them, so they had all signed a petition. Papa said the most important thing was that the Nazi army needed oil; the police needed oil; the SS needed oil. He hoped that his job would buy us enough time to find a way out.

Just like Papa, Mr Melman and Mr Patrontasch had also been spared by their work at the factory. The men got together and started a business in contraband oil. Papa and Mr Melman kept the factory open several nights a week while Mr Patrontasch would liaise with the black market. Word spread quickly among the peasants. The farmers who had been bringing their family grain to the press for generations now came at night. They paid with a sack of potatoes, eggs, cheese, onions, anything that could be sold on the black market. The Russians had moved part of the factory from across the street to a building six doors down on our side. Papa would go out the back door and cut through the backyards to get to work.

Uchka's armband hadn't been worn enough to get one speck of dirt on it when she showed up at our front door weeping. She was crying so hard that we knew something must have happened to Hersch. She told us a peasant from a small village who brought his grain to my father's press had heard that Hersch Leib had been killed just a few days after marching out of Zolkiew. His unit had been headed to Tarnopol when they were bombed by German fighter planes. If not for this peasant, we never would have known anything of his fate. In their engagement photo, Uchka and Hersch shared the same dreamy expression, the same half smile on their lips, the same dark eyes looking off together. Their wedding was only a few years ago. I could see Hersch in Zygush's face as he was struggling to make sense of this new world in which he would have no father.

I was beginning to understand that when we grieve, we not only grieve for the loss of a loved one but also for the part of us that is lost with them. The Hassids say that we perform the mourner's *Kaddish* for the prescribed eleven months because the souls of the departed linger, still hungry for those they have left behind; with words unspoken and deeds undone; with the spark of their transgressions still burning. It is only with *Kaddish* over that period of time that they will understand that our love and devotion is enough to free their souls to ascend to Heaven.

We were all in a state of shock. Hersch Leib was the third member of our family to die and we knew there would be more. Uchka was heartbroken, but brave. Without a husband and with two small children to support, Uchka needed to earn a living. She borrowed some money from my father to start a used-clothing business. She would sell Jewish clothes to non-Jews.

As the summer wore on, we started to emerge from our state of numbness. Uchka had such a good reputation that women were now coming from other towns to buy from her. Mania and I were together more than we had ever been in our lives, but we rarely went out of our front door. Like Papa, we travelled from one backyard to another, passing through fences where we had pulled out the nails so we could move the slats. We'd either go to my friend Genya's house or down to the orphanage three backyards away where we'd play with the children. I read anything I could get my hands on.

As desperate as we were, I knew we were privileged: we were together, we had enough to eat, we lived in a rich town. The elders in the Judenrat had come to an arrangement with the commandant of the SS in Lvov. Almost every Saturday, month after month, the commandant drove to Zolkiew to collect his tribute. Jewels. Gold. Coins. Ingots. Family silver. Watches.

Fabric. Furs. Lumber. Clothing. Stamps. Art. Rare books. Somehow we scraped enough to buy us another month. Others weren't as fortunate. Town after town around us was being decimated; the inhabitants either slaughtered or moved to ghettos in Lublin or Lvov. We knew that our safety was a matter of whim. We were in the eye of the storm.

In the autumn, Mama decided we needed to learn and she organized a school. There were five or six girls: Mania, me, and my friends Giza, Genya, Klara and Lipka. We met in a different house every day for our safety. We studied Hebrew with Gershon Taffet, mathematics with a famous university professor from Warsaw who had fled to Zolkiew. We even had Latin. I don't think any of us studied harder in our lives then we did in those months.

When the United States entered the war after Pearl Harbor in December 1941, there was a burst of optimism that died within weeks. The American involvement changed nothing for us in Zolkiew. By February 1942, there was nothing left in Zolkiew with which to bribe the SS. The commandant had bled us dry. On 25 March, every category-C man and his family was herded like swine down the mansion-lined street that led to the train station. The cattle cars were waiting for them. The Nazis were sending them to the camps. Mama saw it all. She told us that the streets were red with blood. Those not moving fast enough were shot on the spot. From the balcony of the biggest mansion on the street, the wife of the head of the Gestapo was pulling out her hair and screaming, 'Who will pay for this? Who will pay for all this?' She knew there would be a day of retribution. At least a dozen girls I knew from school were on that transport. I didn't know how to begin to mourn them.

Sooner or later everyone would share the same fate as that

of the category Cs. But we didn't know exactly what that meant. Nobody knew where the train was headed. Somebody, I don't know who, hired some peasants to follow the train. They reported back a few days later, telling us that the train had stopped near Belzec, where the Nazis had built a camp in the deep woods. They said they couldn't get near the camp because there were too many soldiers. Although they were still kilometres away, they said they could smell the stench of burning bodies.

There were no more illusions for us. Every family we knew was trying to find a way to get out of Zolkiew, either with false documents, or escaping to Romania or Hungary, which hadn't been overrun by the Nazis. We continued to live our day-to-day lives, but we knew that time was running out. The oil press would not save us for ever. Mania would not let up on Mama and Papa. She drove my parents crazy.

'Papa, Papa, please, stop ... listen to me. We need a hiding place. We need to find a way to get out of here. Papa, please, tell me we'll get out of here ...'

My poor father was trying to get papers, trying to find a place to hide or a way out, but without success. I could see the pain in his face as he listened to Mania's incessant demands. 'Enough! Please, Mania.'

'Did you find something? Did you find something? Just tell me, just tell me we'll get out.'

'I'm doing everything I can.'

'What does that mean? What does it mean, Papa? Does it mean we'll get out, or does it mean we'll die trying?'

She would be waiting for him when he came home from work with an expectant look in her eyes, hoping. Every time someone managed to escape, she would tell Mama and Papa. It wasn't information, but an accusation.

Hiding, escaping, papers cost a fortune. I didn't know how much money we had, but I knew that the underground business had been making the three families rich. The Melmans and the Patrontasches saved their money. But Mama was spending as fast as Papa could make it, buying food and running the soup kitchen to feed the refugees as well as the poorer Jews who had already run out of money. The town was starving. The Judenrat had a soup kitchen, but it wasn't enough for Mama, who started one of her own. We had a gigantic pot, almost as big as the stove, which we usually used to boil our sheets to make them white. Every day Mama would make soup in this giant pot with buckwheat groats from my father's press and whatever else she could buy and put it out on the back porch above the stairs. Mania and I were her helpers. The hungry came, lining up for hours before the soup was ready.

Mrs Mandlova, one of Mama's closest friends, saw the crowd outside our door and cried, 'Salka, the Gestapo!'

Mama simply said, 'If God wants to strike me dead for feeding the hungry, then let Him.'

My father begged, argued, reasoned, but she was stubborn as Dzadzio, although she would always deny it.

Mania and I now devoted all our time to helping other Jews. School had become a luxury since the category-C transport. There was a war and we could not sit in the false security of our house while other Jews suffered. Over the course of the winter and spring, there were more and more transports. Soon there was a train every day that would pass through Zolkiew on the Lvov–Lublin line. After each train *skoczki* – jumpers – would wander into town. Teenage boys patrolled the tracks near the station for injured jumpers. Those who were near death, sometimes with broken bones protruding from their skin, were taken to Pepka Fisch. But often the jumpers had perished in the fall;

entire families would be found scattered over hundreds of metres; sometimes dead mothers were found with living children in their arms.

Mania and I started to work with Pepka. I had learned a lot during my time in the hospital the year before. As soon as I was able to get around, I had wandered the hospital following the nurses, trying to be useful, watching and learning. When I started with Pepka, I wasn't squeamish like some of the other girls. I was soon doing the work of a nurse. The stories the jumpers told were simply too horrible to believe or comprehend. Yet the truth was sitting before me, bloodied, terrified, broken. There was a death camp at Oswiecim, a small town less than 150 kilometres north-west of us. A report on the radio claimed a million Jews had already been killed. Special SS death squads were murdering thousands of Jews at a time. I listened to the stories that fell from their lips like poisoned prophecies.

Pepka was tireless and quickly earned a good reputation. Some jumpers had been told to try their luck near Zolkiew because they had heard about the hunchbacked nurse who was as good as any doctor at setting bones. We learned to make splints and bandage and clean wounds. One day my friend Genya Astman came running to the house and said I had to get to Pepka's right away. A jumper named Hela Ornstein and her mother were there. I couldn't believe they were alive after jumping off a train. Mrs Ornstein's face was half torn away. Genya's family took the two of them in.

In June 1942, Josek and Rela had a baby boy. Handsome Josek, the family Don Juan, had surprised us first by marrying a plain girl with a big heart, and then again last winter when they had announced Rela was pregnant. We were stunned that anyone would think to have a child. But no one said a word to her. Their son was named Moshele. The baby was healthy and blond with blue eyes. We couldn't resist having a small family celebration, and a *bris* eight days later to circumcise the child, as is prescribed by our law. My mother had baked a honey cake, the traditional sweet to celebrate a birth. A sweet life; that's what the honey cake was supposed to ensure. The party was lavish. If we had known, if only we had known what would come, we would never have celebrated his *bris* and marked him as a Jew. He could have easily passed for an Aryan, and then he would have been spared.

We all loved the baby and couldn't get enough of him, especially Mania and I. There was something about the way he looked at us, just happy to be held by someone who loved him, so content and unaware of the hell he had been born into.

Things were grim. Papa hadn't been able to find a way for us to escape, so he was now searching for someone to hide us. I took refuge with my girlfriends whenever I could. Giza Landau lived several streets away, and it was too dangerous for her to come and visit. But there was Genya, Libka, Muschka and Klara Letzer nearby, and still alive. One day at Genya's house, we realized that we were the last of our group. We had already lost so many friends, and we were discussing which one of us would be next to die. We mourned the fact that we had nothing, not one photo, to remember our friends by. We decided to go to Mr Domanski and get our pictures taken to have something to remember each other by. We wanted a token of our friendship to survive the war, even if we didn't. But as I left my house to go to the studio a boy called me a dirty Jew on the street. I was terrified and went back inside. When we eventually went, Mania schlepped along with us. She didn't want to miss anything, even having what would perhaps be her last photograph taken. We decided not to dress up, but we braided each other's hair. We had a group picture taken as well as individual portraits of each of us. Mr Domanski had the prints for us the next day. I was shocked at the picture. I had been trying to smile, but I wasn't. It was the only picture of me in which I wasn't smiling. We sat in Genya's living room and exchanged the pictures, writing our names and the date on the back. We thought about writing a message on each picture, but what was there to say?

Papa hadn't been able to find anyone to help hide us. Neither had the Melmans or the Patrontasches. Having run out of options, the three men decided they needed to build a temporary hiding place in the crawl space under the Melmans' house. Their house was the biggest of the three and would hopefully be able to hold all of us. Mr Patrontasch, who was a wonderful carpenter, built a jigsawed trapdoor in the bedroom's parquet floor. When the door was in place, the seam, like the opening to a Chinese box, was impossible to find. The crawl space was too small for the grown-ups to enter so Mania and I, and Igo Melman and Klarunia Patrontasch, who were both eight, inched our way through the tight space. Our job was to hollow out a passageway to the far corner of the house where we would be able to dig a pit large enough for all of us to hide in.

It was high summer and hot in the crawl space. There was no ventilation, so we were dressed only in our underwear. Mania and the other children always ran around in their undergarments through the baking hot days of summer, but I was modest and never took off my dress. Not once. But I had no choice now, it was just too hot otherwise.

We dug for two weeks straight with our hands and then with pots and pans and shovels. My hands looked like those of a peasant, raw with blisters and broken fingernails, dirt wedged under the nails and tattooed in the lines of my palms. We had to dig to Mr Patrontasch's exact specifications. We couldn't take the dirt outside, so we had to lay it out evenly all over the rest of the crawl space. We worked by the light of kerosene lamps, which fought us for every molecule of oxygen. There were times I almost passed out. There were times I wanted to stop and weep. There were times when the dirt walls seemed to be caving in on me while I dug. I wished I was dreaming and would wake up with the lovely breeze of a summer morning cooling my sheets and pillow. But this wasn't a playhouse and I was no longer a child.

We were proud of the work we had done and yet looked at it with terror. The bunker was three metres square and a metre and a half deep. There was just enough space for the ten of us to lie next to each other. In the event that anyone should become aware of the trapdoor in the bedroom floor and enter the crawl space to look for evidence of people hiding, Mr Patrontasch designed a cover to disguise the underground bunker perfectly. First he constructed a square of wood, three by three metres square. On each of the four sides he attached planks a third of a metre deep, which made the cover look like an empty sandbox. We then filled the box with dirt and, when we were done, placed it over the bunker. It fit exactly. Once it was in place we couldn't tell the cover from the dirt floor. We had built a tomb. Inside it we placed matches, candles and water.

Our time was running out. Some nights Papa would come home from the factory almost in tears. The fact that Mama continued to spend money on the soup kitchen threw him into a panic. Mania and I would be in our beds, listening to the same argument, again and again. It was an argument born of despair rather than anger. The words weren't spiteful or meant to hurt; I had never heard Papa's voice so desperate. He was worried about our future and having the means to save our lives. 'Salka, Salka, you're killing me. As fast as I make it, you spend it. And more!'

'We should eat when someone's hungry?'

'The Judenrat runs a soup kitchen.'

'Oh well, we both know that there's not enough to go around. They do the best they can, but their soup is like water. I don't think you'd sit still and be happy if all Clara and Mania had was a bowl of watery soup a day. And what about the dozens of families too proud to beg? To go to the soup kitchens? They should go hungry too? Why? Because the men would rather see their children starve than accept charity. You'll make more money.'

'Salka!'

'No more "Salka"! If God wants to strike me dead for feeding the poor, then let Him. In fact, I dare Him to!' It was what she said to anyone who suggested she stop.

That was the end of the argument. Papa knew there was no talking to my mama. My aunt Giza had said that she was a *tzadakess*, a righteous person, and God would protect us because of her.

Once they stopped yelling and everything went quiet, Mania and I would fall asleep. Me in the same thick, dark mahogany bed that was as sturdy as any ship, under the same goose-down comforter that was so light it seemed to float like a cloud when you shook it out to make the bed. Mania lay in the little baby bed, in which she looked like a big doll. We looked out through lace curtains at our fruit trees. And despite the fact that we lived in a different world during the day, sleeping side by side brought us close in a way in which words are almost superfluous, perhaps even redundant. How could nothing, nothing be out of place in this house and outside the world be so upside down?

Mania wanted to talk. 'I've been thinking about going to the nuns. Lots of our friends have already gone.'

'I know.'

'We'll be safe,' my sister argued. 'Mama and Papa want us to be safe.'

'I know they want us to be safe. But I'm not sure about going to the nuns.'

Mania was capable of making big decisions, of rash actions, of decisive and independent thought. I was used to living in this protected cocoon of a world where Mama and Papa made all the major decisions for me. I was content not to question because I knew they loved me and had my best interests at heart. But now, in this ever-shifting world, Papa seemed over-whelmed. To go with the nuns would mean perhaps to lose them, perhaps for ever. 'I don't know. I don't know if I want to leave Mama and Papa.'

'Clara, everybody's disappearing. Everybody's going some place. We're being murdered at every corner. We know what happens at the camps! We know what's happened in other places!'

Mania was honest, blunt and direct as always. If we wanted to go to the nuns, I know my parents would allow it. The deci-sion was now mine to make. We lay awake a long time that night, but we didn't say much more. Mania's proposition was a weight on my chest and it crushed all the air out of my lungs so it was hard to breathe. Whatever happened, it would happen to us as a family.

Shortly after that argument, the summer ended and the Nazis ordered us out of our house. We moved into Uchka's tiny house, where she lived with Hersch Leib's aunt, who raised him after his parents died. We didn't talk about it; just like we hadn't said anything to Josek about Rela having a baby. It was simply too painful to talk about. We didn't sleep at Uchka's, however. We started sleeping at the Melmans' and going back to Uchka's during the day. The Patrontasches slept there as well. We wanted to be prudent since we knew the Nazis preferred to come early in the morning, hoping to catch their prey disoriented and vulnerable.

Papa spent all of September and October still trying to find someone to take us in. Even with all the families we had helped over the years, all the families we had employed, all the farmers we had given credit to and whose grain we had milled for nothing in hard times, we couldn't find one person to help us. We understood their reasons and didn't think any less of them. Josek and Rela were in the same situation as us. We built a bunker under the factory in case they would be forced to hide there. At least Uchka had managed to find a Polish family named Skibicki willing to take her and the children in. It was a relief to know that they would be safe.

There were rumours of an *akcja* – a mass deportation or a slaughter. I don't know where the rumours started or how they got to us. The town was full of rumours. Mr Patrontasch was an insomniac and seemed never to sleep at all. One day, 22 November, when we were still at the Melmans', I woke up to Mr Patrontasch screaming, 'Get ready! I just saw two trucks and the Gestapo and the Jewish Police! From Lvov! They're heading into town.'

While we scrambled to wake up and put on our shoes, he ran out again and came back just a moment later. 'It's an *akcja*! They're driving us up the street!'

I heard gunshots and the Gestapo running and yelling. Mr Melman ran out to warn his friends, the Britwitzes next door. They were sitting at their table, eating breakfast. They also had a bunker, but the Gestapo was already banging on the front door. Mr Britwitz held his front door closed with his body until the family had time to hide. Then he let go and started running down the street away from the house. The Gestapo shot him, but his family was safe. Mr Melman was lucky to get out and safely slip back into his own house undetected.

We didn't have time to run to the hiding place in the factory. Instead we all crawled through the bedroom trapdoor to the tomb under the Melmans' house. The darkness was suffocating. We couldn't burn the candles we had stored; there wasn't enough oxygen to keep them lit. I had never sat in the bunker even for a minute while digging. I wasn't prepared for the closeness, the terrifying darkness and the smell of damp earth I inhaled with the thick air. As the bunker heated up with the warmth of ten bodies, my pores opened and sweat soaked my clothes until they clung to me, like a second skin.

We stayed there for two days, with no pail for our refuse, a few pieces of bread and a little water. There wasn't room enough to move. When things seemed calm upstairs, Mr Melman and Mr Patrontasch crawled outside to see what was happening. They scrambled back after just a few minutes. The *akcja* was still on. They had killed Mr Lockman, a neighbour who tried to escape. We sat another night in the bunker. At dawn, Mr Patrontasch's younger brother Laibek walked by the house. He knew we were in here and whispered that it was over and that the train had left already. We sat for another hour to be sure before going out.

Our city was in desperate mourning. Carriages loaded with dead bodies were taken to the cemetery. Everyone was in shock as they described family members who had been killed while trying to run. Or else they had been shot trying to get up when they were told to kneel in the centre of the town. Or they had been shot while jumping off the trains. Or else they had been shot when betrayed by the Poles whom they had begged to hide them.

Aunt Rela lost her mother, brother and sister-in-law. Mr Patrontasch lost his youngest sister Pepka (the girl Josek had flirted with before marrying Rela) and her child. She had been running to the house of a Polish friend who had promised to hide her, but the friend didn't let her in when she got there. Papa's friend, Mr Taube, saw her lying in a puddle of blood. They went for her body, but couldn't find her again. My friend Klara Letzer and her family were taken, but she and her mother had managed to jump off the train and make it back. Her father was shot and killed as he tried to escape.

We were thankful that all of us had survived, but didn't know what to do next. It was only a matter of time before they returned to get those they had missed. Mania looked at Papa. Even she didn't have a word to say. The nuns were just up the street. We could see the steeple of the convent from where we were. But we didn't talk about the nuns any more. Our only hope was to find a Polish family willing to take us. But my father had already exhausted that avenue again and again.

We went back to Uchka's. She was in the same bad straits as we were. After the *akcja*, the family that was going to hide her had gotten cold feet. But she told us that one of her Polish clients from another town had offered to take Zosia, thinking that she could pass for a Polish child without any trouble at all. The woman loved Zosia because she was such a delightful little girl. Uchka gave Zosia to the woman at the train station, and was going to spend the night in Lvov before travelling to her home town. Zosia cried and cried as she was separated from her mother. Uchka felt as if her heart was ripped out, but she was grateful to know her daughter would be safe.

The next morning the woman brought Zosia back to Uchka. Zosia had sobbed all night and couldn't be consoled, she said. She wanted her mother.

While my father looked in vain for a place for us, the Nazis announced they had taken Stalingrad, the city Stalin named in his own honour and the very symbol of the Soviet empire. Papa knew the Soviets had to defend this city with all their might. If Stalingrad fell, there would be no hope for us.

A new decree followed shortly thereafter. All the Jews in Zolkiew were ordered to be in the ghetto by the first of December, only a week away. We knew the ghetto would be the end of us. There was nowhere to hide there. Two days after the decree, there was a knock on Uchka's door in the evening. Papa opened it to find Pavluk standing on the step. He was a strong man whose giant hands were curled around his hat. His pants were shabby and he wore a soiled homespun linen shirt. He had one of those big moustaches that so many of the Ukrainian peasants had. Pavluk was a murderer. After being released from jail he had come to the factory looking for a job. Papa had gone to my grandfather to ask his advice. Dzadzio hadn't hesitated for a second. He said, 'Hire the man. I promise you, you will have a grateful man your entire life.'

Pavluk told Papa he wanted to hide us. Papa didn't say a word. He just took Pavluk's hand and invited him into the house.

'Thank you. You don't know what this means to us. But we can't.'

I didn't understand why Papa was refusing the offer. Mama, Mania and me all looked at each other and at him. I could see the protest forming on my sister's lips. Her dark eyes expressed the most profound disappointment. Papa went on in a kind voice: 'You have six children, Pavluk. And your house. Two rooms with no place for us to hide.' As much as we wanted him to say yes, we knew Papa was right. We couldn't put six children at risk. Out of all the Poles and Ukrainians that my family knew and had helped for generations, Pavluk was the only one who had come forward to help us.

Pavluk was upset that he hadn't properly thought through his plan for our survival. He muttered, 'I want to do something, anything to help.' Mama was moved by his sadness. Even though we had already put everything of value we had left behind the stuccoed false wall in the basement of our spinster neighbours, Mama gave him two down pillows and a feath-erbed to keep for us.

Our down bedding would survive the Nazis.

Chapter 3

THE HOUSEKEEPER

End November to the beginning of December 1942

There are terrible tragedies, unbelievable tragedies... a stone would cry, but I'm sorry to say, the Gestapo is not touched by Jewish tears. They shoot at the people who jump indiscriminately, old or child... Carriages bring dead bodies that were killed on the spot trying to run, or trying to get up when they were told to kneel in the centre of the city. Also the people who were killed while jumping off the train and the ones that were betrayed by the gentiles.

*

There was nothing more to do. There were just a few days left. We would have to find a place in the ghetto. My father's brother David had found a studio, but he had six children and there would be no room for another four.

Aunt Giza had gotten married to a man named Meyer. They had left Zolkiew for the tiny little farming town of Mosty Wielke. There was a work camp there that was considered safe. The German commandant Krupp protected the Jews. He made sure they had enough to eat and that they lived as normal a life as possible.

Josek and Rela had found a place to live in the ghetto, but they were afraid for their little Moshele. Thankfully, because of his fair skin and blond curls, they were able to find a Polish peasant named Sluka who was prepared to take Moshele in exchange for money. Josek had secured a job as a Jewish policeman, which would allow him to leave the ghetto and check on their son. Uchka and the children were going to live with Hersch's aunt, who had found a place on Turiniecka Street, which marked the border of the ghetto. One side of the street was the ghetto. The other side belonged to the Poles and Ukrainians. We were all packing, and Papa did all he could, searching everywhere for somewhere we could hide.

It was late November, Uchka's yard was barren and the house exposed. Through the window I could see Bolek, a boy from school, coming down the lane with his horse and cart made from scavenged wooden planks. Bolek was a year ahead of me and his sister, Anka, was in my class. They were both small for their age, a couple of pixies with reddish hair, green eyes and noses covered with freckles. I was surprised when he stopped the old horse in front of Uchka's house. He jumped down and with the expression of a little man walked into the house. Bolek didn't say 'Hello, Clara' or even acknowledge with his eyes that I was there when he stopped right in front of me. He simply picked up a wicker trunk that held our belongings and carried it out as if he were retrieving something that belonged to him. He loaded it on to his cart, which was already filled with dressers, trunks, lamps, chests, rugs, beds and bedding.

We watched with resignation. There was nothing we could do. Bolek could have done whatever he liked with us. This child, no bigger than a Bar Mitzvah boy and with skin as smooth as a girl's, could have just as easily come in and beaten or shot us. Nobody would have lifted a finger. Without thinking, I followed him outside. I surprised myself when I heard my voice asking, 'Please, Bolek, there's a wooden box with pictures in it. Can we keep it?' He hesitated, then opened the trunk and took out the box. He still hadn't said a word, but he finally looked me in the eye. The box was hand-carved from Russian birch and inlaid with an intricate pattern. He could tell how valuable it was. I didn't care about the box's value; I just wanted to keep the photos that proved that our family had once existed in an almost divine state of happiness and love. Our life was all there. The weddings, the *brises*, vacations in the Carpathians, trips to Rosa's in the country. And even the picture of the four of us on our way to Paradise Hill. There were dozens and dozens of photos.

Bolek stared at the box as if it had been in his family for years, and then handed it down to me. He left with his carriage, stopping at another house down the street. This theft was just one more humiliation in the chain that started with the armbands and there seemed like there would be no end to it.

Only a few days after Bolek we had another Polish visitor, while Papa was out again. We were surprised to see Basia, one of Uchka's Polish friends, at the door. It was dangerous to be outside on the silent streets by oneself. Nobody went out now unless they had to. Uchka was so happy to see a friend that she insisted on making her tea... Of course the conversation quickly turned to matters of life and death. The house was so small that we could hear every word. Basia seemed to be mourning the death of so many Jewish friends. She said that she would be inconsolable if anything should happen to Uchka or the children. 'If something were to happen, I would be so grateful to have something to remember you by. The bedroom set maybe...'

I could hear Uchka exhale. It seemed as though she couldn't speak. Basia went on: 'The Nazis would just take it.'

Mama and I saw Uchka drag Basia by her neck to the door and throw her down the steps.

Mama cried out, shaking her sister by the shoulders: 'What have you done! Why did you do that?'

Uchka said in Yiddish, 'I have to take it from the Nazis, but I don't have to take it from that piece of shit!'

I had never seen my mother this frightened. Nobody dared talk about what had just happened. Mama went back to the kitchen to continue making her soup in silence.

When Papa rushed in the door later that afternoon, he was talking way too fast for us to understand. He stopped to catch his breath and slowed down to tell us that Julia Beck and her husband had agreed to hide us, the Melmans and the Patrontasches. We couldn't believe what we were hearing. The Becks of all people. We hadn't even considered approaching them because Mr Beck had such a bad reputation. My parents discussed the implications of going under their protection. I had never met Beck. Everything I knew about him I had picked up from whispered conversations. He was a drunk. A philanderer. Couldn't hold on to a job. Owed money to everyone and never paid back a zloty. He was also reputed to be an anti-Semite. Could we risk putting our lives in the hands of a man who was known for a vicious tongue, his anti-Semitism, for his affection for drink and his failed businesses?

The decision was made to accept their offer. We knew that hiding only meant a reprieve. But we didn't have any other alternative, and we trusted Julia Beck. She had been our housekeeper, and her mother had been my grandmother's before that. Once to twice a month she would come to our home and stay for as long as three days, or however long it took to get the laundry washed and the rugs beat. She was a tiny woman but a tireless worker. Together with Mama, she would boil the kilos of sheets and laundry in huge pots and then crank them through the wringer by hand. It was hard work, and it had taken its toll on Julia, whose hands had been worn raw and were now also tortured by arthritis. Mama didn't see Julia as a maid; she was a helping hand whom we could gratefully afford for many years. She and Mama would chat for hours as they worked, but I was spared, and would usually sneak off to read a book by myself. I had probably never said more than five words to her in my entire life, but now, as we embraced, I wished Julia were with us so I could embrace her too. We hadn't seen her since we had to let her go after the Russians came. And now this Polish woman and her *Volksdeutscher* husband were saving our lives. It might be an hour, a day or a month. But in that hour, day or month, something else might happen. The war might end. Papa might find papers. Something. Some miracle I couldn't even imagine.

But our good fortune would be ours alone. The invitation hadn't been extended to Uchka and the kids. Up until that moment our good fortune was their good fortune. If we would be saved, they would be saved. Dear God, how we could make such decisions… I looked at my little cousins and my heart broke with love for them. They didn't understand. How could they? In all our hearts, we knew there was no other choice. It wasn't our decision to make. Very young children couldn't be counted on to be quiet and would put the Becks and the others in danger. There was no argument or discussion. Uchka and the children would have to go to the ghetto. There was nothing we could do.

We were quiet now while Papa explained the details of what had been decided. We would expand the partially built bunker under the Melmans' house. Since Beck was ethnic German he could choose any house he wanted. Beck had gone to the

German housing authority and said he wanted the Melmans' house. Without a word of discussion, he was given the house. It was that simple.

Papa was suddenly confident again. Papa suggested that the Becks start a rumour that we went to the Janowska camp in Lvov because we heard there was work there. We hoped the authorities would not get suspicious because it would be easy for them to check if this rumour was the truth or a ruse.

Not having to go to the ghetto filled us all with more energy than we had had in the last 18 months. My father, Mr Melman and Mr Patrontasch were very smart men and watching them applying their intellects to our survival allowed me to feel like a girl and a daughter again. I could once more look into the dark eyes of my father and feel the warmth of his protection. Feeling that our survival was back in our own hands restored a sense of dignity to us all.

It was only a few days before everyone had to report to the ghetto. Uchka's tiny lane was busy with families, moving what was left of their belongings on pushcarts past us in a slow migration. Their lives had been reduced to what could be carried in their suitcases. Their faces were blank. They dared not look at the uniformed soldiers with the death's head on their collars who seemed to be everywhere.

Throughout Zolkiew, almost as if by edict, old people went to the ghetto and allowed the young to hide. Parents said what they knew might be their final goodbyes to their children and grandchildren as they entered the ghetto and their children entered whatever hiding places they might find. Parents' final gift and their legacy to their children was to take away the burden of their care and the threat to their survival. Honoured, beloved parents would not allow themselves to enter the promised land of the bunkers or to eat a precious crust of bread that might mean life or death for their children. If their children had to run, they wouldn't be slowed down by parents who might be too weak even to walk. Poor Dzadzio was dead, but Babcia was alive in Kazahkstan and our family was spared the awful decision the Patrontasches were forced to make. While the Nazis and the SS revelled in their courage behind their machine guns, which they pointed at the unarmed and the defenceless, they had no idea of the real courage all around them as family after family said their silent farewells. As we had to live with the shadow of Uchka and her children, the Patrontasches had to live with the shadows of their parents, and Mr Melman with those of his half-brothers Hermann and Gedalo.

Eleven of us would be living under the floor: the four of us; the Melmans and their son Igo; the Patrontasches and their daughter Klarunia, and Mr Patrontasch's widowed sister Klara. Klara and Julia were best friends and Mama thought that it had been she who had convinced Beck to take us in.

I was happy and grateful that Klara was coming. Klara was one of the most beautiful women I had ever seen, but her beauty was tinged with sadness since she had lost both her husband and daughter. Her husband had died a year after Luncia was born. Luncia had been the only child in the house and there was nothing that money or love could buy in Zolkiew and even Lvov that wasn't bestowed on her. She was the good, sweet child that every parent wanted. We had been best friends until she died in the diphtheria epidemic of 1938 that swept through Eastern Europe. Klara had had to watch her child slowly suffocate to death.

Mama had felt the burial of one of my best friends would be too distressing for me and so she left me in bed that day. But the procession passed in front of our house and woke me up. Mama reluctantly said I could go as far as the synagogue. Klara walked next to her daughter's coffin. Because of the epidemic and the fact that so much time had passed between her death and the funeral, Mr Patrontasch had had to put Luncia in a wooden coffin, which was then placed inside another coffin made of zinc. Klara was afraid that Luncia's soul would not ascend to Heaven. She was surrounded by her family, Mama and Julia Beck, who were there to catch her should she collapse. I held Mama's hand; I could barely see where I was walking through all my tears. I had known people who had died, but Luncia's death brought me grief, mourning, heartbreak and loss for the first time. Everybody said a part of Klara died when her husband died and now the rest of her was gone too.

Klara was also one of Mama's best friends and after Luncia died Mama wouldn't walk down the block, go to a store or visit a friend without running across the street to take Klara with her. For a long time after Luncia's death, when I saw Klara across the street, Mama told me to hide, to keep out of sight, because Mama didn't want her to be reminded of Luncia.

There was much to do for us to make the bunker inhabitable for eleven people. The men sent Mania, me, Igo and little Klarunia back underground, where we started digging now with even more fury to open up the crawl space between the trapdoor hatch and the original bunker. The air was cold and damp and my fingers were numb but after only minutes we would be sweating again.

Mr Patrontasch was concerned that the floor above would collapse and bury us alive. Papa and the other men cut down a tree in the Melmans' backyard, which they fashioned into columns to support the ceiling. He told us how to dig shelves into the walls. Mr Melman cut planks to fit the shelf space. Every family had identical shelf space. We brought down old enamel, tin plates, two pots and a frying pan. Nobody wanted to bring anything of value to a hole in the ground, except Mrs Melman who brought with her a lovely earthenware pitcher and a few other reminders of her life upstairs. Through a small hole drilled into the floor behind the Becks' bed, Papa drew a wire into the basement. We would have light and a spiral clay hotplate. When there was a search, he would be able to pull the plug down through the hole. He also calculated the exact amount of electricity the Melmans' house would use in all seasons. He knew how to rig the meter so the authorities wouldn't be aware this house was burning more electricity than normal. Mania, I and the other children stuffed straw into mattresses. Mr Patrontasch took precise measurements of the bunker and worked out where we would all sleep.

We were frightened of lice and typhus and knew that our survival depended on keeping as clean as we could, despite the dirt we would be living in. Mama said Mania and I had to cut our hair to avoid catching lice. We both had hair that went almost to our waists, which each morning was put into a long braid and each night was brushed till our arms hurt. We all wept as Mama took a pair of scissors and cut the braids off. There was no need for beautiful hair; it was a threat to our survival. My mother placed our braids in shoeboxes lined with tissue paper, corpses in tiny coffins, like a child might bury a pet kitten or a bird.

Over several nights, we would wait an hour after every house on the street had gone dark, and would move our belongings to the Melmans' house. Beck was waiting for us at the door, his eye up and down the street. We didn't speak at all as he led us to the bedroom where we slipped down into the bunker and arranged our things. Then, again without a word, we would slip out the door and retrace our way through the quiet and deserted lanes back to Uchka's.

I had hardly seen this Valentin Beck before, and yet we were trusting our lives to him, and we were grateful to do so. As gaunt as Julia, with light, wolf blue, bloodshot eyes, and cheeks and nose road-mapped with tiny broken purple capillaries, he looked much older than his 40-odd years. He had grey hair and a thin goatee; I thought he looked like the woodcut on my copy of *Don Quixote*.

We had been so busy that the moment we were to leave Uchka and the children came upon me before I realized it. It had been dark for hours, but we wanted to wait until all the lamps had been turned off in every house in the neighbour-hood. We sat in silence, weeping. Mania and I had taken care of Zygush and Zosia every day since Uchka had started her busi-ness selling clothes. I felt like their mother. Zosia clung to me. I could not look into her eyes without weeping and yet I could not look away. Such was our grief that we were without shame. This was the only life Zosia and Zygush had ever known. I had memories to cling to. But what could Zygush and Zosia cling to? What did they know of this life except hunger and fear?

Nobody said it would take a miracle if we ever saw each other again. As we kissed Uchka and the children, nobody said this might be the last embrace, the last goodbye, the last time I would feel Uchka's soft hands on my cheeks. My father moved the curtain one more time and looked out. All he did was nod and get up. It was time. We disengaged like mourners after a funeral. As we walked out of the door that my father held open, I looked back and there was Uchka. Uchka, who in better times couldn't stop smiling, was smiling once more. From the bottom of her heart it told us she was thanking God that we had this chance.

Papa again led us through the tiny back alleys. The neigh-bourhood was deeply silent. Not a person spoke or a radio played. I used to love being out at night once the houses had gone dark and the sky swallowed everything up in its vastness.

Starlit nights were magical, with a carpet of lights that staggered the imagination of a young girl. But tonight I didn't look up. I didn't know if the night was dark or moonlit or starry. All I took in was the beat of my own heart and the sound of my shoes on the cold earth. It seemed to take an eternity to reach the Melmans' house. I felt like I had left the better part of my life with Uchka and the children. I could not believe I was walking away from them.

Beck was waiting at the back door of the house and had it opened for us as we slipped inside. He smiled and shook my father's hand. His daughter Ala was with him. I had seen her but never met her before. She was 18 and pretty, and if harbouring Jews under the floor was a problem she looked absolutely unconcerned by it. She had brown hair, styled like a city girl, and welcomed us, also with a smile. Julia was behind them as well. This was a house I had been in hundreds of times. It was filled with beautiful dark furniture and Mrs Melman always made sure the parquet floors were polished until they shone like mirrors. Her china, hand painted, was in the breakfront, which also contained the tiny china dolls; ballerinas and Dalmatians, shepherd girls with their sheep; almost an entire world that she had collected over the years. But it wasn't the Melmans' house any more and I felt alien in it. The Becks had been there only a matter of days, but their presence filled it now. Without much conversation, we walked through the kitchen and into the hall. There was one lamp on, otherwise it was dark. In the bedroom the big mahogany bed had been moved back and the trapdoor that Mr Patrontasch had made was open. The others were already there, only Klara was missing. She had gone to the ghetto with her parents to make sure that they were properly settled before joining us.

I had gone down into the bunker many times. I had built it. But going down that night was different. I didn't care about the dirt. I didn't care about how close it would be with the other families. I didn't care about the lack of a proper bathroom. I didn't care that I wouldn't go to school or see the sun or run in the streets. That life was gone. All I wanted was for that trap-door to be shut, the carpet to be rolled back and that big heavy wooden bed to be put in place. I wanted to be locked in. I wanted to have back the feeling that tomorrow I would wake and not worry that someone was trying to kill me.

As we crawled down into the bunker, the little light was on and the other families were there, sitting on their pallets, not saying a word. They were getting used to the silence, to not speaking unless it was necessary. Besides, what kind of small talk could we have?

Now that we were in the bunker, the three men had to decide whether or not to bring the Torah down with us. As soon as the Russians invaded Zolkiew, my father had hidden the Torah in the attic of Mr Melman's house where there was a reservoir, encased in wood, for the water pumped up from the well in the backyard. The men had wrapped the Torah in a tarpaulin to keep it dry and placed it in the reservoir on a shelf above the water, where it had stayed for the last three years.

We would be underground but we would still pray, and for the men, for all of us, to have the Torah near us would be a balm. The decision was taken to leave the precious scroll safe in its hiding place, but its close presence would console us. Only someone like my father who was an Orthodox Jew and lived his religion with every breath could understand what having this Torah near us would mean.

Sitting in the dim light of a single bulb in which we were all mere shadows, it was impossible to consider anything other than a feeling of safety, or the illusion of a feeling of safety. How long would we be here? Would we survive? Would someone find out? Would the Becks be betrayed? Would we be discovered? I tried to put all those thoughts aside and be grateful to this family who were risking their lives to save ours. Did Beck and Julia have a conversation about the danger to Ala? Did they ask her about it?

There was nothing left to say. Mr Patrontasch turned the light out. I was lying next to Mania. We were afraid even to whisper to each other that first night. In the darkness, I could only think of Uchka and the children in the ghetto. I prayed for them, the first of many prayers I would offer up on their behalf. But what good would prayers do when we were here in safety and they were not. I knew all the reasons, the brutal logic why they couldn't be with us. But knowledge is never enough. It didn't cease the ache in a heart or stay the incessant haunting sound of our own voice, ricocheting from one part of the mind to another, asking, demanding: why us and not them?

Chapter 4

A GIFT FROM MR BECK

December 1942

The days pass in monotony, one day the same like the other. Downstairs, we make breakfast and supper. Everybody washes once a week in the kitchen upstairs because it's cold downstairs… Christmas Eve, they closed all the windows and doors and they invited us all for dinner. It was wonderful. We sang Christmas carols, we almost forgot all our troubles, but most of all we ate a lot. We had to run down and hide again because somebody knocked on the door.

*

After two days in the bunker the reality of our confinement gripped us. The men's optimism that the war would be over in a matter of weeks was gone. They had thought the German army wouldn't be able to withstand the freezing Russian winter and would retreat. But they had been wrong. The Germans still held Stalingrad and were advancing in the Ukraine and the Crimea.

The men followed the war with the interest and passion of the generals who were actually running it. Beck had an illegal radio in the attic that would result in his execution if found, but he was determined to know what was really happening in the war. He brought Patrontasch up from time to time to listen with him. Beck also brought the newspapers and the men would sit around them in a haze of cigarette smoke, charting the front lines on a map and circling the cities taken with a pen. But very little was happening to encourage us. They came down to tell us about a conference in Tehran where Stalin, Roosevelt and Churchill were meeting to discuss the war. It wasn't clear what they were discussing. Tehran was so far away, it might have been a tale from the Arabian Nights. The only thing close to good news was that the Russians were starting a winter offensive to take back Kiev, 500 kilometres away, and there were reports that the German advance had started to stall. But this was happening so far away. It didn't seem like anything was going to change for us for a long time.

We had prepared to come into the bunker for a few weeks. I hadn't brought more than a few books with me. We hadn't brought enough clothing or food or, most importantly, things for the Becks to sell. Our furs, Mama's jewellery, the Persian carpets, the down comforters and bedding, the family silver and china were all safely hidden behind the false wall in our neighbours' basement. We worried they might be stolen by the Nazis, but who knew if we would ever be able to enjoy them again? We were freezing and not more than 50 metres away was everything we needed to sustain us.

Only Fanka Melman had brought china and silver into the bunker. I understood why she did it. Of course, it was very human for someone to want to have something personal, something of beauty with them. Poor Mrs Melman, driven to living below the floor of her own home. She was a tiny woman and perhaps it was her obsessive affection for her precious water pitcher that made her the object of some derision for us. Mrs Melman's affection for, and devotion to, her pitcher, which would have barely raised an eyebrow in our former life, was now grating. I wanted to break the pitcher at times, smash it, and I'm sure Mama did as well. She laughed and whispered to Mania and me, 'The thing should be in a museum the way she takes care of it.'

Mama would now never say such a thing to Mrs Melman's face, but Mrs Melman knew this was what Mama and everyone else thought about her. Before the war, such a remark would have been taken as some good-natured kidding and kibitzing among the women. I don't know how many times I heard them in our kitchen laughing so hard they're kvetching, they're splitting their sides and they've got to loosen their girdles. If I walked in to see what was so funny, they'd laugh even louder because what they had been discussing was not something for my 'little ears' or ask me when I became such a *koklefl*: a ladle and the slang for busybody.

But more than the lack of comfort or food or even the reality of the war, what gripped my heart and crowded my mind were the blistering recollections of the last ten days, from the *akcja* on 22 November, during which the Nazis murdered three thousand of us, to our frantic search for a protector and our desperate goodbyes to our families. In a town like ours, in the best of times, the death of one of us affected all of us. In our tradition, one death tears the fabric of the world. We were all connected. Through marriage. Through business. Through friendship. Through work. Through the dozens of organizations that sustained our community.

Out of nowhere, Mama looked up at me and said, 'Clara, you're going to write a diary.' I was stunned.

'What for? They're going to kill us anyway.'

'If they kill us, somebody will find the diary and they will know what we went through.'

Mama looked at me. She wanted me to start that moment.

She found one of the pencils Mr Patrontasch used to chart the war and gave it to me. I had nothing to write on, but I didn't even bring that up because I knew it wouldn't make any difference to Mama. This was Salka the Cossack talking. I looked around and picked up one of my books and started writing in the margins. But as soon as I started writing, I embraced the task. It would be a record. It was something for me to do every day, something with purpose. It was a way of fighting back.

While I was quickly filling the margins of my books, in those first weeks, we had to figure out a way for eleven people to live almost on top of each other in a space no larger than a horse stall. A set of rules evolved that had the authority of commandments.

Rule number one: Mr Patrontasch was the only one allowed to open or close the trapdoor. For some reason, when he closed it, the door went smoothly into place without a squeak. When anyone else tried it, the door protested with noises that could mean death.

Rule number two: Privacy and propriety were now things of the past. The 'bathroom' was in the trench around the corner from the main living space. The first time I used the bucket, I was mortified. A few days later, there was no sense of embarrassment.

Rule number three: Always be polite. A new formality emerged in our relationships. We had known each other as long as anyone could remember, but now everyone was a Mr or Mrs, and every request was preceded by 'if you please' and 'would you be so kind…' All this transpired within moments of our arrival.

Rule number four: No complaining. Not about the cold, the damp, the dirt. Mrs Melman made one comment about the filth and the looks she got made the rule clear.

Rule number five: Each family was responsible for their own food and water. We'd take turns to use the hotplate. We wouldn't share. The men felt this would prevent tension among the families.

Rule number six: No talking unless it was absolutely necessary. Even when only the Becks were in the house and there was not an absolute need for silence, it was a matter of discipline. As it was, we could hear the footsteps upstairs like they were inside our own brains and we could also hear the Becks' conversation. The wooden floor above us acted like a sounding board, collecting the sound waves and magnifying them down to us. We could hear every word. We could even hear a light switch go on above our heads. Who knew what our conversations sounded like upstairs? There were neighbours on both sides of us, not more than 10 metres away, and we never would know if they were outside in their yards, or close to the Becks for one reason or another. There was only one way to be sure we would not be discovered: silence.

The main living space we had created was immediately under the Becks' bedroom, and was no more than three square metres and a metre and a third high. The planking of the parquet floor above acted as our ceiling. When we had begun work, it was crisscrossed with generations and generations of spider webs. The recesses that edged the floor above us were used to store our clothes, which we rolled up in bundles and tied with twine. The flagstone foundations, which followed the map of the house room by room, were our walls. Right behind the hatchway to the trapdoor we dug out a space for a wooden plank table, which was used for food preparation and storage. On the wall to the left of the hatchway and along the adjacent wall was our sleeping area. We had made platforms of dirt, which we covered with planks. On top of the planks, we placed our straw mattresses. The Patrontasches were on the wall next to the hatch. The Melmans and our family were on the adjacent wall. During the day, we would roll up the mattresses to give us room to sit and eat with the plates on our laps.

Opposite the hatchway was another flagstone foundation wall, which ran under the centre hallway of the house above. We built another small plank table for a hotplate against the stone wall here. We didn't want the hotplate anywhere near a surface that could catch fire. We had taken out enough of the stones to create a 'doorway' to the corridor between the two support walls, which formed a tunnel, a metre and a half wide, under the hallway above. To the left of the tunnel, we placed our pails for refuse. Further down the tunnel we had made another 'doorway' on the right that led to the original bunker with the dirt cover.

One morning, shortly after Klara joined us, Mr Patrontasch woke up as if his mind was on fire. Without a word he grabbed the shovel and started digging a small hole in the very centre of the bunker.

Nobody said anything but we all watched with curiosity. Anything to break the routine was appreciated, and short, round Mr Patrontasch digging with the fury of the possessed was very much out of the routine. We had our Talmud of understandings down in the bunker. Since we were three families living on top of each other, when one of us scratched their head, dandruff from all filled the air. If one of us set our foot on fire, nobody would have blinked an eye. So for a long time we just watched, through a haze of the men's cigarette smoke, Mr Patrontasch digging with the smile of a self-satisfied genius on his face. His wife, Sabina, couldn't take it any longer. 'I'm not going to even ask what you're doing. Just tell me what you're planning to do with the dirt?' But Mr Patrontasch didn't answer and took out a tape measure, gauging the depth of the hole. He grunted and kept digging.

After a few more shovels, he measured again and, not paying any attention to any of us, he put his feet in the hole and gradually unfolded his squat body until he was standing straight, his head just beneath the roof of the bunker. This could have been a scene from a silent movie. But it wasn't. It was our life. I felt like applauding, and we all had to take our turn standing in the hole. To unfold my body, which had been compressed like a little concertina for days, was a pleasure I was never required to experience before. I wouldn't have got any exercise except for Julia, who thank God brought me and Mania upstairs once a week to help her clean. Scrubbing floors. Cleaning the kitchen. The bathroom. I didn't care. It was all gold to me.

The first time Julia called us upstairs to wax the floors, Mania and I got down on our hands and knees with big sheepskin buffers that went on our hands like mittens. Ala came home from work and saw us on our hands and knees and gave us a smile.

'That's not how it's done.' I wasn't an expert on polishing floors, but I certainly had an idea how it was done. The first thing Ala did was turn on the radio and find a station with dance music. Then she took off her shoes and put her feet in the buffers and started to dance to the swing music on the radio. Mania and I followed her example and we started dancing, alone, with each other, shyly at first, faster, slower, comically, showing off, dancing wildly and madly until we were too exhausted to move another step and the parquet floors gleamed. Julia rewarded us with rolls and with fresh cold water from the well outside. The food I would share with the children downstairs, but the water I savoured for myself.

And once in a great while we went upstairs to wash our hair. I cannot tell you how much pleasure that gave us. The smell of soap and the luxury of hot water were almost too delicious to bear. Julia poured hot water over my head and dug her fingers into my scalp. I wished it would never end. Downstairs, water was measured in teaspoons, and usually cold; we often had to make the choice between drinking and washing. But upstairs a white-tiled wood stove threw off warm dry heat and the smell of fresh baked bread, borscht and mushroom and cheese pirogies filled the air. Even if it was only for a few minutes, it was enough for me.

Our family, with the exception of Mama, who had asthma and a thyroid condition, had always enjoyed the best of health. I used to take this for granted. But with an epidemic in the ghetto, and with eleven of us living on top of each other, washing once a week, breathing in dank, mouldy air, I was concerned about Mama. We had been lucky enough to live with a hospital just on the other side of the backyard, as well as plenty of doctors only a short walk away. But now if there was a medical emergency there would be no doctor, no hospital. We hadn't even an elementary first aid kit. But so far, Mama didn't even have a sniffle or a wheeze. She wasn't hot when we were cold or cold when we were hot. Her throat wasn't sore; her poor muscles didn't ache; her hair wasn't dry or falling out; she wasn't even cranky. All of us were the picture of health.

We had got into the habit of expecting to see Beck once or twice a day. He, not Julia, who couldn't climb into the bunker, brought us our food most of the time. I could tell he enjoyed the company of the men and he loved to talk. But he rarely said much to the children. I was intimidated by him and nervous to be around him, no matter how comfortable he seemed. I was afraid of saying something that might upset him or in any way jeopardize our place in the bunker. Of course, I didn't think I had ever said anything in my entire life to upset a grown-up. That was Mania's job. But I could tell he noticed me and made a silly comment or two about me always having my nose in a book. My reaction was embarrassment. I just wasn't used to strange men talking to me. I was starting to realize just how sheltered I was. The adults I had conversations with were my family, my teachers and friends of my parents. Even though Zolkiew was populated with hundreds of Becks, up close he was as exotic as a lion to me.

In the middle of December, Mama started worrying that we didn't have proper presents to give the Becks for Christmas. We went through our things and nothing seemed good enough. They were risking their lives to save us and we didn't have anything decent to give them.

A few days before Christmas, Mr Beck knocked on the hatch, his blue eyes twinkling with mischief. There was something about this war that spelled adventure to Beck, and if there was anything that gave us hope, it was this sparkling look in his bright if often bloodshot blue eyes. He invited me and Mania, Igo and Klarunia upstairs without telling us why. When we didn't budge, he insisted. 'Hurry, hurry, hurry…' Mania was up in a second. Mr Patrontasch shooed Klarunia up the hatch while Beck leaned down to help us up, one by one. My mind was racing. It was Julia who asked me up to clean. Neither Beck nor Ala ever asked me up. What did he want? Did I have to go? Of course I did, and I let his strong hand haul me up like a sack of grain into the above-ground world of polished parquet floors and oriental carpets where we had once been at home. It felt especially foreign to me today because it was Beck bringing me here and not Julia.

Beck led us out of the bedroom and across the corridor up to the closed bathroom door where Julia and Ala were waiting. With a flourish, Beck opened the door. My eyes went straight to the window that was high enough not to be curtained and filled the eggshell blue room with the melancholy winter light of late afternoon. But a splashing in the tub quickly drew my attention back down. Swimming in the full bathtub was the largest carp I had ever seen. It had to be 8 kilograms. Christmas in Poland without a carp was unthinkable; even the scales were passed out and kept as good-luck charms. This one was a beauty, fat and sleek. The dorsal fins were the bluish grey of dried lavender and the side fins were bright orange and red like Chinese fans. In the years before the war, the streets would be filled with fishmongers with live carp swimming in washbasins, buckets and small tanks, anything that could hold a fish. Little Igo and Klarunia couldn't believe its size. The fish was almost as big as they were. It was too big and good-looking for them to afford. We asked Mr Beck if he had caught the fish.

'Better you shouldn't know.'

Julia was now curious. 'You didn't catch it?'

Beck shook his head. He was either teasing us or he didn't want his wife to know where he got the fish. But she was persistent. 'Where did you get it?'

'From Von Pappen himself.'

We couldn't believe what he was saying. Von Pappen was the German SS commandant, Beck's boss and the most feared man in Zolkiew. It was he who had created the ghetto, ordered the murders, extorted our money. Beck had met him through two of his card buddies, Krueger and Schmidt, who were German policemen. Beck had presented himself to the commandant as a loyal *Volksdeutscher* and Von Pappen had given him the job of overseeing the German army's alcohol supply. It was like giving the fox the keys to the hen house.

Julia persisted. 'A gift from Von Pappen?'

'Not exactly a gift. Let's just say I caught it from the commandant's cook.'

Beck refused to give a straight answer. All he would say was that Von Pappen was without his Christmas carp and we were going to eat it. I didn't know if Beck had got Von Pappen's carp because it was his way of asserting his independence and authority, or simply because it gave him pleasure. Whatever the reason, Mr Beck grew taller in my eyes in that small bathroom.

From my few brief interactions with Beck, I was beginning to understand that he was full of contradictions. He had a reputation for anti-Semitism, but he never acted with anything but friend-ship towards us. The only word I could think of to describe this rough-hewn man was charming. He was charm itself to every one of us. He was not supposed to be educated, but he was a proud patriot and had well-thought-out opinions on everything, which displayed his hatred of the Nazis, the Ukrainians and anyone and everyone who abused their power or authority. To listen to him talk about greedy landowners and the corruption in government, you'd swear he was a communist, but he hated them as well.

Beck let Julia lead us back downstairs and as we went down the hatch, she invited us to their Christmas dinner. I hadn't even thought about an entire dinner. I thought we would get some scraps, some leftovers. But of course Beck wouldn't show off the delightful carp just to taunt us. I wasn't ashamed of my reaction, but I had forgotten what it was like to be given such a gift by a non-Jew. For three years I had become more and more of a shadow, a broken heart, an empty stomach, the single mono-chromatic thought of survival, and here was this woman who wanted me at her Christmas table. The invitation reached my ears in an alien language. 'Why? Why were they doing this?' I silently asked myself. For a moment, and only a moment, this one sliver of light engulfed the darkness. A feeling of joy, which I had felt so often in my life and which had fled from the Nazis, was briefly back. I experienced a powerful sense of gratitude, peace and trust. The carp in the bathtub had become a token of the Becks' commitment to our lives. I also knew that I would love this fish, not because of where it came from or what it signi-fied, but because I was hungry. It would be pickled like herring; jellied in aspic and deep-fried like catfish. But the more I had looked at the carp in the bathtub, the more I thought about the Christmas dinner and wondered what we had that could possibly demonstrate even the smallest part of our gratitude to the Becks.

On the afternoon of Christmas Eve the bunker was filled with the wonderful smells of Julia's cooking and, for the first time in months, we had something to look forward to. Ala brought Igo and Klarunia upstairs and gave them a piece of candy, which was a gift in itself. We decided to give Beck one of Papa's sweaters. Mama's leather handbag would be for Julia and Mania's tortoiseshell comb would be for Ala. Even though they were hand-me-downs, they were the closest thing to real pres-ents we could find.

That evening when we went upstairs I don't know why we were taking such a big chance on leaving the bunker, but perhaps Mr Beck thought the SS and the Gestapo would leave us alone on Christmas Eve. None of us was prepared for what was waiting for us as we climbed up from underground. The curtains were closed tight and the rooms were filled with the soft light of candles. There was even a Christmas tree, which Ala and Beck had chopped down in the forest on the other side of the train station. The tree was decorated with candles and the Beck family ornaments, glass balls, angels and wise men made from shaved wood and paper.

Julia and Ala had set the table for 14 with Mrs Melman's finest china and linen. Julia had cooked all the traditional Polish Christmas dishes. I had no idea where they could get such things during the war, but all Julia said was, 'Beck has his ways.' She loved him very much and was proud of him and called him her magician. There was a huge *challah* on the table. There were the traditional dishes of borscht and pirogies with mushrooms and sauerkraut as well as the many carp dishes. Julia pointed out the dishes one by one, naming them. One of them was actually called *ryba zwdowski*, 'Jewish fish', which was *gefilte* fish. Of course I had seen Julia helping Mama make *gefilte* fish on dozens of occasions, but I had no idea it was eaten on Christmas or eaten by Poles at all. I kept all the wonder to myself, but I'm sure it was there in my eyes as I followed Julia's fingers around the table. I don't know why this surprised me so much, considering carp was such a staple of our diets.

Even though I went to a Polish school and had Polish friends, this was the first Christmas dinner I had ever been invited to. The table was filled with many things I didn't understand. I counted all the place settings and noticed then that there were not 14 settings but 15. I wondered who the extra guest might be, since no one knew we were 'guests' of the Becks. Julia saw me staring at it and told us it was for the 'unexpected guest'. All over Poland, their Christmas dinner tables were dressed with empty plates, waiting for a knock on the door that might bring a hungry stranger. It was an old Polish tradition. 'When there's a guest in the house, then God is in the house,' Julia told us.

I had lived in Poland my whole life and I never knew of such a tradition. It was hard to believe there was so much we didn't know about each other.

My father was very moved. He raised his glass. 'Then I know your house is filled with God tonight.'

The room was lit only by the candles, and for these few moments the war seemed to recede into the darkness beyond the glow of the candlelight. We all knew the war was still there. We had been in the bunker for three weeks and, as bad as our situation seemed, we had no idea of the horror ahead of us. The ghetto was only three weeks old. We had heard of the camps and the deportations; we had witnessed the murder of our Jewish leaders and head rabbis in Zolkiew; we knew we had ransomed every day of our lives with the wealth of our community, but there was nothing in our collective imagination to prepare us for what would come and what we would learn. So the feelings of goodwill, gratitude and fellowship pushed our fear to the furthest recesses of that lovely room and our minds. I wasn't thinking of the war at all, just what I saw in front of my eyes as they moved across the table.

Julia then reached into the centre of the table and took a satin-embroidered covering off a plate, revealing a huge loaf of bread. 'Before we get to the dinner,' she said as she picked up the platter and put it in front of my father, 'we each eat a piece of this bread.' Another tradition I had never seen, but which echoed our tradition of starting our meals with a blessing over the bread.

Mr Beck explained the custom. 'When we eat the bread, we forgive the sins made against us over the last year and wish for happiness for all in the upcoming year.' Papa then explained to the Becks our Jewish traditions of the extra wine cup for Elijah at Passover and our yearly expiation of sins at Yom Kippur. We had always seemed so different from the Poles, and as much as I knew about their religion – the stories of the saints, the mass in Latin, the cloistered abbeys, the nuns that lived behind bars, the rituals of holy communion and confession, the idea of resurrection, the piety of the Polish peasants – it was both familiar and alien; comforting and frightening. It was strange and wonderful and disconcerting all at the same time to have their customs reflect some of our own.

Mama said, 'I'm sorry to say that in all the years we've known each other, this is the first holiday we've spent together.' In these words were an apology for all the times she treated Julia like a servant and not a friend.

Julia only smiled, but she understood the deeper meaning in Mama's words. All of us who owed our lives to these people understood. But our gratitude, even unspoken, made the Becks uncomfortable. Mr Beck stood up and said in a loud voice, raising his glass, 'May there be many more.' I started to love the Becks like a mother and father. Because now, even more than my own mother and father, Mr and Mrs Beck were responsible for my life, and for all our lives. They were risking their lives for us, and risking their daughter's life as well.

There were laughter and jokes and toasts. Vodka was one thing Jews and Poles had in common – the men at least. The streets outside were filled now with carol-singers and their voices just added to the wonder of the evening. The Poles were deeply religious and the carols were usually sung with not only spirit but deep devotion and love. After the *kutja*, which is a traditional Polish dish made from barley, nuts and honey, and one of my favourite dishes since a spoon first entered my mouth, Julia and Ala cleared the table and now it was time for our own singing of Christmas carols. The curtains were closed and our voices raised with the Becks wouldn't have attracted any attention. For the first time in years, I felt I had a reason to sing, and was safe enough to do so.

Ala, Mr Beck and Julia started singing: 'Jesus, Heaven's Infant' (*Jezus Malusienki*), 'To the Town of Bethlehem' (*Przybiezeli do Betlejem*), 'Let Us All Go' (*Pójdzmy Wszyscy*), 'Rejoice Bethlehem' (*Dzisiaj w Betlejem*), 'God is Born' (*Gdy sie Chrystus rodzi*), 'Midst Quiet Night' (*Wsrod Nocnej Ciszy*), 'Hush-A-Bye Little Jesus' (*Lulajze Jezuniu*). They were all songs Mania and I had known for years. We went to Polish schools, which were taught by nuns, and we had sung these carols since we were five years old. Mania and I had never bothered to share this part of our education with our mother and father, so you can imagine their surprise when we joined in. Mania's voice was so beautiful as she harmonized in, above, below, within and without the rest of us.

For three weeks, we had been sitting as quietly as we could, with every word's consequence weighed and judged before it was spoken. There had been so little of the normal way of speaking, with words added here and there to convey love or affection, amusement, anger or frustration. And now here we were, singing, if not as loud as we could, with as much emotion and joy as Mania and I had ever sung anything. Looking at my parents' faces, and the Melmans' and Patrontasches' as well, gave us the feeling that we had played a wonderful joke on all of them… as if we two little Jewish girls had conspired for years to play this joke. For the few hours we were upstairs with the Becks, there was no war, no ghetto, no hunger and no fear. After the end of a song, Beck leapt up from his chair, a man on fire, and ran to the closet, extracting gifts wrapped in simple tissue paper or newspaper. We were stunned. It was their holiday. We had our second-hand gifts for the Becks, but Catholics giving gifts to Jews was something I had never experienced or even heard of in my life.

Beck had made a dancing bear for little Igo and Ala gave Klarunia one of her stuffed dolls. Beck had packs of cigarettes for the men and in no time at all the packs were ripped open, matches lit and the room full of smoke, the men puffing and sucking like there was no tomorrow, content, full, drunk and happy. Ala had given Mania one of her combs, which she immediately put in her hair. She ran to the mirror to see how it looked. Beck gave me a package wrapped in newspaper. It was flat and at first I hoped it might be a book. I was crazy for a new book. I opened it. Inside was a composition book with a black cover and filled with lined paper, just like all the many composition books I had used in all my years in school and never given a thought to.

'For our little writer,' he said. 'I know you'll be a famous writer some day, Clarutchka, I just beg that you only say nice things about me.' Mr Beck knew that I was keeping a diary and had no book to write in. He also gave me a blue pencil, which he had sharpened to a fine point with his penknife.

Mr Beck could see how pleased I was. I was still so shy in his presence that I am sure my thanks didn't correspond with how deeply I was feeling. All my life, I had honoured my father above all men. I grew, I felt safe and happy, in both the shadow and light of his life. He and Mama and the rest of my family were enough. I thought Beck had barely noticed me, if at all, and somehow he had found for me what would become my salvation. No longer would our lives be written in the margins of discarded books. Whatever happened to us would be properly recorded on lined paper with a sharp blue pencil in a book with hard cardboard covers. Whatever his past and whatever his shortcomings, Beck was emerging from the circumscription and diminution of gossip and prejudice and becoming someone in my life who knew me. None of us was thinking beyond the war or beyond living just another day, but Beck knew that what was happening to us was important. Our lives – our stories, and his – had meaning. Even if all we had to fight with were a composition book and a blue pencil.

There were more gifts. He had dried lilies for Klara Patrontasch, which he presented to her with a smile that was embarrassed and off kilter, as if he was trying not to smile or didn't know if he was giving too much away with it. This was Poland in 1942 and a married man didn't give flowers to an unmarried woman, widowed or not, unless she was on her deathbed or already in a coffin.

Then came a knock on the door that silenced the conversation, brought the terror of the outside inside and sent us all through the bedroom and down through the hatch, one after the other. We listened to who it might be. It wasn't the SS, the Gestapo or the Blue Coats (the Ukrainian police, who were vicious in their persecution of Jews). It was carol-singers, friends of the Becks who knocked on the door wanting to sing for them and wanting the Becks to join them in a song. Of course the Becks joined the carol-singers, and we listened to their voices in darkness. I sang along in my head until I fell asleep.

Christmas Day was spent downstairs as the Becks entertained Beck's brother and sister-in-law, and his nephew Wladek. There was nothing threatening to us upstairs, so I wasn't listening to the conversation. There was laughter, loud talking, lots of toasts, many more than at our party last night. I was writing in my diary. And then words that caught all our attention. Whatever we were doing we stopped. Potatoes dropped from hands. Books were put down. Knives were placed gently on our makeshift wooden counter. The men, however, kept puffing on their cigarettes and the smoke swirled around the bunker with every turn of the head and floated up towards the ceiling to meet the words coming from Beck's voice, a voice that was at once quiet and conspiratorial, proud and defiant, a voice slurred, which meant that Beck was extremely drunk. We all knew that voice and now it was calling for more vodka. We heard Julia's steps across the floor and the clink of the bottle on the glasses and then Beck started...

'Have I got a Christmas story for you!'

His brother was laughing. 'I hope it's not a long one.'

Beck's voice dropped to an almost whisper that we could still just about hear. I could imagine him leaning in to talk to his brother whom I had never met. I could imagine the looks on the faces of Ala and Julia, looks that I knew would be as terrified as ours. But of course, they wouldn't interrupt Beck or change the subject. They would sit there as we were sitting, dumbstruck by Beck's folly.

'You know the Schwarzes, the Melmans, the Patrontasches?'

'Of course I know them. Where the hell have I been taking my grain to be pressed? We're in Melmans' house, for Christ's sake. They're nice people. All of them. For Jews. What? Are you drunker than usual?'

Then there was a long silence. I was hoping Beck had changed his mind and wouldn't continue. That he would get another drink or go off on a tangent and tell another story about us.

Then his brother was speaking again, his voice loud, his tone incredulous, 'Downstairs? Are you crazy? Are you out of your blasted mind?'

I knew that Beck must have smiled and gestured with his head to the bunker underneath the floor.

'You worry too much. You're going to kill yourself with worry. What was I supposed to do? Give them to the damn Krauts?'

'But we're *Volksdeutsche*!'

'Are we? You know how the Nazis treat us. They wouldn't piss on us if we were on fire. We're just a step above the Slavs – not even – a half step. You think I'm going to let them come in and tell me what to do, to kill the Jews? Merry Christmas, fellow Nazis, and for your present we're hiring Ukrainian dogs to kill you if you take one step out of line!'

'You put all of us in danger for them? Your wife? Your daughter?'

'Whose idea do you think it was? My wife! Julia! She's got more courage than the both of us!'

'You don't owe them a damn thing.'

Now Beck's voice was rising, rising loud enough to travel through our walls to the neighbours'. Thank God it was freezing and the windows were closed.

'I don't? I don't?'

Finally, finally, Julia said, 'Please, Valentin, not so loud.'

His voice dropped, but not the intensity. 'In '39 when the god-damned Soviets shipped us out to the colony in Bazalia, and Bandera sent in his thugs and started burning us out, we were lucky to escape with our lives. Then the damn Soviets were going to ship us to Siberia for abandoning the colony, and you know who buys me out?'

Now his voice was starting to rise again.

'You, my beloved brother? You, my fellow *Volksdeutscher*? NO! IT WAS THE JEW MELMAN DOWNSTAIRS WHO BRIBED THE FUCKING COMMUNISTS! I ABANDON THEM, I ABANDON MY HONOUR! I HATED JEWS MY WHOLE LIFE. I STILL DO. WHY? HOW THE HELL SHOULD I KNOW? But it was a Jew saved my worthless-piece-of-shit life, my sacred wife and my beloved daughter... Come over here, Ala, sit by your father. I want my Ala to look at her father and see a man, not a coward. They can kill me ten times over…'

Then there was silence and some words we couldn't hear and then his brother and his wife were gone.

My father whispered, 'Oh my God… we're dead…'

My poor mother tried to counter what everyone was feeling. Optimistically she said, 'He wouldn't betray his own brother.'

Then Mrs Melman was whispering: 'His wife's another story. She thinks she's descended from Polish aristocracy.' Mrs Melman was the pessimist to Mama's optimist and Mama was not intimidated.

'She just says that to make herself feel better… A hunchback always feels better when he sees that the next fellow's hump is bigger.'

Well, what can we do if Mr Beck trusts them? We have to trust them too. We have no choice in the matter.

Chapter 5

I GO TO THE GHETTO

12 January to February 1943

In the meantime, the news from the ghetto is bad. Mr Melman's brothers and also Mr Patrontasch's brothers sneak out at night and come to us. There is a terrible epidemic of typhoid fever. People are dying 10 to 15 a day. Mostly the young and the strong are victims. That is how we lived until 12 January. That day, Mr Melman's brother, Hermann, came and said somebody by the name of Lewicki found out about us. We decided to go back to the ghetto.

*

Panic spread through the bunker. We would have to leave. If Lewicki knew, it would be only a matter of time before the Nazis or their cohorts the Ukrainians would be at the door. It would probably be the latter, since Lewicki was Ukrainian himself. We knew that they would kill us and the Becks. We couldn't put their lives at risk.

There was no time to be upset that we had been betrayed by a neighbour whose children had been my classmates. At great risk, Hermann had been able to sneak out and warn us. Uncle Josek, in his role as a policeman, would escort Mama, Mania and me to the ghetto, while Papa and Mr Melman would hide in the factory bunker and plan another hiding place for us. The others would go to the ghetto with the Patrontasches later.

We left early in the morning before the light of day. Uncle Josek told us that if we were to be stopped we should say we were a work detail. I hadn't been outside or smelled fresh air for 43 days. It was 20 degrees below zero. Mama, Mania and I marched in terrified silence behind my uncle Josek, our eyes downcast. We had all thought that when we came out of the bunker we would emerge to freedom and our old lives. But now, on this freezing cold morning, there were only Nazis and Ukrainian policemen on patrol. The streets in my neighbourhood were bereft of even one Jewish soul.

In the past, walking these same streets to the ghetto, I might see Uchka, Zygush, Zosia, Rela, Dudio, Josek or a hundred other friends or relatives. We would stop off at one of the stores in the colonnaded plaza for a sweet, or buy some chestnuts roasting on a coal fire that would fill my nose with the smell of wonderful smoke mixed with fresh winter air. There was no smell of roasting chestnuts that morning. On a normal day we would be holding hands, the three of us, or walking arm in arm, and laughing and gossiping. Women would come up to Mama asking where she got the material or design for our latest dresses. There were socials and fundraisers to be planned; food kitchens for the poor to be organized; clothing drives, the sewing school. All the things that required Salka the Cossack's attention were organized on our walks to town. A walk was not a walk, but a social event. But that morning we walked as prisoners, not allowed the luxury of conversation or the simple gift of holding a mother's hand. Luckily the Nazis out on the streets, with their fresh faces, were laughing and not paying any attention to us. They looked like conquerors without a care in the world. We were invisible in our shabby clothes and stooped demeanour. I was thankful for that.

Josek led us past the 12-metre-high fortified stone walls of the cathedral and monastery. The border to the ghetto was at the next corner, where the wall made a left turn and continued up Turiniecka Street. Up ahead were the barbed-wire gates of the ghetto. I looked up only for a second and saw the guards before I looked back down at the dirty snow under my feet. Josek smiled and nodded at the guards as he walked us inside. We were nothing. Beasts of burden driven from one place to another.

The ghetto encompassed most of the Jewish section of town. It was like a nightmare. Walking corpses swollen from hunger intermingled with the fatted calves, sitting in the cafés in their best clothes, eating and drinking with money made from the black market or worse. There was laughter. I could see it through the windows, but it was grotesque, as grotesque as their faces. I wasn't judging; I didn't get that far in my reaction. It was fear, plain and simple, and everything around me was at the periphery of that fear. How I wanted to get back to the bunker, where, as frightened as I was, I felt safer, less exposed, away from the eyes of blue-coated policemen and fresh-faced German boys and my former Polish friends, not knowing who would sell us out for a few litres of vodka.

Two days after arriving at Uchka's, we got word that it had been a false alarm. We could return to the bunker. Mama decided to stay behind for a while to sell some more of our things. Little did we know that all the silk underwear Mama used to buy over afternoon cups of tea and slip into the chest of drawers before Papa came home would one day save our lives. I don't know how many kilograms of potatoes we got for one silk slip, but it was substantial.

Josek led us back out of the ghetto. We now had the additional fear that someone might see us go into the house. The houses in the neighbourhood were close together. In the spring and summer, they were hidden from each other by the large shady trees that lined the street. But now, in the dead of winter, the houses were exposed as every branch on every tree. I felt there were as many eyes as windows on the street and they were all looking out at us. I looked for any movement of any curtain, but couldn't see anything. Beck, who was waiting for us, opened the door and we were safe and inside. The others were already there. Mania and I collapsed from exhaustion.

I woke up early the next morning. It might sound crazy, but sometimes early in the morning was the only time I had to myself. Eleven people in a bunker, even when they were not saying a word to each other, could be very distracting. It was easier to write while the others were asleep, without their curious looks. No one asked what I was writing, though I'm sure everyone wondered whether I was being too 'personal', or recording, for some unknown reader, the pettiness that sometimes overwhelmed our desire to get along.

Mania was up next and she looked over to me, crawled over and gave me a kiss, and then there was a kiss for Papa. We were hoping that Mama would come back from the ghetto today.

We heard a knock on the trapdoor and Mr Patrontasch crawled over the bodies to open it. As always it went up on its hinges with the satisfied sigh of a door on a Rolls Royce. Mr Beck looked down at us from above, his face framed by the hatch, like an austere and foreboding portrait. Klara looked up, thinking he might be calling for her. Mr Beck had got into the habit of asking beautiful Klara to join him upstairs when he was alone. But I knew he wouldn't this morning because I could hear Julia and Ala's feet moving across the floor upstairs.

We waited for the news of the day. If he was in a good mood, he'd join us with a bottle of vodka which he had 'liberated' from the German alcohol depot along with cigarettes and an armful of newspapers. But he didn't come down. His hands were empty. He said simply, 'Mr Schwarz, a word please.'

My father moved to the opening. I had never heard this tone from Beck before. Never before had he selected just one person to talk to. There could only be one reason why he would ask to speak with my father alone. Something must have happened to Mama. Mr Beck said, 'Please, Mr Schwarz, please feel free to stand.' The bunker ceiling was barely four feet tall and no one could stand up, not even Mrs Melman, not unless they had their legs in the hole Mr Patrontasch had dug. My father stretched his long frame up through the opening of the hatch. His pants were much too big for him now and were held up only by the suspenders.

Mania grabbed my hand. She was as frightened as I was. How many thoughts raced through my mind in the few seconds my father and Mr Beck spoke. Mama was dead, captured, deported, shot, in jail, dying. As with the many moments of panic we had, this one, knowing it involved the fate of Mama, set my heart racing. Other mothers were killed. Other fathers, brothers, sisters, but they weren't mine and so this selfish guilty gratitude that my family was intact while others were destroyed was, I felt, coming to an end.

I strained to hear what Mr Beck had to say, but there was so much coughing and shuffling that I couldn't hear myself think, much less what Beck was saying to my father. How much noise a bunch of people can make without saying a word! The inhalation and exhalation of air sounded like the roar of wind. It might have been my own breathing.

My father bent down back into the bunker and Mr Beck closed the hatch. Papa crawled over towards us. For a moment he forgot where he was and stood up, smashing his head against the wooden beams and floor above. His head began to bleed but he didn't notice.

In that matter-of-fact tone he would get when compelled to tell us the worst of news, Papa told us that Uchka had contracted typhus, and that Mama had decided to stay there to take care of her and the children.

Everyone stopped whatever they were doing. Not a potato was being peeled, not a glass of water drunk. The first cigarettes of the day remained unlit in mouths, and even Mrs Melman put down her precious jug.

Mania broke the silence. 'Typhus! Typhus! When will she be back? Papa, you can't leave her there. Mama will die!'

My father simply said, 'Mr Beck is afraid of what would happen if typhus got into the house.' The typhus-bearing louse was the Nazi's ally. They had marched hand in hand into Zolkiew. We had all become experts on typhus. There wasn't a louse alive that wasn't our enemy. We examined each other constantly, checking our hair, our bedding and even the lining of our clothing, where they liked to lay their eggs.

These words were a death sentence for Mama. Mania refused to accept them. 'Just like that, Papa? Just like that? NO!'

Perhaps I was just selfish and stupid to want Mama back so desperately. I begged my father: 'We have to get her back. Papa. Papa!' I was afraid to stop talking because as long as Mania and I argued and begged and pleaded there was at least some shred of hope. We knew that there would be an end, an acceptance, a resignation, once we ran out of words.

My father was already resigned as he told us: 'I begged. I offered Mr Beck money. I offered him our business, everything we had, but he had to say no.'

Mama's death sentence meant life for everyone else in the

bunker and I saw the relief on their faces, especially Mrs Melman's. A part of me hated her; a part of me understood her. Panic and fear for her life and that of little Igo. As much as they loved Mama, who would be willing, knowing the consequences, to bring a woman infected with typhus into this 10- by 14-metre, dank, unsanitary place? The rules for mutual survival set us at one another's throats, if not physically, at least in our hearts. And yet we were condemned to live with each other for who knows how long. If, God forbid, anything should happen to Mama, Mrs Melman would have to look at me every day we shared this dirt bunker.

I heard my voice telling my father that I could get her back. I heard my father asking me how, and then I was telling my father that I would talk to Beck. Surely this was not me speaking? I had never really argued with my father about anything. Never contradicted him. Never raised my voice to him. Honour thy father and thy mother, and I did. Yet, how could I face a life without Mama? I knew in my bones that a part of me would die if she died; that if I had any will or courage at all I would need it now. And if I didn't, my life was nothing. I could see the questioning in his eyes and hear the hollowness in my voice. I didn't know what I could ever say to Mr Beck to change his mind and allow typhus in this house.

A day or so later, Mr Beck had gone out and I sat at the kitchen table with Julia. She didn't say anything because we both knew she had no voice in the matter at all. It was Beck and Beck alone I needed to talk to. I guzzled a glass of water and Julia was ready with a pitcher to give me a refill. It was a ritual. If for any reason I had to come upstairs, Julia was there with fresh water and rolls. I can't tell you how delicious that water was and how guilty I felt for drinking it.

My mind was racing and Julia was walking across the kitchen and back again with a roll. I tore the roll apart with my fingers and was putting part of it in a napkin to bring down to Igo and Klarunia. Not even Mama's impending death could stop me getting scraps for the children. The Nazis could be breaking through the door and I would be still gathering crumbs for the little ones. It was a simple reflex. Julia had seen me and brought over what I thought at first were more rolls, but turned out to be some potato and *kasha knishes*. Her dark brown eyes were full of compassion. 'It's typhus, Clarutchka. Mr Beck is afraid and it's all on his shoulders. But as far as he knows, Salka doesn't have it yet.' I looked at her. I wanted her to tell me that she would talk to Mr Beck and make it okay for Mama to come home to us, but she didn't. She kissed me on the head and walked out of the room. I was watching the clock, knowing that I had to get to the ghetto before it got too late. Ala's head appeared in the doorway. With a finger to her lips, she gestured for me to come into her room. I wrapped up the *knishes* and followed her.

Ala whispered, 'I'll take you.'

I couldn't believe what she was saying. I could barely manage a response. 'Your father won't let her back into the house.'

Ala's voice was as light as if she were inviting me to see a film at the Eagle. 'You know he can't say no to me. And if we bring her back then he'll let her in and nobody downstairs can say a word to him.'

I can't imagine the expression on my face as Ala kept on talking. 'We'll be two girls out for a good time.' In Zolkiew? In Nazi-infested Zolkiew? Was she crazy? And she was laughing. 'What could possibly be dangerous about that?'

I lived in fear of Mr Beck's approval and disapproval. We all did in the bunker. We would never argue with him, or even disagree.

Ala was the only one of us who had no fear of Mr Beck. Ever since she had been old enough to walk, her father had taken her with him whenever he went to Lvov or Warsaw or Krakow. He taught her how to haggle in the markets and how to play cards. They spent evenings together laughing and dancing to music on the radio. They never walked anywhere without her arm through his, and if anyone could defy Beck, it was Ala.

I don't know how I convinced my father. I was expecting an argument, but it was a measure of both his desperation and his sense of defeat that he simply nodded his head. My father, who had laid *tefillin* all his life and could argue with the rabbi for hours about the most obscure applications of the Talmud, had nothing to say. Perhaps he believed in miracles still. He was sending his daughter out of her safe hiding place into a world where her discovery might mean not only her death, but death to everyone in the bunker. I was surprised as well that there were no objections from the other families. Had we all become crazy? My capture would bring perhaps even more danger than Mama's return. I didn't look for the logic in their silence. I was simply thankful. I was going into a world with signs plastered on every wall and every building that harbouring Jews was *verboten* and punishable by death; that being in the streets past curfew was punishable by death; that going into the ghetto was punishable by death; that aiding and abetting Jews in any way was punishable by death. On our last trip to the ghetto with Josek just a few days ago, I had seen all these signs composed in that brutal Gothic typeface that was as hateful to me as the swastika on the Nazi flag. There was no time for my father to reason out his decision.

It was eight at night when we left. Ala said we had nothing to worry about. She repeated that we were just two girls out for a good time in Zolkiew. I had taken off the armband. It was a cold clear night. My heart was beating so loudly I was afraid it would wake the dead in the cemetery. There was a fresh layer of crunchy snow that went off like fire crackers under our feet. Despite my warm coat, I was freezing. Anything exposed, nose, cheeks, the tips of my ears, were hard as porcelain and felt as if they would break if someone touched them. My feet were frozen even in soft thick felt and two pairs of woollen stockings. But we were thankful for the bitter wind and polar temperature. No one was in the streets.

My face was hidden under my hat and my features were masked by my scarf. I tried not to think about the SS and the Gestapo, whose headquarters were in the old governor's villa just across the park from where we used to ice-skate. Or the brutal, Jew-hating Ukrainian policemen. They were even more gun-happy than the SS and the Gestapo combined.

Ala and I hadn't thought about this or much about anything else in the way of a plan.

When I saw my house across the street, I was filled with longing to go through that big brown wooden door into the living room where my bed was placed close to the stove so that even in the coldest winters Mania and I were warm as toast. I would go to sleep and when I woke up it would all be the way it was before. Ala caught me looking at the house. She pulled me up the street and we walked past the pink walls of the convent.

There had to be patrols around, although we hadn't seen any. It would be hard to hear anything at all over the crunch of our boots on the snow.

My teeth were chattering, more from fear than the cold. And Ala kept whispering, 'Talk, Clara, talk, it will stop your teeth from chattering.' Ala hadn't stopped talking since we left the bunker, about anything and everything, telling me about all the men who had crushes on her, so many I couldn't remember their names; so many lonely boys with guns looking for kindness, warmth and even love from the people they conquered. Ala talked about the films she had seen and what the actresses had worn and how she had styled her hair after this actress or how she wanted the same dress as that. Who could suspect that this beautiful girl with her light talk was risking her life by leading a Jewish girl through the streets to rescue her mother in the ghetto? Even I hardly believed it.

The ghetto was just up ahead. The synagogue loomed above us, the white-washed walls gleaming in moonlight. The silhouette of the citadel looked like a ghost ship in the night.

When we reached the barbed-wire fence, I told Ala that she could leave me now. Uchka's place wasn't far and I didn't know how long I was going to be upstairs. It might be hours and I didn't want Ala waiting in the freezing cold, alone, past curfew. She had done enough, but she insisted on staying with me.

Once we were stopped and facing the ghetto we were no longer two girls out for a good time on a cold night in Zolkiew. If we were stopped now, there would be no talking our way out of it. Not even all of Ala's charm would help us, or the music of her laughter or the irresistible light in her eyes.

Uchka's flat was only three doors down from the Judenrat. There was always something going on at the Judenrat at night. And that meant the SS and Gestapo wouldn't be far.

Again I told Ala to go home. She whispered she would. I slipped between the barbed wire and walked as fast as I could. But soon I heard footsteps behind me. I was afraid to turn around, but I had to. It was Ala. Her eyes and her mouth were set and I knew I couldn't argue with her.

As I entered the building, Ala hid in a doorway across the street. I was scared to death to knock on the door. I could barely lift one leg after another. I didn't know what was on the other side of that door.

I knocked. There was a long, long silence. I heard Mama's cautious voice. 'Who is it?'

'It's me. It's Clarutchka.' Mama opened the door. I couldn't tell if she was infected. The pustules don't affect face, palms or soles of the feet. All she said was, 'GO HOME!' Her expression was full of fury and disbelief that her smart daughter could have been so stupid.

She tried to shut the door in my face, but I held it with my foot and edged into the room, closing the door behind me. Mama didn't let me come more than a few inches inside the door and blocked my way.

The room was full of people in pain. I could see Uchka and her husband's cousin. But I couldn't see anything else because the room was dark, to protect the sensitive eyes of the typhus victims. Any light causes them excruciating headaches. The stench was so thick I could almost taste it and I had to fight to keep the rolls I had had at the Becks' in my stomach. Mama's face was red and she was sweating. 'Mama, Mama, you have to come home,' I was crying. I was looking at her face and trying to look at her arms and hands but couldn't see anything. I was too petrified to ask. Mama repeated the same words over and over: 'Go home, go home, go home…'

'Mama, please, you can't get sick. You can't get sick.' I grabbed her hands and tried to push up her sleeves so I could see if there were pustules on her arms. Mama pushed my hands away, grabbed me by the neck, forced me through the door and threw me out. She threw me so hard I fell down several of the steps. If I hadn't caught the banister, I would have fallen all the way down.

Mama was frightening me. She seemed like a crazy woman. Mama would never scream at me. But this woman was still yelling: 'You think I can leave her? You think she'd leave me? You think you'd leave Mania? You think she'd leave you? GO! Go home before you get caught! Does your father know you're here?'

All I could manage was a nod. Mama was shaking her head, a look of non-comprehension, more a look of bafflement turning her flushed face a nauseated white. 'He let you go? He let you go!'

I nodded. Mama didn't say another word. She didn't tell me if she was sick or not sick. She didn't tell me if Uchka would live or die. I couldn't see Zygush and Zosia. I didn't know if they were in that sick room or if they were safe somewhere else. She didn't tell me if she was going to come home or stay in the ghetto. Without a word of goodbye, without a kiss or a nod or a touch, she walked back inside and shut the door.

I stared at the door. Mama had never spoken to me with such fury. Her commands were usually delivered with pats and smiles and kisses. She never had to raise her voice to me ever. I don't know if it was that I was such a docile child or lived in a benevolent world, protected on all sides from anything that might hurt me. But now I had to walk down the stairs, through the frozen streets to my father and sister without my mother. I had never considered for a moment that Mama wouldn't come back with me.

In the street, Ala saw I was alone. I told her Mama wasn't coming. She took my arm and started chatting again. Again we were two girls without a care in the world. On the way back, I didn't hear a word she said. I was scared to death and crying, the tears freezing on my face immediately. But I didn't care about that. I didn't know if I would ever see Mama again. I didn't know how to tell my father and sister. And despite my grief and fear for Mama's life and Uchka's, all I wanted to do was get back to the bunker where I would be safe. And I was not ashamed to have such selfish thoughts.

*

When Ala unlocked the door, Beck was waiting for us. 'Better get in before the entire Gestapo sees you!' he said angrily. Ala kissed her father and pulled me over to the stove where we took off our gloves to warm our hands. Ala kept chatting, treating our misadventure as if we had been out buying a fish at the market.

Whatever anger Beck had felt had disappeared now that his daughter was home safe. 'Look at you both.' His hands were feeling his daughter's nose and ears and warming them. 'Icicles. There's soup. Have something hot.'

But I didn't wait for the soup. I went straight to the hatch and knocked, whispering, 'It's Clara.' The hatch opened right away and I saw my father's face right behind Mr Patrontasch's and Mania's right behind him. I didn't have to tell them as I climbed down into the bunker alone.

My father wanted to know how she had looked. I told him that she had looked fine and that I hadn't seen any signs of the disease. Later when we had all gone to bed, Mania whispered into my ear, 'Was she really okay? Is she still alive? I know you. Maybe you were afraid to tell Papa.' I told her how mad she had been and that she had thrown me down the stairs by my neck. I could see that Mania was trying to conjure up Mama whole and healthy as if the image would be enough to sustain us if she never came back to us. There was a smile as Mania thought about how angry Mama must have been at our father for having let me go.

I tried to fall asleep, but it was impossible. I was not tired at all. I wanted to sleep so that I could stop thinking what a world without Mama would be like.

Chapter 6

THE FINAL SOLUTION

February to early April 1943

It's the 20th century. It's unbelievable. They pulled trucks below a window and threw the people and children into the trucks. Some of the Gestapo were using axes. One of them hacked to death Nusick Lichter, a 12-year-old boy, a nephew of the Patrontaschs. The rest of the Jews were herded to one street, Josek, Rela and Uchka and the children were lucky this time.

*

Mr Beck was kind enough to keep running back and forth to the ghetto to keep us informed of Uchka's condition and how Mama was faring. He told us of waiting outside the ghetto for hours and hours, drinking and talking to the policemen and his friends while waiting to get a word from Josek. He tried to cheer us up with the news that the Russians took back Stalingrad in the bloodiest battle of the war. But Stalingrad was far away and we were more concerned with the people who died in the ghetto every day. Beck watched as they were piled on to carts and pushed to the cemetery; he looked to see if Uchka or Mama were on the carts, buried under the bodies on top. He waited for the news of which Jews had died so he could report to us that Mama was still alive. Josek told Beck that he and Rela were trying to find someone to take care of Uchka so that Mama could leave. We were lucky that the ghetto bordered the main street of Zolkiew, otherwise Beck wouldn't have been able to spend so much time within sight of Uchka's window while drinking and gossiping with his friends on the way home from work.

Although Beck would share with us everything he learned, he always reminded us that there was no way he could let Mama back into the house. Each time he said that the survival of the group was more important than the life of any single person, I felt like screaming at him, as well as at Mrs Melman and Mrs Patrontasch, who whispered to each other after each report. But on the outside I was a vision of calm. We became even more formal with one another, addressing each other with titles. I knew the rules, and I did not argue, beg, plead or bargain for Mama's life. I was cooking our potatoes, doling out the water instead of Mama, washing the dishes, putting away our pallets every morning when we got up, but it felt worse than a lie, it felt like I was betraying Mama. The days blurred together as I went through the motions. Mania and I whispered at night to each other and we prayed.

Three days after my journey to the ghetto with Ala, we heard the front door open and Beck's steps coming towards the hatchway. He wasn't alone. He knocked on the trapdoor and Patrontasch hurried to open it. Mama was staring down at us. Beck helped her down and we were in each other's arms. The four of us. I just said 'Mama' over and over again. Out of the corner of my eye I saw Mrs Melman about to say something, but before there was a word, Mr Beck's voice was invoking a certain authority. 'Not a word. If God chose to bring her back, then it's His will. Not a word.'

Then he went. There was no discussion of typhus or lice or soaking Mama in disinfectant, although she did go upstairs shortly after she arrived to take a bath. She told us that sick as she was, Uchka was saying she couldn't die and that Zygush and Zosia were her medicine. She told us that Beck didn't move from across the street for hours at a time and she thanked God for him. Then she asked my father where he got the money to buy soup for Uchka and the others. Every day Josek had brought a pot of soup for them saying it had come from us. My father hadn't given Beck a zloty.

Upstairs Beck started humming a popular German song, 'All's Well That Ends Well'. This tune would become his trademark, the signal that everything was all right; that the Nazis were gone; that we could talk; that whatever danger we faced was no longer a threat. To hear him whistle that tune lifted my heart almost as much as Mama's return because in its simple melody was a promise that all would be okay; that Beck's faith was greater than ours; that despite his reputation and his sins that were the source of so much gossip and disdain, he was proving himself to be not only a *mensch* but a *tzadik*, and that when he said we were in God's hands it wasn't an expression of, or a longing for, faith, but faith itself. I thanked God for Mama and that He had given us Beck.

After hugging us and telling us over and over how much she had missed us, Mama looked around the bunker and laughed. 'How I missed this place!' This was the funniest thing any of us heard since we came into the bunker and, in that moment, everything was forgotten. I no longer hated and resented the other families. We were united once more. That night Mania and I both slept with our arms around our mother.

One day after Mama's return, Josek brought Rela to the bunker, with Beck's permission. The uniform protected Josek, but life in the ghetto was worse than they had expected. Josek promised to watch over their son and bring Rela news of him through Beck.

Mr and Mrs Beck weren't just our protectors, they were also our messengers. They even went to Mosty Wielke from time to time to check on Giza and Meyer for us and to relay news. Giza told Beck that every time there was a call for deportations, the German Commandant Krupp would stand up to the SS and not let them have even one of his Jews. 'The work was important to the army. They are all skilled workers. The production schedule doesn't allow him time to train new people,' and on and on. Jews in every village in Galicia were being exterminated but the Jews of Mosty Wielke were safe. Then Beck told us that in early February the commandant had been replaced by an SS officer. Within days, he had murdered 1,500 Jews, Giza and Meyer among them. We were inconsolable. Giza, who loved the theatre and performed in every amateur theatrical in Zolkiew, whose laughter rivalled Uchka's, whose round face and dark eyes were as warm as any stove and as sweet as the darkest chocolate was dead. It was hard to imagine our world without her. Just like after every other calamity, Mama said, 'Write, Clara, write!' There was simply nothing else we could do. This sense of loss and amputation was now our way of life.

A few days later, Julia's sister, Maria, came over, hysterical. She lived in the Beck's old house outside of town. We could hear every word she was saying as she spat out her story in gasps and halted breath, her voice rising in panic. The Nazis had knocked on her door looking for the Becks and the Jews they were hiding. Thank God, she hadn't been home. She had missed them by minutes and only found out from a neighbour. The police had left without searching the house once they had been told that the Becks no longer lived there. Maria had taken a short cut and run through the woods to warn us. I knew the woods and fields this poor woman had crossed, slogging through snow up to her knees, soaking and freezing her feet. The large expanses of fields would have exposed her to any German or Ukrainian policeman, who, if they had seen this woman running across an empty field, would have stopped her to question her. But even with the short-cut, the Nazis in their cars should have beaten her here.

Then we heard the banging, the pounding on the door, with the Nazis screaming, 'WIR SUCHEN JUDEN!' Julia's sister slipped out the back door as fast as she could. Patrontasch extinguished the light and we sat in the dark silence, each of us alone with their terror. I held my sister's hand. We were afraid to breathe. Every noise from the rooms above sounded louder than usual. I silently prayed that when the Nazis came downstairs for us, they would shoot us. I prayed for the Becks. I didn't know how they were facing the Nazis or what they were thinking or if they were cursing us.

I heard Ala's light step across the floor and the door open and then her voice, in its fearless 18-year-old breathiness, say, 'What can we do for you?'

I had no idea what the faces of these Nazis looked like. 'We're looking for Jews. We know they're here.' And then Ala was laughing, almost giggling. 'Jews? Here? Don't you know who my father is? He despises Jews. Go to any tavern in town and ask how Beck feels about Jews!'

Sweat fell from my forehead into my eyes. The policeman's voice was threatening. 'You have one chance to survive. Where are the Jews?' Ala was laughing, actually laughing. 'All right, all right, I'm Jewish, can't you tell, take me away.' The policeman wasn't amused and threatened her with arrest. Ala's voice was contrite now. 'I'm sorry. The idea is just crazy. You think I'd be joking if there were Jews here?' Julia was frightened now, with more reason than the Nazis might suspect. She was asking them to forgive Ala because she was just a girl. But Ala still wouldn't be quiet. 'Oh, Mama, it's just that we never get any visitors and I was just kidding with our guests. But why would they think a loyal *Volksdeutsche* family would harbour Jews?' The German said, 'We're not at liberty to say.' And this remark seemed to set Ala off.

'You have no idea what it's like for us. The Poles, the Ukrainians, everybody's informing on each other. Twenty years ago, somebody buys a sow. It's barren. And now, 20 years later, the seller of the barren sow is guilty of hiding Jews. Oh my God! Look at the time. I'm late for my job at the post office. May I go?'

Then we heard the second policeman speak for the first time. His voice was young, melodious, and I could hear that he was taken with Ala. 'I'm sorry for the inconvenience... We'll leave. We have other reports to check.'

Ala didn't miss a beat. 'Then are you walking to town? Perhaps I can walk with you.'

After a few more flirtatious words, the policemen left with Ala and we heard the door close.

Beck left the house shortly after Ala. When he returned, he came immediately to see us in the bunker. He told us that we would have to leave. He had no choice. We could see the torment on his face, the deep sadness. He had to think of his family. Papa told him that under these circumstances there was nothing else the Becks could do. Beck left to get Josek to take us back to the ghetto. There was no place else to go. Nobody got hysterical or cried. We knew that this moment was coming sooner or later. We were drained and exhausted. The conversation with Beck had taken less than a minute. Never had a death sentence been delivered with so much kindness.

We had barely started to gather up our things when Beck knocked on the trapdoor again. We were shocked to see Melman's half-brother Gedalo Lauterpacht instead of Josek with him. Beck looked at all of us with eyes that were burning more than usual. 'We're all in God's hands. You can stay and Gedalo will be joining you.' I didn't know if he was a madman or a saint, but we would live another day. He got his bottle of vodka and the men drank.

What we didn't know was that Julia's sister had been hiding Gedalo and his brother Hermann, as well Hermann's fiancée Lola Elefant and her little brother Icio, when the Nazis had come to her home. Gedalo told us that Hermann, Lola and Icio had gone to the ghetto, and he had come here.

The situation in the ghetto worsened over the next few days. They stopped letting anyone out. Even policemen had to have a special paper in order to leave. Then on 15 March, two trucks of Gestapo arrived and took away all the people from morning *Appell* to Janowska camp in Lvov. We heard the details from Lola, who had been able to escape. A few days after the deportation, Beck brought Lola to us.

The sight of her hair caused a communal gasp in the bunker. When she took off her hat, snow-white hair tumbled out in an avalanche. She was only in her twenties. Lola started to tell us in a voice no louder than a whisper what had made her hair turn white.

When she, Hermann and her brother Icio had returned to the ghetto, they had been told that the Nazis had designated Zolkiew an official labour city. This would save all their lives. The Nazis had increased the number of Jewish policemen to help run this large labour detachment and had organized rehearsals to demonstrate the skill of the Jewish workers to the commandant. On the morning of the 15th, the Judenrat encouraged all the men to look good for the selection, where they would be given 'W' (*Wehrmacht*) or 'R' (*Rüstung*) patches. Close to 700 men, fathers, husbands and sons, had gathered in the square and were marched to the sports field next to the theatre where Mania had her concert.

Lola said that in her heart she knew something was wrong. Hermann had told her to stay in the apartment, but she left and was in the street, watching. Suddenly the gates to the ghetto had opened up and her heart had stopped. Hundreds of German police and Blue Coats had rushed through the gates, surrounding the men and forcing them into a tighter and tighter circle. An official car had driven up, followed by a convoy of trucks. SS General Katzman had got out and watched as the Blue Coats and German police mercilessly beat the men into waiting trucks.

Lola had seen them push Hermann into a truck. He had looked up to catch her eye. That was the last time she saw him. She hadn't been able to find Icio in the chaos. After the convoy had left, the women had rushed the Judenrat, screaming for answers. Lola said she had felt the ground slipping from under her feet.

For days and days she had been too grief-stricken to sleep. She learned that the men had been taken to Janowska camp. On the day of their arrival, a Jew had killed an SS guard. Two hundred of the new arrivals had been gunned down. Lola didn't know if her fiancé or her brother were alive or dead. Finally exhaustion had overtaken her and she had collapsed. When she woke up, her hair had turned white. She hadn't known what to do with herself. She hadn't been able to stand looking at the walls of her family's flat. She said there were too many ghosts and too much grief. She had gone outside and had walked the perimeter of the ghetto, back and forth.

After an hour, she said she had heard her name being called.

She had turned and seen Mr Beck standing by the fence. He had come to find out how they were. He whispered for her to come that night; that he'd be waiting for her. She had no idea he was so honourable.

I had my family with me and together we could mourn Dzadzio, Giza and the others, but Lola alone held the memory of her family. There would be no *shiva*, there would be no funeral for the people she had lost. The only thing she could do was write in her diary what had happened to her family on the night of the November *akcja*, and then one day find the strength to tell us.

Her mother and sister Genia had been out of the house when the *akcja* started. She had run to the basement with her father, while her brother Icio had hidden in the attic.

After the gunfire had finally died down, she and her father crept up the stairs. They found Icio trapped beneath some metal pillars that had fallen on him. He hadn't had time to put on any warm clothes, so he had been stuck in the freezing cold with his face pinned towards the window that faced the main square. He had seen everything. He couldn't turn away if he wanted to. He saw it from the beginning, how the commandant of the Gestapo set up positions on all the streets and shouted for everyone to come out into the streets and then the hunt for the Jews began. Whoever did not see it with his own eyes would never believe it.

Lola had ministered to him until he could move his feet a little. Then they heard a noise, as if someone was throwing a hand grenade in a building nearby, and a woman's voice screaming, 'Run!'

It turned out the head of the Gestapo himself was going house-to-house searching for more Jews. They were able to run down and get out through a small hole in the wall in the back-yard and by some miracle were not seen or heard. Later on they crept back to look for Lola's mother and sister. In the middle of the square stood a taxicab surrounded by Jews who were forced to kneel. This went on until nightfall when the Gestapo marched them to the train station.

Lola wrote in her diary:

Something in me dies when I look at all that. I know that in the formation being led to the train is my mother and my dearest sister. My heart is broken. My mind cannot accept the fact that they are being led to their death.

Oh, the blowing of the whistle as the train departs. I do not know what happens to me next. I think I am losing my mind.

Her father had tried to calm her. They looked for jumpers, like Mania and I had with Pepka Fisch. They were able to find some who had been on the same transport; they had seen Lola's mother and sister. Genia had been calm and was comforting the others and encouraging them to jump off the train. Her mother hadn't wanted to jump and Genia refused to go without her. Finally her mother had agreed. She had helped open the window and pushed her daughter out.

A few days later a couple of jumpers had heard someone yell out in Yiddish from the courtyard of a farm. The woman's clothes were in tatters and she was so cold and weak she could not move, but she had recognized the girls. She begged them to find Lola and tell her that her mother was alive. She had been shot at but the bullet had only grazed her head.

I am overjoyed that my mother is alive... I begin to look for a carriage but there are none to be hired. Every carriage is used to transport the corpses. What a terrible sight! Every carriage is filled with corpses and the blood is seeping from there. The streets are covered in blood. It looks as if a battle took place in our town. I feel that the ground is giving under my feet. I feel that I am falling down... I have to find a carriage as soon as possible. My mother has been waiting there since last evening... Every moment drags on... Finally I find one carriage driver, I promise him a hefty payment and off he goes. I can hardly wait for him to return. I go out to meet the carriage and what a terrible sight awaits me. Instead of bringing me my mother alive, I see a carriage full of corpses and on top is my mother. Ordnunger Shultz asks me: 'Do you recognize your mother?' I cry out in despair. My mother is lying on top with her head hanging down, she has only her dress on and a thin sweater, she is barefoot.

Horrible people not only did not take her in and look after her, they robbed her of her clothing. It looked as if she was asleep. It was obvious that she only recently passed away, simply because she was out in the open, weak and frozen, with no one to look after her. I cannot imagine the terrible death of my beloved mother. She was at most three kilometres from our home... We buried Mama in a mass grave with 70 others.

Lola found out from the stationmaster at Glinsko, a tiny town on the way to Belzec, that her sister was dead. She had been shot. Her father, mad with grief, later died from typhus in the ghetto.

Listening, I couldn't help but thank God for my family; that we were still together. But who knew for how long?

*

Only a few days after Lola's arrival, Rela received a letter from Uchka telling her that Josek had contracted typhus, but that she and Dudio were taking good care of him. The news of her husband's illness ignited the otherwise calm Rela. No argument convinced her to stay. We tried them all: she couldn't take risks. She had to survive because her son would survive the war. It was like arguing with the roar of the wind. Rela loved her husband and wanted to be with him, to take care of him, to nurse him back to health. She sent word to Laibek Patrontasch to come and get her. As soon as he arrived, Rela barely said a goodbye to any of us before allowing Laibek to lead her back to the ghetto.

The weight and swiftness of Rela's departure was stunning. There were no simple things in our lives any more. No easy comings and goings. So few casual conversations.

Julia was gone much of the time, often to Lvov to find out what was going on at Janowska camp. One day she was able to bring us good news. She had found out that Hermann was still alive and working at the oil factory at the camp. Lola's fiancé had been spared: this was more than Lola had allowed herself to dream.

Always gracious and a hard worker, Lola now had renewed energy. She was an excellent seamstress, and she started making new dresses and sweaters from used material and worn-out clothing. Julia also began to bring home German socks for us to darn. Lola was a good teacher. She taught us how to take old clothes apart and make new ones. How to darn, and do cross-stitch. Soon we had our little sweatshop in the bunker, quite literally so, since the weather had become warmer. Mama, Mania and I all took to the work. Finally we had something to do that could earn us some money. Julia took what we made to Lvov to sell in the market.

And Lola brought something else to the bunker. Good spirits. Despite everything she had been through, she always had a smile for me and Mania. She loved teaching us, and each of our efforts was rewarded with great acclaim as if we were designers from Paris.

Klara was being kept busy too. Whenever Julia wasn't home, Beck would ask Klara to come upstairs to help him with something. His shirts needed ironing. Something needed to be cleaned. Sometimes he would come almost as soon as the door closed on his wife and daughter's backs. Klara received stares as she left, and worse ones when she returned. She would come down, crawl over to her pallet and sit, her face defiant, defiant and sad at the same time. I didn't know what was going on. There were whispers from Mrs Patrontasch to her husband; whispers among the women; whispers among the men. 'Someone has to talk to her.' 'Patrontasch, you talk to her, she's your sister.' 'How can she do it? Right under his wife's nose?' 'She'll get us all killed!'

One day the men were smoking, waiting for Klara to come back down to the bunker. Something had been decided and I didn't know what. When Klara came down, the men went over to her right away. I had never seen anything like this in the bunker. They looked like judges. But judges too frightened to judge the accused. Too afraid she would defy their sentence. Too aware that they had no real power. The women continued to peel potatoes. I looked up from the book I was reading for the tenth time.

Patrontasch spoke, his voice quiet, nervous, uncomfortable. 'We've been talking, Klara.'

Klara's voice was flat. 'I'm sure you have.'

Patrontasch was equally understated. 'I don't know what's going on upstairs, but whatever it is, you have to end it.'

'I don't want to talk about it.'

'Our lives depend on the goodwill of Mr and Mrs Beck.'

'It's not your business.'

'Of course it's our business! Are you out of your mind? You could get us killed.'

At this point Klara looked away as her brother went on.

'We're three families down here. The Becks are our lifeboat.'

'Just leave me alone. I don't want to talk about it.'

'Klara…'

'Enough. Leave me alone.'

She turned away from the men. Patrontasch and the others stared at her, not comprehending her behaviour.

Someone asked her to think about the children. 'You don't think I'm thinking of them? You don't know anything. Now leave me alone.'

The men went back to their cigarettes and their newspapers. Lola whispered to me: 'I just thank God he doesn't want me.'

This is how I found out that Beck and Klara were having a love affair. I couldn't comprehend such a thing. Nobody had affairs. I hardly knew what an affair was. I was nearly 16 but I had never been out with a boy, hardly danced, held hands or even been alone with one. In the bunker, I wasn't thinking of the things that a normal teenage girl might think of. Besides the Nazis, the Blue Coats, the SS and the Gestapo, we had something else to worry about. What would happen if Julia found out about Klara and her husband. That she would find out was inevitable. But like everything else we had to worry about, it was out of our hands, and just added to our sense of resignation and helplessness.

From now on, every time Klara went upstairs, I would hold my breath, as did the grown-ups, until she was safely downstairs again. Nobody would say anything. Occasionally, an eye would glance upwards if the radio was turned on or if there was a creak in the bedspring or the shuffling of feet, or, worse, if the shuffling stopped. Nobody could say anything to Beck. The only thing I knew was that no matter how bad things were, they would get worse.

On 25 March, we were lying on our pallets. It was five in the morning and we felt it was safe enough to let in some fresh air. To do this we removed a brick in the foundations. Daffodils and irises with their graceful green shoots were already coming up, and between them and the bushes, the opening couldn't be seen from the street. Mrs Melman had been so proud of her garden and worked so diligently in it. The tulips would be up in a month or so, war or no war.

Mr Patrontasch sat up and said, 'Listen!' That was all we needed and all of us were listening, ears alert for the slightest sound. The word was an alarm. There were footsteps, many footsteps, but not marching, shuffling, and then over the footsteps, voices, German voices yelling, '*Weiter, weiter!*'

Then we heard the trucks, coughing, moving slowly. We could hear the early morning backfires and the grinding of the gears. Patrontasch remembered to shut off the light, even though it couldn't be seen from the street. We were lying in the dark and listening. Every one of us had family in the ghetto. Everyone was praying. We listened to footsteps and the shouting. There was an occasional gunshot that sounded like it was right outside. We would all flinch, not knowing if the gunshot was meant for one of our loved ones. Between the three families, their immediate family, their extended family, their in-laws, there had to be 200 souls that shared our blood and our lives.

The cries and screaming and shooting went on all day, stopped during the night and started again at first light. We were afraid to say a word. We didn't eat. We didn't cook. I don't know if I had a sip of water. How could we? All our tears were silent and our hands twisted and re-twisted themselves into grotesque contortions. Our hearts were breaking. This was the end. The end of the world. The end of the Jews of Zolkiew. It was our Tish'a B'Av, the ninth day of the month of Av, the worst day in the history of the Jewish people. The day of the five calamities and many more. The day God decreed the Jews would wander in the Sinai desert for 40 years so the entire generation that was saved from slavery in Egypt could die out; the day the First Temple was destroyed and ploughed under by Nebuchadnezzar in 585 BCE; the day the Romans destroyed the second temple 665 years later; the day Hadrian wiped out the Jewish rebellion; the day Jerusalem was levelled one year later; the day the Jews were expelled from England in 1290; the day that Isabella expelled the Jews from Spain in 1492. But what was happening now was worse than anything in our 5,000-year history. Such a thing to witness, sitting in darkness. On Tish'a B'Av, we were admonished to recite the lamentations and the words of Jeremiah. We are proscribed any kind of enjoyment for a period of three weeks. No weddings. No dancing. No sexual relations. No one had to proscribe anything in the bunker as the Nazis committed their desecration. To hear the screams of your loved ones and the gunfire in the distant woods where we played as children; the marsh filled with cat-tails and long weeds, with fish and songbirds and wild flowers. It was the Borek, the woods where many summer afternoons were spent with picnics and laughter. We uttered our own lamentations, silently. We prayed silently. We fasted. We rent our clothing. All these things were as natural to us in those dreadful hours as breathing.

Finally, towards the evening of the second day, no more footsteps marched towards the Borek. There were no more screams. No more gunfire. No more '*Schnell! Schnell! Weiter! Weiter! Los! Los!*' And now the silence was worse. We still couldn't speak to anyone in the bunker. We didn't know who was dead and who was alive. I didn't count the bullets and the gunfire, the sound softened by the distance. I didn't know what had happened to Uchka, Zygush, Zosia, Josek, Rela and Dudio. How I prayed. Without words. I prayed with a broken heart. How I loved them all.

Julia told us that she was staring out the window and she saw Mr Patrontasch's father look towards the house as he was driven past in a truck. He was too weak to walk to his death so the Nazis were kind enough to drive him. I could hear the sob that rose from Mr Patrontasch's breast, which he caught before it reached his lips.

Beck was our window to the world. He was our eyes and ears. And as much as I saw in his eyes that he would like to spare us the worst, he could not. Hiding us, feeding us, risking his life for us was one thing. But by sharing our grief, I think he had become one of us.

He told us that the common grave covered over with sand was heaving and that blood erupted from the soil. He told us that Mr Astman, the father of my best friend in the entire world, Genya, who lived across from the church that took in the Jewish girls to save them, had crawled out of the grave, not wounded at all. Not a scratch. It was a miracle. And, like *Hatikvah*, the song that so many of us sang on the path to our deaths, he had every reason to hope that he would be saved because a Polish man he knew found him. I didn't know if this man was a friend. I imagined Mr Astman crawling out of the grave, looking at a spring sky with trees starting to bud because it was too horrible to look around him, and seeing the face of a friend on the man who found him. I could imagine this hope that springs forth into eternity because that is the direction all hope runs to; this hope that was destroyed in the moment Mr Astman saw his fate in this friend's eyes. He took Mr Astman to the police, where he was shot on the spot.

That evening, Mr Beck brought Herr Doktor Professor Steckel and his wife into the bunker. We were now 14. We had created more sleeping space in the area under Ala's bedroom: space in which to crawl and lie down. Herr Steckel was the only pharmacist in Zolkiew and so had been allowed to live outside the ghetto. This had saved his life. I had never met them before and they were an austere-looking couple. I didn't want to think they were haughty and stuck-up, but those were the words that came to my mind. What must they think of us in our rags with our faces and eyes swollen with hunger and grief; our limbs mottled with sores and infected scratches that oozed pus? They in their clean clothes; he in his wool coat and wire-rimmed glasses and she in her mink coat, looking around the bunker, looking where to sit without fouling herself?

Beck introduced us, all of us. And there wasn't one word of solace, friendship, solidarity, gratitude or grief. They knew what had happened. Yet to look at them, they could have just arrived back from a vacation. Only money could allow them to look at us as if we were so beneath them.

I was smart enough to know Beck brought them here for their money. It was written all over their faces. There had never been any formal discussion between Beck and our families about money. The Becks had never asked us for payment in exchange for protection. All they wanted was for us to cover expenses for food. Not a zloty more. But from the very begin- ning our three families felt an obligation to give the Becks whatever we could because we knew they were risking their lives for us. No matter how much we were able to give them, it could never be enough.

Beck was going on and on with a smile, extolling the Steckels, letting us know we were their last resort and that Beck had a moral obligation to save them. 'How could I turn them away?' was what he said, and I knew there was no arguing or protesting. They were Jews. The Nazis wanted to kill them. We would make room. Life was very simple in the bunker. They had recently come to Zolkiew so I didn't know if they had any family or if they knew the positions my father and Melman and Patrontasch had held in our community. Or if they knew the breadth of my father's scholarship and generosity and the compassion of Mama. We who gave away most of everything, we had to provide for others. I could see the diamonds sewn in a special pocket in the lining of Frau Steckel's blouse.

Through it all my father started to explain how we took turns cooking, washing; he informed them of what the families kept to themselves and what they shared; where the buckets were; how they were emptied. Frau Steckel interrupted and said that Julia would be doing all their cooking. Okay. We all understood. It would be us and them.

We had to eat. It had been days since any of us had put anything in our stomachs. The women were ladling out the boiled potatoes onto our enamel plates.

There was a knock on the hatch. But even before Patrontasch opened the hatch, the smell of roasted chicken and pirogies assaulted us. I can't describe it any other way. Julia kneeled at the hatchway with a tray in her hand. Chicken, pirogies, vegetables and bread. Fresh bread. The tray had to be passed from hand to hand, from family member to family member. The tray had to run the gauntlet of starving human beings, past the noses of Igo and Klarunia, two starving children, to the Steckels, who took the tray eagerly and started to eat without a word or a look at any of us. Why we didn't take their food, I can't tell you. But my father and the other men, their decency was transcendent. They knew we were all hungry and I'm sure felt that, in time, without urging or any coercion, the Steckels would share their food, at least with the children. Poor Igo and Klarunia, their eyes bigger than their shrunken stomachs. What must they have been thinking? We had our rules, and we had to live by them to ensure our survival. Sometimes they were brutal, as brutal as any Nazi edict. But at least they were ours. To deny these children a bite of their food told me everything I needed to know about the Steckels and their character.

Beck continued to bring us news of the ghetto. Uchka and the children were still alive, as were Josek, Rela and Dudio. But over 4,500 Jews had now been murdered and the ghetto had been reduced to two streets: Perec and Sobieski. He said there were all sorts of rumours now being spread by the Nazis and their agents. The surviving Jews were in no danger. The murders were over and, on 6 April, bread and marmalade would be distributed in the ghetto. After the murders, that any Jew would believe such lies was impossible for me to accept, but I knew on that morning of the sixth, many of the remaining Jews would wander from their hiding places and assemble, exhausted in every way, wanting to believe that this time the Nazis weren't lying, at the same time knowing they were crazy to leave whatever shamble of a hiding place they had.

On the assigned day, as the remaining Jews assembled in front of the store on Sobieski Street, where the food was to be delivered, there was no bread and marmalade. There were only the killing squads from Lvov.

*

Beck couldn't go into the ghetto or knock on doors to find out the fate of our families. It was too dangerous. We didn't know where they were or if they were alive or dead.

That same night, Kuba and Artek, two of Patrontasch's brothers, arrived at the house. They had been able to escape from the camp at Mosty Wielke. At the same time that we were worried for Uchka and Josek and the children, I couldn't help being thankful that two of Mr Patrontasch's brothers had been returned to him. Kuba was a quiet boy who kept to himself, as silent as Gedalo, but Artek was like a part of our family too. He was Uchka's age and one of her good friends. He had had polio as a child and was balding and asthmatic and, in his own words, not much to look at. In the summers, since they were both asthmatic, he and Mama would often find themselves together at the same resort in the Carpathians, where there was fresh cool air far away from the baking heat on the western border of the steppes. The doctors used to laugh and say, 'What woman wouldn't feel better taking the waters and getting waited on hand and foot for six weeks?'

At five o'clock every day at the spa, they danced on wooden dance floors laid in the park, with orchestras brought in from Warsaw, Prague or Vienna. Artek always begged Mama, who was a fine dancer, to dance with him so the other young women could see the bald little man with the withered legs was still good on the dance floor. The scheme always worked. Mama lost her dance partner for the tangos, foxtrots and waltzes that filled the crisp mountain evenings as the setting sun cast its golden light through the tall pines. These asthmatic dancers, perhaps cured more by the music itself, whirled and smiled through light and shadow. Swarms of tiny mites were turned into golden clouds and the pine and wild flowers scented the air. Artek and Mama dancing, more brother and sister than friends, co-conspirators in a plot to make Artek more attractive. Mama would throw herself into such a task with joy. She loved Artek, and I knew they would have been showing her off in her silk and satin dresses, and how she would have loved the admiring glancing of the other women.

Now Artek was sitting in the bunker. He had witnessed Giza's murder in the 10 February *akcja* at Mosty Wielke and needed to tell us about it.

It was the same day that the SS officer named Hillebrandt had taken over the camp. His first order to his troops had been to surround the men's camp. Some of the men, including Giza's husband Meyer, ran off. Meyer was shot as he tried to jump over the barbed wire. His body was left there, bleeding. Then the Gestapo brought in the women and paraded them in front of the lined-up men. Many of the men saw their wives being led off to their deaths and were helpless to do anything with the Gestapo armed and waiting for them. Artek was in line with the other men. He saw Meyer killed and he saw Giza staring at her husband's body. Artek wept as he told us he tried to hide from Giza's eyes. He was ashamed he could do nothing to help her or Meyer. But she saw him and cried out to him. He had no choice. He had to step out of the ranks and go to her.

The rest of the men and women were marched away to another side of the camp where they were told to halt. Artek and Giza were left there, alone on the roll-call ground, guarded by a single SS officer, who somehow found the heart to let them say goodbye. Giza embraced Artek and she told him she loved him and began kissing him all over as if she were grasping on to the last acts of humanity she would ever express. She had no life left. Only her love, which she gave to Artek, asking him to give this same love to us, her loved ones who she knew were alive in a bunker. Artek said she wept and told him there was nothing left for her to live for anyway. She had just seen her husband killed. She asked Artek to avenge their deaths. The SS officer allowed them to stand that way, holding each other and saying goodbye, for 15 minutes.

Then the Nazi told Giza to take her coat off. It was a beautiful coat, styled like a man's, of dark blue tweed with an Afghan lamb collar. Uncle Hersch had made it for her. The soldier liked it and she took it off. Giza was then taken back to the other women and Artek rejoined the men who remained in the camp. The women were marched out of the camp to the woods, where the SS had taken 20 men earlier that day and ordered them to dig the graves. Artek didn't know if the women decided themselves or the Nazis ordered them, but they marched to their deaths singing *Hatikvah* (hope).

Three centuries ago, Sobieski laid cobblestones in our town with the command that they welcome Christians and Jews equally. Our forefathers walked down these streets with a new hope, a *Hatikvah* of their own, that they could live and flourish and pray and raise their families here in peace. For most of those 300 years, Sobieski's legacy was a canopy, a *chuppah*, which wed us, Christian to Jew, and protected us. And now, blood washed down these same cobblestoned streets.

Before the day was over, we learned that Uchka, Josek and Rela were dead. Our mourning, our grief, would know no end. In whatever time we had left, our hearts would be rent, as our clothes would be rent.

Zosia's fourth birthday was on 6 April, the day she lost her mother. Mania and I decided that we would fast and pray until we knew what had happened to the children. And if God gave them to us, we promised to fast until our liberation.

Chapter 7

THE ARRIVAL

10 to 17 April 1943

They left only 50 men and 10 women to clean the ghetto. They are forced to go to the forest to add soil because the mass graves are sinking. They are forced to sing while they march. Imagine they have to sing over the mass graves of thousands of people, otherwise they are hit over the head. One of the people left to work is Rela's brother Dudio. Mrs Beck saw him.

*

It had been several days since the *akcja* and we still hadn't heard what had happened to Zygush and Zosia. Our fasting and praying didn't bring the children to us. All the hopes I had had for the survival of our loved ones were now concentrated on Zygush and Zosia. Their survival might assuage some small portion of our suffering. If Uchka knew her children survived, she would accept the pain of her own death, would be at peace. Those two small precious bodies, if they survived, would mark some kind of victory over suffering and terror and senseless death.

I had gotten used to sitting on my pallet for long periods of silence. I always had my nose in a book. It was my escape, but there was no escape now. Before Uchka's death and the last *akcja*, I could just about shut out the others and leap into another world beyond the 50 or so square metres of this one. But now I could not even read. The book lay on my lap, open. I looked at the pages but the letters didn't form words that made sense. I couldn't stop thinking about what had happened to little Moshele. I needed to talk. To my mother. To Mania. To anybody, but before I could utter even one word there were looks telling me to shut up, especially from Mrs Melman and Mrs Steckel. My mind started to race. He was such a darling little baby, all blond curls and blue eyes. I could still see the joy in my uncle Josek's eyes. Moshele, the first son born to a Reizfeld of Josek's generation! His *bris* was the last party we had as a family. As usual Mr Beck spared us no details. And as he was compelled to confess, we were compelled to beg for details. It was insanity. We hungered for every word. Wanting to hear every horrible word that painted the vivid pictures of these deaths. The colour of the sky, the weather, what they were wearing, last words, their expression, were they buried or left to rot, who was with them, how many died, did anyone survive and a hundred other questions.

Beck had told us a German SS officer came to the ghetto and asked for a volunteer to bury a Jew out near the marsh. Dudio offered himself up. He had never volunteered before, but for some reason a feeling came over him that he had to go. He didn't know why. The two of them walked to the marsh. As they got closer to the common grave, Dudio could see the rain had washed away much of the sand. Parts of bodies, arms and legs and the occasional face, were visible. Among them, Dudio could make out a red-faced, feverish infant boy with bright blue eyes and unmistakable blond curls. Dudio immediately recognized Moshele. The baby's cries were weak, hardly more than a whisper, and he was choking and gagging on his own tears. It was a cold and raining spring day. God knows how that poor child was suffering or how long he had been there. Poor Dudio. *God heals the broken-hearted and binds up their wounds. God numbers the stars, giving each one their name...*

He had volunteered for this mission knowing he would be burying the body of Jew, so that at least a fellow Jew and a friend could say a prayer for his soul. What Dudio hadn't prepared himself for was to witness this child's murder, his sister's son; a child he had held on the day of its birth, his *bris* and countless other times. The SS soldier swore and cursed as he shot little Moshele. He had enough human feeling to curse his fate that he had to commit such a crime, but not enough to save the inno-cent child. Who would have known? Dudio and this officer were alone. Nobody would have known.

Great is God and full of power, with wisdom beyond reck-oning. God gives courage to the lowly and brings hope to the bereft.

As I sat and thought and prayed about little Moshele's short life... *Shield us from enemies and pestilence, from starvation, sword and sorrow. Remove the evil forces that surround us...*

...I expected Mr Beck to knock on our trapdoor with a bottle in his hand, climb down and report upon the last moments of Zygush and Zosia. They were alone and probably starving, in a basement, an attic, a closet. *Shelter us in the shadow of Your wings, O God, Who watches over us, and deliver us, O merciful Ruler.*

For the past week, Mania and I had been reciting these prayers, which my father had taught us: a prayer for those who suffer a major loss, and a prayer begging God for protection. Over and over, together; we whispered them; we mouthed the words; we said them silently staring at each other; we said them before we went to sleep and when we woke up. We knew we were annoying everyone in the bunker. Those of us who felt guilt at the decision not to allow children in the bunker were especially affronted. They knew who they were. Mama screamed at us (as much as she could scream down here) and begged us to stop our fast, which we started as soon as we heard about the *akcja*. She begged my father to make us stop. 'It was a sin to fast if we were in danger of bad health,' he argued. He told us that the Talmud said we could give to charity after we got out of the bunker instead of fasting and praying. Mania told my mother we might not get out of the bunker, and this was not something my mother needed to hear when she just got the news her sister, her brother and nephew were murdered and nobody knew if Zygush and Zosia were alive or dead. The grief was thick, a fog we couldn't see through, as heavy as a blanket of wet snow, a fog that attacked limbs and lungs so it took effort to move or breath or speak. My poor mother. I don't know how she could find the will to keep living, never mind peel potatoes, make tea, clean the crumbs from the dirt floor and wash the dishes.

I was reciting the prayers now, silently.

A knock on the door shattered my thoughts and prayers and brought back the knot in the stomach that arrived at every knock. If the Eskimos could differentiate between hundreds of kinds of snow, it was the same for us and knocks. Mr and Mrs Beck, their sisters and brothers, in-laws, friends, Ala's boyfriends, Schmidt the German policeman, the SS who came for drinks and cards, the Blue Coats, all had distinct knocks. But even if it was one I recognized, I was still terrified that I might be wrong. Mr Beck's familiar step crossed the floor. Nobody moved or breathed. My mother had been peeling potatoes and sat frozen, only a potato peel dangled from her peeler. Mania grabbed my hand as the

door opened and we heard a voice... a familiar, small voice straining to sound all grown-up and serious. 'Dudio said our mother was here.' Oh God, it was Zygush, he was alive!

I could barely hear Beck's voice as he whispered harshly, 'Get in here, before anyone sees you.'

Dear, dear Zygush. I could practically see the serious expression on his tiny old-man face, which he had had even as a baby, as he said, 'If you don't have room for me that's all right. I can take care of myself. Please, Mr Beck, please just take care of my little sister, Zosia.'

Mania threw her arms around me in relief and whispered *praise God* over and over, while there was a communal wringing of hands as to what could be done with four-year-old Zosia in the bunker. Zygush was old enough to be counted on to be quiet. But of course we couldn't condemn Zosia to her death and take Zygush without his sister. How I hated the Nazis for making us even think such a grotesque thought. Immediately, there were looks being exchanged and hushed words, too shameful to be uttered out loud. Yet. They were gathering their courage. I knew what Mrs Melman was whispering in Mr Melman's ear; Mrs Melman, who woke up every day and accused us with words or her eyes of stealing her water. And the Steckels, who were as cold as ice in their silence, were even more so now. But I didn't have time to think, because even as Beck was crossing the bedroom and banging on the hatch, I was looking deep into my sister's eyes, which were filled with a joy and gratitude I had never witnessed in my entire life. The joy of thanksgiving, creation and answered prayers were in those dark shining brown eyes. Patrontasch opened the hatch. Beck's face was even more swollen and red than usual. I wondered how he could see us, his eyes were so puffy. He was hungover and angry. I started to say something, but he cut me off. 'Not a word! Not

a word from any of you. Clara, get up here.' I didn't know why Beck called for me instead of my mother or father, but Mania looked at me: 'Make it all right.' God help me. Whatever would be pleaded, begged or argued on the children's behalf would be pleaded, argued and begged by me.

I crawled up into the bedroom and he slammed the hatch door down after me. He wouldn't look at me, perhaps to avoid seeing the pleading look in my eyes. I followed him up the stairs into the attic where Zygush and Zosia stood, dressed in their coats and hats and scarves, so bundled up they could hardly move. They both ran to me and embraced me, happy to be with someone in their family, relieved for one small moment to be safe, even if it was an illusion they weren't aware of. I had to hold my emotions in. I was afraid I would scare them to death with what I was feeling. Through the layers of clothing, Zosia's half-starved body was shuddering against me, crying and stunned, not understanding what was going on, looking over my shoulder and all around the small room for her mother.

Zygush said it for her. 'Where's Mama? Why can't she come up here? Dudio told us she was here. Where is she?' Little Zygush looked at Beck and then at me. Beck didn't know what to say, but he looked at me to tell them something.

We knew their precious mother was dead, and they didn't. But I knew Beck didn't want me to tell them and whatever lie I made up would be the one we had to live with. I had never lied to Zygush or Zosia before, and it would be a lie we would have to keep up every day in the bunker if Beck relented and allowed them to stay.

I don't know why I said what I did, but I heard my voice as if it were someone else speaking in a reassuring, matter-of-fact tone: 'Your mother had to go to Lvov... you'll see her as soon as the Nazis leave Lvov.' The news hit Zygush like a hammer.

His face went from joy to despair. Zosia burst into tears. She was crying that she wanted her mama. I held her as Beck looked on. The more she cried, the angrier Beck looked. I whispered over and over that it was all right and she would see her mother very soon. I told her that she was safe and my mother and father were downstairs. I didn't know what else to say. Beck's usually expressive face was now a wall. Zygush put his arms round Zosia and in his stoic little voice also told her it was going to be all right. He'd take care of her until they got to see their mother.

Beck was still silent. Instinctively, he took off their hats, revealing two heads full of lice. His face went from red to purple. His hands were shaking and veins were throbbing on his forehead and his neck. I knew what he was thinking. Lice! Eighteen people living in close and barely sanitary conditions. The typhus epidemic that was doing the Nazi's work in the ghetto could kill us all. The children could already be infected. Cleaning them up was a matter of survival, even if they had been in the house for only five minutes. He must have realized the impression he was making and somehow found a smile for the children.

'We need to give them a bath.' Then in a whisper, as he leaned into my ear, 'No way in hell they're staying here and don't even ask. Not one word! Not one word out of your mouth about this.' Zygush was dark and very Jewish-looking and no gentile family in their right mind would take in such an obviously Jewish child. There might have been hope to find a Polish friend to take care of Zosia, but how to even think of such a thing after what happened to little Moshele.

As I undressed them, Beck went downstairs. He returned with a washbasin and some bread, which the children devoured. Beck made several more trips up the stairs with buckets of hot water. Zygush took off his coat. He was a little Charlie Chaplin! Underneath were silk nightgowns, slips, stockings, brassieres, corsets and lingerie of all kinds. Even in the best of times, he was a skinny boy and I had wondered why he looked so stout in his coat. He had tied the nightgowns, slips and stockings into knots and struggled to get them untied. He was like one of the clowns at the circus: as soon as Beck and I thought we had all the garments, there were more hidden in pockets and even in his long underwear. I thanked God under my breath that Beck started laughing. Zygush grinned at Beck's laughter.

'Mama hid us up in the attic at the Judenrat. Mama and the other women used to dry their underclothes up there. I thought we could sell them. Did I do good?'

Beck agreed with a smile. Poor Beck. Every day, another life or death decision, relentless. And here he was on his knees, a raging argument and rising anger in his drink-ravaged face, which he tried to hide with a smile for frightened children.

Despite all this, he couldn't stop himself from asking Zygush how they managed to avoid a town full of SS, Gestapo and Blue Coats. Zygush informed us: 'We hadn't seen our mama or anyone in days and days and we were really hungry when Uncle Dudio came and explained that Mama was hiding at the Melmans'. Uncle told us it was Sunday morning and all the goyim were in church so it was a good time to go to Mama. He said not to be afraid because there would be Jews hiding all over the place to help us in case the Fascists or the police saw us.

Whoever said the Jews went like sheep should know a story like this! The last 50 Jews out of 5000, armed with only their fear and hunger, risked their lives to save perhaps the last two Jewish children in our town. It was a miracle two Jewish children walked two kilometres in broad daylight and didn't get arrested. Beck muttered that Dudio was damned clever. 'The SS, Gestapo and the Blue Coats like their Sunday mornings at church after a week full of murder. And damn the priests that hear their confessions.' He punctuated his statement with a giddy toast to Dudio's bravery and a long drink from a glass of vodka.

Beck asked the children if anyone saw them. Zygush shook his head. Beck turned to me. 'Burning's too good for these clothes.' I tried to read Mr Beck's face as he stared at Zygush and Zosia, all protruding bellies and swollen joints. In my mind, I was saying, *Please, please, please…* I wanted to beg him, grab his hands and kiss them, but I knew if I asked he would say no. Without one more word, he turned and walked downstairs to get more hot water, yelling for Mrs Beck to make soup for the children. I prayed Julia would say something, but good a person as she was, it was Mr Beck who made the decisions of life and death for all of us. He was God in this house.

When he came back up, I was already cutting their hair and shaving their heads. Zosia had the most beautiful blond, curly hair that everyone, family and friends, fussed over. She wept inconsolably, still asking for her mother. Even in the bath, she held on to me. I kissed her again and again and again, told her that her hair would grow back as beautiful as ever and she would see her mother very soon. I also whispered in her ear that it was very important for her to be quiet, quiet as a mouse, and that we all played a game in the bunker of who could be the quietest mouse. I was sure she would be the best mouse of all. I said this for Beck's benefit as well as Zosia's. I knew what the rule was. I knew that a small child in a house of hidden-away Jews risked everyone's life, especially the lives of our benefactors. I wanted to ask Beck with every fibre of my heart. But I also knew I didn't have to. I knew he was in as much torment as I was. Maybe even more. We were testing his goodness and generosity and courage at every step of our confinement.

I don't know where, but he found the children fresh, clean clothes. I helped them get dressed. Beck still gave me no indication what their fate would hold. Beck said he would burn their clothes outside. I could see Zygush's eyes. I knew he wanted to go outside with Beck and watch. Witnessing an immolation of so hated an enemy would, I knew, be morbidly fascinating and satisfying to Zygush. *Zygush!* I was screaming in my head, *for once in your life could you please restrain this incurable love of mischief! And don't ask Beck.* He looked at Beck and said nothing. Somehow he knew that his life was on the line and he was remarkably silent. Again, Beck looked at the pile of lingerie and underwear at the children's feet and then at Zygush. I thought I saw a trace of a smile in Beck's eyes. I tried to read him the way I would read a book or study a painting. Looking for any indication, hidden or otherwise, of what he was thinking. Sometimes his feelings poured out of him like sweat. But in moments like this I knew he didn't want to betray a thing. In that moment, I had the giddy and absurd thought that the two of them had become a small army. General Beck and Private Zygush. *Hatikvah!* Hope! But then it was gone. Beck's eyes were blank and empty. Empty of everything.

Without a word, Beck marched us downstairs and into the bedroom. He moved the bed away and Zygush watched, his big brown eyes wider and wider, as Beck removed the rug and knocked on the hatch. Zosia's hand kept going to her shaved head and she continued crying even as I whispered that it would grow back prettier than ever.

Patrontasch opened the hatch. My mother, father and Mania were waiting, faces looking up in apprehension. Beck handed the children down to my mother, father and Mania, who embraced them and covered them with kisses. Beck and I hopped down into the bunker.

Before my mother could ask the question, 'Do they know about their mother?' I said, as if I was giving away a small piece of gossip, 'I told them how Uchka was in Lvov with Rosa, and Zygush and Zosia can't wait to see her!' This was the lie that would be their reality until the end of the war. Until they found out the truth. What would they feel when they found out that their mother was shot one step outside their doorway as she was trying to bring them food? Would they hate us for the lie? Hate me?

Mr Beck found out from Dudio that poor Uchka had been going crazy knowing that her children were starving, frightened and alone two houses down the street where she had hidden them in the attic of the Judenrat. She knew it was risky to try to see them, but Dudio said she felt she had to take the risk. He and Josek tried physically to stop her and she fought them until Dudio realized he had to let her go. Josek said he would go with her. He wouldn't let her go alone. As soon as Dudio heard them go out the front door downstairs, he heard two shots. By the time Dudio got downstairs, they were dead. He took off their coats. They were both shot in the head and he knew that their coats would keep one of the few remaining Jews warm. Beck also found out that as soon as Sluka heard that Josek and Uchka were murdered he threw away the child. That's how Moshele had ended up in the common grave. For almost six months Sluka's wife held this boy, fed him, changed him! How could she have allowed her husband to commit such a crime, a child who without doubt looked upon her as his own mother? The coward waited until the baby's father was dead before he murdered the son. I had never heard my father speak of revenge before, but he prayed he would survive to see Sluka shot.

The Melmans and Steckels were looking at Beck to sentence the children to death, although I knew Mr Beck would never be cruel or callous enough to condemn the children to their fate in front of them. But the Steckels were shelling out good money to the Becks for their safety. Their zloty, deutschmarks and dollars were payment in full to get the children out of the bunker before a solitary cry gave us away. There was not a milligram of pity in their eyes. I didn't want to say it was hatred. I wanted to find fear and anxiety in their eyes, some kind of human emotion, but their eyes were cold. Beck looked right at the Steckels. 'The children are staying.' I don't know how he made up his mind. Perhaps it was the hatred in their eyes that set Beck off or perhaps it was Zygush and his underwear that allowed him to leap once more into the abyss for us. Who even knew if Beck understood what he was saying when he said it. I thanked God for these words, because I knew once given, Beck would never take them back. With these four words he bound all our fates together as much as blood. *For this one act, God should save and protect them.*

Professor Steckel couldn't get a single word out before Beck cut him off. 'Throw the children out? If God brought them here, who is Beck to turn them away? Whatever will be will be.' It was Beck who brought God into the conversation and it was through the miracle of Beck that God had answered our prayers. The children were with us. Part of Uchka was now alive and in my sight and arms, and even if we perished we would perish together. My prayer was answered.

I saw Mrs Melman holding her tongue. Steckel couldn't help himself. 'I don't think it's wise—'

But Beck was quicker. 'You don't like it, you know where the door is… and don't you dare insult me with money.'

Thank God the children didn't hear the exchange. They were too busy getting kissed and hugged by my mother and Mania. My mother was immediately moving the pallets around so the children could sleep between us.

In a few minutes Julia brought down their soup and for once the Steckels could watch while someone else enjoyed a meal. Zygush, alert, looked around, taking in his surroundings. Zosia was exhausted, more concerned with holding on to Mania.

Zygush stared at Klarunia Patrontasch across the bunker. I knew he didn't care for the girl, who was a year older than him, and took every opportunity to torment her in some way. I knew he would do the same in the bunker. The same brave boy who marched down the middle of a town full of Nazis and told Mr Beck that he could take care of himself was thinking he was going to make Klarunia's life a living hell. I whispered to him, 'It's very important we all get along down here. No being mean. No teasing her. Understand?' He didn't answer. 'Understand?' He finally nodded. But that wasn't good enough for me. I made him promise. We were now 13 in this tiny corner of the bunker.

As Zosia's eyes were closing from exhaustion, a full stomach and relief, she noticed Mrs Steckel on the other side of the bunker and called out, 'Aunt Giza!'

I explained: 'That's not Giza. That's Mrs Steckel, the pharmacist's wife. He makes the medicine that makes you better when you're sick.'

Zosia was insistent. 'It's Aunt Giza.'

The pharmacist's wife was annoyed already.

'It's not Aunt Giza, Zosia,' I said.

'Well, Clarutchka, the other name is way too long and too hard for me to say. I'll just call her Aunt Giza.'

Mrs Steckel was about to say something, but even she knew to keep her mouth shut, at least for a little while.

Zosia looked at Mrs Steckel for another few seconds, 'If she's not Aunt Giza, but looks like Aunt Giza, then I know Aunt Giza is still alive.' I was stunned that a four-year-old child could look for signs that her loved ones were still alive. Zosia lay down on a pallet and fell asleep almost immediately. Nobody told her that Aunt Giza had died.

As much as we mourned our lost family, the survival of these two children brought all of us such joy and relief.

The next morning, everyone except Zygush was still asleep as a faint light came in through the tiny opening that Patrontasch would fill with brick as soon as he awoke. The light was mine to enjoy for a few more moments as I was writing in my diary, trying to put into words my gratitude for Mr Beck, because I knew this might be the only chance I had. In the few moments we had upstairs, cleaning, it was an adventure. Upstairs, there was never the quiet moment just to talk without the fear of a knock on the door or a strange face in the window.

Zygush was staring at my sleeping sister. He pulled a feather from his pocket – where he got a feather, only God knows – and started to tickle Mania under the chin. She brushed at her chin with her hand and rolled over. Zygush waited a moment and tickled her under the chin again. Mania again brushed her chin.

I knew I should put a stop to Zygush's game, and he was now very excited, but quietly so, for the moment. He moved his hand out ever so slowly above her chest, barely breathing, and tickled her again with the feather. This time, Mania's hand darted out like a snake and grabbed Zygush's hand.

The commotion woke up Mama. She looked at Mania and Zygush and the first words out of her mouth were: 'Clarutchka, I think it will be your job to be the schoolmistress.'

'Me?'

My father opened his eyes and said, 'We were talking about it after you fell asleep last night. The children need to learn to read. You know what the *rebbe* says: "When we had to choose between building a sanctuary and a school… All you need to pray is ten men... If you have to build one thing, build a school.'"

A school? That's why I loved my father. We were scared to death, hiding in a four-foot-high bunker with dirt walls and slowly starving to death, mourning our relatives, and the way my father phrased the task is that we were going to build a 'school'. It was a task in the coming months that I would take very seriously, as much necessitated by Zygush's low tolerance of boredom and the need to keep the children occupied and quiet as their need to learn. Such was my father's wisdom. Teaching the children would benefit all of us in the bunker. People who had normal lives had schools; therefore we would share this normality with them. And if a school implied normality, the everyday preparations of lessons implied that children needed to learn for a future, and if they had a future, then we all had a future. And who could not watch with joy the face of a child as he learned to read?

Left to himself Zygush would find the one thing to do to drive every grown-up *meshuggehdik*. The only toy he had was a small penknife which he repeatedly threw into the dirt, hundreds of times already and he'd only been up a couple of hours. Zosia held on to a small piece of bread, wanting to eat it, but not knowing when the next piece of bread would be on the enamel plate my mother gave her... Mrs Melman and the Steckels looked at poor little bald, skinny Zosia as though she were a bomb, ready to go off and kill us all. Keeping the children busy would keep us all busy.

The school would start tomorrow. We still had to worry about what to do with the children that day. I don't remember if it was me, Mania or Lola who came up with the idea of our doll factory.

We supervised the children as they cut people and animals

out of our old newspapers filled with news of German exploits. They coloured the newspaper dolls with my blue pencil and pens that the men allowed us to use, which was no small gift because ink was precious. We scoured the bunker for candle drippings, scraping the wax from the wooden pallets, shelves and our enamel dishes. We kneaded the scavenged wax in our hands. Once the wax was soft, we showed the children how to make a base for their paper dolls that allowed them to stand.

Zygush had made a soldier, Zosia a milkmaid, Klarunia a mother and Igo a dog.

We worked for hours, and now we had the satisfaction of watching the children playing quietly with their new toys. Nobody said anything, but as we watched, we thought that perhaps having the children here wouldn't be our death sentence.

I didn't know what or who started it.

Little Klarunia was yelling at Zygush, 'I'm the mummy. You all have to listen to me!'

Zygush pointed his soldier's paper rifle in Klarunia's face. 'If you boss me around, I'll shoot you.'

Klarunia burst into tears. I told Zygush to be nice to her for a change. Zygush complained that Klarunia was always bossing him around. Klarunia said that Zygush needed someone to boss him around because he was a troublemaker and everybody said so and besides she was older. The bunker was suddenly very small. The Steckels couldn't find anything better to do than stare at us and the children as if we didn't exist at all. As many years as I've lived, I've never seen such coldness towards other human beings. I'm sure if the Steckels weren't there, we could have just distracted the children or they would have got bored or Klarunia would have retreated to the arms of her mother. But that look from the Steckels that went from my parents to the children to the Melmans and the Patrontasches was a lit match.

As Zygush informed Klarunia that at least he wasn't a crybaby, she threw down her doll and informed Zygush that she wasn't going to be the mummy any more. She took Zosia's milk-maid doll and little Zosia started crying. Eight-year-old Igo picked up his dog, shoving it in their faces. Mania and I tried to intervene without raising our voices and alerting Mr Beck upstairs to this commotion that could be our ticket to a camp. But the children paid no attention. Patrontasch grabbed his daughter and slapped her across the face. I felt the imprint of his hand on my own face it was so hard. Poor Patrontasch wore the face of a murderer. He was not a man ever to hit a child. He loved poor Klarunia, whom he had always spoiled. She was an only child and had never quite learned how to be happy or get along with other kids. In Klarunia's world, Zygush's arrival was another blow. The war, the Nazis, life in a bunker, starvation and now Zygush. His arrival made her beloved father raise his hand to her. She was inconsolable. Zygush was stunned. He didn't live in a world where parents struck children and I could see the knot of guilt in his throat. Can you imagine? With all he's been through, to have this final remnant of his innocence ripped away.

Mr Patrontasch apologized and put his arms around his daughter. He said, more to himself than anyone else, 'After the war, I'll spoil her again. Just like I used to.'

In the middle of the night, I felt a hand shaking my shoulder. I knew it was Mania's. I opened my eyes and I knew she was staring at me, eyes bright and wide awake, even though I couldn't see her in the utter darkness of the bunker at night. I could feel the soft breath of her words on my face. Everyone else was asleep. She talked about the fight for a few minutes, but there was something else on her mind. There was always something on my sister's mind. That night it was: 'I'm so happy the children are here.' I was too, I said.

And then the question and conversation that still haunts me. She whispered, 'Do you think God answered our prayers?' I wish I had a better answer, but all I could say was: 'He must have. The children are here. Why?'

Mania was not a child given to introspection or philosophy, so I knew she must have been thinking about this since Zygush and Zosia climbed down into the bunker. This was what she said: 'I don't want God to think I'm being greedy.' Dear, dear Mania. My poor sister, so grateful for the children that she was wondering if she even had the right to pray for her life, for our life, for food, for safety, for a new dress and clean clothes.

Ninety-nine remarks out of a hundred you can and do reply to without even thinking. But how could I even begin to respond to this that came from the depth of my sister's heart? All I had to offer was what I thought my father might say: 'If you're not being selfish, I don't think God minds at all. I think He likes it when you pray for the good of the people you love.'

Mania agreed. 'Papa says that the best prayers are good deeds.' She snuggled closer to me, putting her head on my shoulder and letting it rest there a moment. We could hear the quiet breathing of Zygush and Zosia, between us. Mania's voice was now in my ear. 'We were never so close before the war.'

My sister, who without a care sped through life on a bicycle with a skipping rope wrapped round her neck, was now cutting my heart open with every word. All the famous and learned rabbis in the history of our town could not stand up to the razor's edge of such words. Truth demands truth, but how could I possibly agree to the idea that we had ever not been close? I knew my sister. From Mania it was simply a statement of fact. I didn't say anything. Although she wasn't saying there was anything lacking in me, I knew what was lacking in my bookish, shy self. When did my wild little sister become so wise? She then told me, 'You don't like to talk about your feelings.'

Again, I could not find a single word. In every statement, in every way, especially this last one, she was telling me how much she loved me. We were hiding for our lives, in danger of imminent death from so many different sources you couldn't even think about it without going crazy or wanting to end your own life, and here she was confiding her secrets.

After a prolonged silence she said, 'I'm glad we didn't go to the nuns.'

I finally had something to say. 'Me too,' I said. Her love simply filled me up. Her last words that night were: 'I'll be quiet now. Good night.' She closed her eyes and in a moment I could hear her steady breathing. I was happy too. Such happiness as perhaps I have ever felt. What is this creature that God has made, that even as our families were slaughtered and each moment might be our last, we could still feel such love? Perhaps this was the greatest miracle of all

Chapter 8

18 APRIL

18 April to May 1943

The day I will remember until I die. Early in the morning, when we were still lying in our pallets with the little 'window' open, I smelled something. Before I could think what it was, Mrs Beck knocked at the trap door and yelled that there was a fire on the street.

*

I don't know what woke me up. I don't know if it was the wind blowing so hard outside, wailing through our little air vent. I can't tell you if it was the smell of smoke or everybody getting up at once, panicking as Julia banged on the hatch, shouting, 'FIRE, FIRE!'

Patrontasch climbed over us all and threw open the hatch. Every one of us panicked and rushed to throw on clothes as Julia kept screaming over and over and over for us to come upstairs. But we were panicked and paralyzed. Something stronger than iron bars kept us in the bunker and from running into the street and to save our lives. We knew what was outside. The SS. The Gestapo. The police. The Blue Coats. Poles and Ukrainians who would gladly turn us in for a few zloty and five litres of vodka. Beck yelled for the men to help him. Papa, Melman and

Patrontasch ran upstairs to help as he dashed in and out of the room with buckets of water, throwing them on the walls. We could hear the pounding of their feet above us as they ran back and forth from the bathroom and kitchen with their full buckets and then the heavy splash of water against the wall. I heard my father screaming that the entire block on our side of the street, one, two, three, four, a dozen, 20 houses, were on fire, flames pouring out of windows, roofs ripping with fire and falling in on themselves. A ferocious wind drove the flames first in one direction and then another and then up into the sky in whirlpools of spark and fire. I heard Melman screaming that the factory was on fire and could only imagine the look on his face as he watched his life go up in flames. Beck yelled that Mr Patrontasch's house was on fire too. Over the roar of fire and wind and Beck screaming, 'More water, more water!' I heard Mania's hysterical cries of, 'What do we do? WHAT DO WE DO?' I was watching and holding Zosia to soothe her and I realized for the first time that Mania had climbed up through the hatch and was now upstairs.

I couldn't hear what my father said to her, if he said anything at all. I knew he had to be thinking what I was thinking and so there was no answer to her pleas. The house he was desperate to save was our life. If the house burned down, we were dead. Smoke was now seeping through the floor above and into the bunker and we heard Beck screaming that the woodpile next to the house had exploded into flames that had ignited the outside walls. Beck and Ala threw open the door and ran outside with buckets, jumping over the flames to toss water on to the walls. Julia, in the kitchen, kept refilling pots and pans from the big zinc water barrel. She handed them to Papa and Melman, who threw them on the flames inside. But even as the house might be burning down above us, we didn't dare step up through the hatch. We huddled together with the children in the bunker, helpless. I listened for Mania, but all I heard was Beck screaming, 'Water, water!' over and over. The men and Ala couldn't get it to him fast enough. The church bells were ringing, calling everyone in Zolkiew to fight the fire. A small army was running up the street, heeding the call...

Every second another fire department wagon pulled up and along with them cars and trucks filled with SS troops, German army regulars and the dreaded blue-shirted Ukrainian police. Dozens, then hundreds of our enemies. Every building to the left and right of us was bursting into flames. Every other person was in uniform. Any second, I expected the entire house to go up. Beck was now screaming that the police were in the yard in the back of the house. They were on the other side of the bunker wall I was looking at, just a few feet away. If there had been any hope of running out and disappearing through the backyard, it was gone. There was so much water on the floors that it started dripping into the bunker, making the smoke almost liquid in our throats and eyes. Papa and Melman crawled back down into the smoky bunker. The grown-ups were all talking at once, over and at each other, voices rising to be heard. Melman: 'We can't go outside! We'll be shot!' Then Patrontasch: 'All of us? Are you crazy?' The argument ran in an endless circle with no resolution in sight. The panic was building as the bunker filled with more smoke.

A dozen half-starved, half-naked Jews running from the house with the hope of not getting shot? Or worse? Insanity. Finally, Melman screamed over the others, 'The bunker under the living room. It's our only hope.' He was talking about the bunker we had built under the far crawl space beneath the living room in case the house was being searched. It was no more than a tomb with a trapdoor roof. But death by fire and suffocation was preferable to being caught by the Nazis. All the children, however, except for Zygush, were hysterical. Mama told me she would go first and that I should put Zygush and Zosia in front of me. Mama was afraid that the children would get crushed as everyone would rush to the bunker to save themselves. Zosia was still in my arms and I put her down in front of me and followed Mama. We crawled on hands and knees as fast as we could, scraping knees and elbows. The smoke was thicker now, acrid, harsh, and black. It burned our eyes and throats. We couldn't see anything, if at all just a glimpse of the body ahead of us. Even the Steckels took their place in line. Lola, Artek, Patrontasch and his wife crawled with Klarunia between them. She was wailing with fear, but no one was telling her to be quiet. Even if we burned to death, the howling of the wind outside would have swept away our screams. I assumed Mania was somewhere behind me in this caravan of bodies.

In this crawl space, my father, Artek, Melman and Patrontasch yanked up the dirt-filled trapdoor that hid our secret bunker. There were water, candles and matches for emergencies. We crowded in, hip to hip, shoulder to shoulder, Zosia on my lap, all cramped together on the dirt floor. Even though we were sitting, we still had to hunch down as much as we could because the roof was so low. The children who weren't on laps sat crushed against their parents' legs. Our feet were pressed against the far side of this tomb that was now teeming with smoke as the men struggled to pull the heavy dirt-filled lid over our heads. The last thing I saw in the dim light was Mrs Steckel fingering the vial of cyanide around her neck.

You can't imagine such darkness. My father had matches and a candle ready. So did the other men. In the darkness, I concentrated on my father's unsteady hand as he tried to light his candle. His match flickered and went out. He lit another match, then another, then another with increasing urgency. Without light this was a tomb. Scratch after scratch of the sulphur match-head against the striker. All the men were working to give us light. But there was just one flicker of flame and then darkness after another. The street was an inferno. The house might be burning down around us and we couldn't light one damn match! There simply wasn't enough air in the bunker to light a candle.

Defeated, my father said, 'It's no use.' Then my mother screamed for him to light a match. He was furious, frustrated. 'Useless!' He tried to calm his voice. 'If we can't even light a match, we shouldn't waste the oxygen. We shouldn't even talk.' She screamed over his explanation: 'I don't see Mania. Mania, Mania?' My mother's anguish was met with silence and the horror of Mania's absence. The men were striking their matches, which gave off light for desperate fractions of seconds, illumi-nating a nose, an eye, a cheek, a chin, an eyebrow. None of them belonging to my sister. I wanted to scream her name as well, but I knew I would just be adding to the panic. I tried to remember if I had seen her come back down the hatch. I hadn't. I tried to remember when I'd last seen her. I ran through the chaos again and again and each time came up with the same result. I couldn't remember the last time I saw my sister.

I knew she wasn't with us, and the lighting of matches was nothing more than a waste of our precious oxygen and a post-ponement of a grief that would never heal. If we could all just keep striking matches for ever, we would not have to accept the truth that we were never going to see her again. My heart stopped when I realized my father was no longer screaming her name, like the shock of noticing the loudness of a clock's ticking when it stops. He knew where she was and couldn't bring himself to tell my mother. My mother was silent now. She knew.

My father lit one more match. Only his eyes and mouth were visible in the dim flickering light. He said simply, as simple and final as death itself, 'Salka, she ran out. She told me she was afraid of the fire. She told me she wanted to live. I tried to hold on to her with all my might. But she pulled away. She's such a strong girl. She said she was going to the bunker in the factory.' This was the factory that had just exploded into flames. His match went out. We were in utter darkness. My mother didn't ask him to light another match. There was no need. She said, 'I don't have a daughter.' Then nothing.

My mother was somewhere in the darkness on the other side of this grave. We were wedged so tightly together there was no way I could go to her or kiss her hand. I couldn't even tell her of my own grief because we could not afford the oxygen. I was so alone that even if it had been light I wouldn't have noticed if the others were sharing in our grief or if they were simply relieved that it wasn't their own child who was lost. What a horrid world we lived in when another's grief reminded you of your own dumb luck. There but for the grace of God go…

Papa should have stopped her from going, but this day was the fortieth anniversary of his mother's death… She had died in a fire as well and Mania was named after her. I didn't know how or why, but I hoped this child's cry was heard by the Almighty.

I have such a strong memory of everything that happened in the bunker for the 18 months we were there. I can still see every detail if I close my eyes. But I have little memory of the rest of that day. I don't know how we survived for so long without air. I know we prayed. We must have prayed. If there was conversation, I have no memory of it. If there were tears I didn't hear them. If the children cried, I couldn't tell you now. Some time later that day, we heard banging coming from somewhere outside the house and Beck's voice telling us we could come out. To this day my heart is filled with love and grief in equal parts for my sister Mania.

It was night-time when Beck came down to help us out of the 'tomb' and back into our regular bunker. I looked out of our little window. The night was bright, lit by a full moon, and the wind was still howling. I couldn't see how many exactly, but Beck told us that about 20 houses to the left and right of us had burned down. The wind blew hundreds and hundreds of burned books, pieces of furniture, children's toys, clothing, curtains, parts of roofs, prams and clouds of ash past us in an endless stream of charred lives.

My mother and I sat together, numb. Everybody in the room, except for the Steckels, loved Mania. More. We were all *in love* with her. There are some people who are simply gifts to everyone they meet. My sister was one of them. Beck poured himself a drink and then a drink for everyone else.

In his usual blunt manner, he said of his drink, 'My courage. I'm afraid I'm going to have to ask you to leave.' Beck's voice was hard because that's the only way he could utter the words.

My father said, 'We understand.'

Then Beck told us that he'd heard Mania had been shot. He didn't know anything more about it. This was our death sentence and we couldn't even express a word of our grief for Mania. We would soon be dead just like her unless we found another place to hide. Mania's death had taken away our own will to live. We were numb, defeated. How could we argue with Beck? Or even beg? There was nothing more this man and his family could do for us that wouldn't be their death sentence too.

Only tiny, cranky Mrs Melman asked Beck if she might have a word with him upstairs. She couldn't look at him as she made her request. She stared down at her shoes, which were covered with mud and ash. He nodded and helped her up through the hatch.

Beck didn't say when we would have to go, but as soon as he left we started gathering our things. I tried to hold Mama, but she shrugged me away. She wouldn't look at my father. However angry my mother got, she never once mentioned that my father didn't stop Mania from running out of the house. The children looked at us, silent, not daring to speak. Zygush's young eyes had grown old. How he had loved my sister, his co-conspirator in all things mischievous, the girl in our family who would defend him from the bullies and ride him on the handlebars of Aunt Giza's bike as Uchka chased them down the street, begging them to be careful.

Then Beck was screaming. 'Get into that damn hole and close the hatch over you and stay there until I tell you! Until hell freezes over if need be!'

Mrs Melman stumbled into the bunker and my mother asked her what she had said to Beck. Mrs Melman said she couldn't remember but she had begged. That was all. We were in such a state of shock that the men couldn't even begin to think about where we would go and the women didn't ask them. The only one of us who would have pushed was Mania and she was dead.

All I could think was where should we go, straight to the Germans? To top it all off, it was still a terrible night outside. The winds were like a hurricane. Blowing 80 kilometres an hour. You wouldn't send a dog out in this weather and we had two small children. Who would blame the Becks? After all, it's we who were their death sentence…

A few minutes passed and Beck jumped into the bunker again. He looked out of the window, the wind howling outside, and said, 'Go to sleep, whatever will be will be.'

'God, please help us,' I prayed, 'that we survive and repay these people for what they do for us.'

The next days were one nightmare after another. Mama's grief was unbearable. She couldn't or wouldn't speak to my father. And it wasn't out of anger, even though in her silence she condemned him. It was because to look at him was to see Mania's eyes in his, her face in his. They couldn't even grieve together. Or out loud. I, however, clung to a whisper of a hope that she had got away, that Beck was wrong. And so I continued to say the prayers my father had taught me. I wanted to talk to my father about the conversation Mania and I had had the night before the fire. My darling sister had wondered if she had the right to ask God for more favours since He brought the children to us, but to ask Papa might open an even deeper wound. The one person I wanted to talk to about it, or about anything at all, was Mania. We had lost so many, yet somehow the four of us had seemed inviolate. Fate had seemed on our side in keeping us alive and together. My burst appendix had kept me from being shipped off to Kazahkstan with Aunt Rosa. Mania and I didn't go to the nuns. The Russians arrested the wrong Meir Schwarz and shipped him to Siberia instead of my father. The Becks came to us. Too many close calls to mention. And now?

And now, we had to go on without her, our lucky charm. We were still alive, whether we wanted to be or not. I now knew there was no such thing as a broken heart. It will go on beating to taunt you and mock you and tell you that even in grief it is indestructible and full of love.

Every few hours Beck came down with another report. He told us that some neighbours down the street had sworn to the SS that they saw Mania run out of the house in the middle of the fire. Another had told Julia that he had seen Mania running to the nuns at the church just five blocks away. If Mania made it to the nuns... I prayed.

Then Beck was taken into the SS and in his presence a Russian neighbour, old Stefaniuk, another drunk, who lived in the Britwitzes' house, accused Beck of harbouring Jews. When the Russians came to Zolkiew, they brought with them workers, spies really, to work with the local businesses. Stefaniuk was our 'spy', but my father treated him well, like a friend, and here he was betraying us. Thank God, Beck's *Volksdeutscher* friend, Mr Lang, a professor of Latin at the gymnasium, happened to be at the SS headquarters at the same time. Lang told the SS it was Stefaniuk himself, a *Moskol*, a hated Soviet sympathizer, who was harbouring Jews.

Beck told us to stay. 'We are all in God's hands.' How many times would he invoke this benediction? He was convinced the SS believed him when he told them that Stefaniuk was a 'lying Russian dog', and how could they believe their enemy when it was Beck, a loyal *Volksdeutscher*, who was telling the truth? Beck told the SS that the Russians, the Poles, the *Volksdeutsche* and the Ukrainians had been at each other's throats for years. And he thanked God the Nazis were now here to bring order to the town. Beck would be damned if he wasn't going to one day piss on this Russian's grave.

We waited and waited for the pounding on the door. But it didn't come. The SS didn't come for us that night.

But the next day, they knocked on the door and took Julia in for questioning. God knows why they didn't search the house as they had threatened. We sat in silence and horror as they took Julia away and still we did not say one word about Mania. Her fate was extraneous to our survival and therefore a luxury in the eyes of the others. We expected Beck to be panicked about his wife being questioned by the SS. We were worried about her being tortured and murdered because of us. Still Beck didn't throw us out. He waited upstairs as we waited downstairs. The worse things seemed to us, the calmer he became. Again, he said, 'It is out of our hands,' meaning, of course, that it was in God's hands.

A few hours later, Julia walked in the door and reported that the SS told her that Mania had confessed she was a maid in the Beck house. Julia denied it, saying the German police, the Gestapo and the SS were all frequent visitors to the house and how could they possibly not notice a Jewish maid. She told them to ask Schmidt or Krueger if they wanted. They would vouch that the Becks harboured no Jews. The two policemen practically lived there. She was sent home and still the SS didn't come. Where did the Becks get such courage to look the SS straight in the eye and lie with such conviction? Beck I could understand. But Julia was so timid and shy she could hardly smile in public, and if she did laugh or smile she covered her mouth, ashamed as she was of her teeth. This was the SS that could break the strongest man or woman if they had the slightest doubt in their story.

After Julia came back, Beck brought a bottle and some glasses down into the bunker and told us what happened to Mania. He said he had gathered his information from different people: friends, enemies, partisans and traitors. He said he wished to hell that he didn't have to tell us, but he did. He had to get it off his chest.

This was the story he told us: 'The entire street was on fire. The police were out in force pushing everyone back. Through the fire, I thought I saw Mania run up the street and disappear into the crowd. But I didn't believe my eyes. I couldn't believe that she would leave us, leave you.' Beck had to take another drink. His eyes were red-rimmed. This was so hard for him. We wanted to listen as much as Beck wanted to talk: not at all. But we knew we needed to hear what had happened to my beloved sister. Beck asked me if I knew two boys, Tilzer and Schitling. I went to a different school, all girls, but the boys were my age and I saw them most days, walking to and from school, playing football in the park or running the streets in a pack. I was shy and so were they. We would never even speak, but now and then we would have a silent nod. We weren't friends, I couldn't say that. But we all used to skate together on the river. Skating was the one sport that I loved. We would form long whips, and if I held Schitling's hand in one of these whips, this was the closest I ever got to him. But he seemed sweet and was always polite to his elders.

Beck continued: 'Mania was walking quickly up the street to the church where some of the other Jewish girls had been taken in by the nuns. Tilzer told me they saw her and that Mania looked back and saw them. She didn't start running, Tilzer said, because they smiled at her and she smiled back. The boys thought that she must have felt safe. The boys were poor as dirt and of course they knew there was a bounty on the capture of Jews. They didn't say anything to each other. They just started chasing her. They said Mania was fast. She heard them running after her and they told me that when she looked back at them, she thought they might help her. But then she realized the two boys were after her. She ran like hell as far as the church steps when Tilzer tackled her. Tilzer was hoping that none of the nuns came out because they all knew him. Even I don't understand why not one of the nuns came out of the church with all the commotion from the fire. Tilzer said Mania was only 10 metres from the convent door. She begged for her life, but then she followed him. She only asked that Tilzer tell her family her fate some day. When they came to the alcohol depot to pick up their bounty of five litres of vodka from me, they felt so guilty that they confessed everything, because they knew Julia had worked for Mania's mother. They had no idea you were here. I wanted to kill them and cry for them at the same time.'

My tears were coming now. Julia was questioned. They told her that they had caught a Jewish girl who had claimed to be cleaning house for the Becks. Julia looked right in their faces and called it an outrageous lie. She asked to see her accuser. Beck had a few more things to tell us. He had heard an SS buddy talking in a bar about a girl they had caught who said she was from Lvov. A maid! Mania had never given us away.

Her last thoughts were to protect us at the cost of her own life. A 13-year-old girl, no more than 40 kilos, stood up against the SS and the Gestapo, whose officers and men represented the collected might of the Nazi empire, and they could not break her. In the bright, bright light of such love and courage, how could I not find the will to live?

Dudio had seen the murder and had given Mr Beck a letter with the date, 19 April. Dudio wrote saying that they had brought her to the old Jewish cemetery, shot her and dumped her body. The cemetery was now a barren field of unmarked graves. Jewish boys had been made to cart away the headstones and break them with hammers, almost as big as most of the boys, into small rocks for paving.

I didn't know what they did to her or how much she suffered. But I did know that this had to have happened in front of dozens of people who had come out because of the fire. This had happened in our neighbourhood where everybody knew and loved her. The Becks had made a choice to risk their lives to save us, but all Tilzer had to do was look away and my sister would still be alive.

Chapter 9

THE LOVE AFFAIR

May to September 1943

Tuesday, 7 September. It's terrible how we are dependent on all kind of factors. When the sister-in-law wants to get married, it's our problem. When Mr Beck plays cards, we are worried. When he drinks, we are panicky. When he has a fight at work, we are desperate. God help us and all the problems should get straightened out. I hope Mrs Beck lets us listen to the news. Maybe the news is good.

*

The bitter truth, the bitter unacknowledged truth about my sister's death was that even as we prayed for her survival and once we learned of her capture, we also prayed she wouldn't betray us. So our tears for my sister were also tears of relief. We were afraid to cry out loud so I wept silently. We couldn't mourn in any of the traditional ways. We didn't say *Kaddish*. We didn't sit *shiva*. Instead, Mania's presence filled the bunker in her absence. The rest of the bunker took their lead from Mama and Papa and never mentioned her name. The children as well didn't ask. She was gone. When I awoke in the mornings, I looked for her. And the memory of her death was new again. It seemed to devour the air around me as if her memory wanted to live so much it required air. It was hard for me to breathe, yet I cherished the pain because it was all I had left of her.

Nevertheless, our lives and needs had to be attended to. We put up our pallets and sprinkled a few drops of the precious water on our faces. Two weeks after Mania's death, I was at the hotplate, peeling and cooking potatoes with Mama and Lola. As the morning wore on, the heat seemed to pour off the walls. Patrontasch had a newspaper open and was emptying out the dregs of tarry but unburned tobacco from the butts of smoked cigarettes. It was painstaking work and Mr Patrontasch constantly wiped his brow with a handkerchief to keep his sweat from dampening the tobacco. The newspaper was from the previous month and the news was both good and bad. The SS had taken over the German assault on the Warsaw ghetto. And Rommel had surrendered in North Africa. We were proud of the ghetto fighters, but knew they were all doomed. We felt like they were fighting for all of us and I wished I could fight with them.

Mama said something she repeated at least 20 times a day. 'It's too hot to eat, never mind cook.' We all laughed as if it were the first time we heard the remark. Mania would have laughed.

We managed to live through the heat of the summer, the prickly heat, the hunger, the boredom and the depressing reality that there seemed to be no end to the war.

Beck came down with a paper and handed it to Papa, who looked at it. 'Italy surrendered! It can't be too much longer now.' He was excited.

Mama couldn't let such a remark go by. 'That's what you said ten months ago, nine months ago, eight months ago—'

My father interrupted. 'Enough already, I get your point. It says right here that the Russian army is at Zhitomir. Even the German papers say it so it's probably true and the Russians are even closer.' Zhitomir was west of Kiev, which meant the Russians were on the way to Lvov. This news was encouraging, but we were afraid to put our hopes in anything now.

Mama changed the subject, suggesting we should pick through our clothes to see if there was anything left for Julia to sell. We did this periodically and never found anything good enough. *Kol Nidre* was in a week or so and we wanted to see if there was anything special left for us to wear. The men were going to pray in their underwear, since the weather had turned warm. They had examined the Talmud and discovered that as long as one's head was covered and one wore a tallith, the rest was optional.

As my mother picked through her clothes, they all fell apart in her hands, eaten away by dampness and mildew. And then she told my father that since she had nothing to wear maybe the women should imitate the men and pray in their underwear since it was so hot anyway. My father said, 'Go ahead'. All the other women threatened to do the same and were quite surprised that their husbands didn't protest.

Julia and Ala had gone to church as they did every Sunday morning. Almost immediately after they had left, Beck called Klara upstairs to perform some fictitious service. Ever since the first day Beck invited Klara upstairs, we lived with this additional source of terror. How long could this affair go undiscovered? We knew, given the closeness in which we lived; we knew about Beck's increasing persistence and obsession; we knew that with his drunkenness came carelessness, and we knew that, sooner or later, Julia would find out that her husband and her best friend, a woman whose life and whose entire family she was saving, had both been betraying her.

Beck had been getting bolder and bolder. As soon as the door closed and Julia's footsteps echoed on the stone walkway to the street, Beck called down for Klara. We said nothing. We did nothing. Nobody could talk to Beck about it. And perhaps we knew that if Klara tried to break it off, there would be consequences as well. Who knew what Beck really felt about Klara? Was it love between them? And what did this say about the character of the man to whom we owed our very lives? If we begged him to stop, would that brave and generous man disappear and leave only the man who would sleep with his wife's best friend? Would that man risk his life every day for us? We were afraid that simply to beg him to stop would be enough to put us on the street.

We heard the front door open upstairs. There was no knock. I listened to Julia's familiar footfall cross the nine steps from the front door to the kitchen. I'd counted them a thousand times. Nobody moved, nobody talked, nobody breathed.

Julia's voice was cheery as it called out to no one in particular: 'It's just me. I forgot my purse. I was in church and didn't have one groshen for the collection plate.' It was only five steps across the small living room to the bedroom. I counted to five and she was there.

All our eyes went to the ceiling. I had never heard Julia raise her voice before, not above her usual pleasant tone, but she was screaming now. 'You bastard! BASTARD! AND YOU! I WON'T HAVE A SNAKE LIVING UNDER MY ROOF! GET OUT! GET OUT!'

Klara's feet staggered across the room and she stumbled down the hatch, face first. She had her dress on, but it was unbuttoned. Without looking anyone in the eye, she buttoned her dress hastily and crawled past everyone around the corner into the furthest part of the bunker.

Upstairs, I heard Beck roaring and throwing furniture around the room. I could only imagine the chairs and pictures smashing against the walls. There were the wedding pictures and the pictures of Ala at her confirmation, her graduation, skating on the river and so many others. Zosia and Zygush crawled over to me and buried themselves in my arms. The worst thing in the world, our world, was happening and we were powerless to stop it. The implications ran through my mind. She was going to throw Klara out. She was going to throw us all out. There was no way any woman could tolerate Klara and Beck's affair. And she wasn't just any woman. Before the war, Klara and Julia were friends, best friends. Two women could not be closer unless they were sisters. It was because of Klara that Julia convinced Beck to take us on. Klara knew it. We all knew it. Even Beck knew it.

Beck screamed now as if he was the injured party, as if somehow Julia had destroyed his happiness, his perfect world and, most tragically, his image of himself. 'Leave me alone! Leave me alone!'

But Julia fought back. 'Get her out of here! Get them all out of here! All of them!'

We were more than silent. This was our nightmare. This was the SS coming through the hatch in the floor; this was our marching with our friends and family to the marsh outside of town to be shot. And really all it was, was an unfaithful husband and an injured wife. This scene has been played out so many times, almost every minute of every day all over the world. But this time it was a matter of life and death to so many. Zosia was weeping and as much as I tried to console her, telling her it would be all right, I knew I was lying.

Beck roared again: 'YOU DON'T LIKE IT? YOU GET THE HELL OUT!' Another mirror smashed against the wall, or maybe it was a picture, I don't know. Then there was the sickening crack of a fist against bone and a body crashing to the floor.

Beck panicked. 'Help me. Help me! Help me! Patrontasch! Help me!'

Patrontasch crawled up through the hatch. He had some first-aid training. Julia was on the floor, convulsive, bleeding from the mouth. Her eyes were rolled back up in her head and she thrashed on the floor. He immediately grabbed a belt and put it in between Julia's teeth so she didn't swallow her tongue.

Beck didn't say anything. He grabbed the bottle of vodka that he and Klara were drinking from and sat on the bed, calm as buttered toast now. Patrontasch wrapped his arms round Julia's body to try and quell the fit, but it went on and on and on. He was a big man but, struggling with all his strength, he still couldn't control the spasms. In the bunker, I was helpless. I didn't know what was happening but I was afraid Julia was going to die. I wanted to tell Mr Beck to run for a doctor, but how could I? Patrontasch finally screamed what I was thinking, 'You have to get a doctor!'

Beck took another swig. 'She has these all the time. She'll be all right in a few minutes. God help me. I hate this house. I hate you all. Most of all, I hate her!' He got up and walked out of the house. He was right. In a few minutes, Julia calmed down and Patrontasch put her to bed and came downstairs and told us what had happened. He also thought Julia was going to die.

A few hours later, after Ala had come home, she, Lola and I sat with Julia at the kitchen table, drinking tea. Her face was swollen, her lips bloated and cut. Even though it was hot, the windows and curtains were closed. Ala held Julia's hand.

Julia wanted to talk, as if she had something to explain or confess. 'I was so happy. I was at church the other week and after the service I was in a hurry to get home to get some money because it's Sunday and I didn't want to miss the bus to Lvov. I was rushing and slipped down the stairs at the church and my dress went up and Mrs Lueczkiewicz – you remember her don't you?' she said, looking at Lola and me and Ala. 'Your sewing teacher at the school? I was so embarrassed to fall in front of everyone with my dress going way up past my knees. You can imagine how I felt. Mrs Lueczkiewicz helped me up and saw how my stockings were stitched with the zigzag stitching that Lola does and she remarked on what a good seamstress I was and that my stockings were so pretty. I couldn't wait to get home to tell you three. I thought it was so funny that Mrs Lueczkiewicz thought I had sewed it when it was three of her students. I wanted to tell her that you and Lola were alive because I know she always liked you, but of course I didn't.' She stopped in the middle of a thought. She took a sip of tea and refilled my cup. 'You know,' she said, 'I can't live with a snake under my own roof. I'm leaving. I have to leave. As soon as that bastard comes back. I'm sorry. I'm so sorry to leave you with him.' She looked at us like she expected us to argue or at least put up some kind of protest. But we just sat in silence drinking the tea that Ala made for us.

Back down in our bunker, we heard her packing a bag and then followed her and Ala's footsteps going across the floor. We heard the door open and close. We were alone, and for how long we didn't know. Both our protectors were gone and we knew we couldn't survive more than a few days without them. From the very first time that Mr Beck invited Klara upstairs, we knew this moment was inevitable, and now it was here.

The house was empty and we were all pretending to be asleep. My head was on Mama's lap; she was fanning me softly, careful not to blow out the candle that would leave us in the dark. Klara was awake. She was staring at the ceiling. Nobody had even mentioned or discussed what we had heard earlier in the morning. It was too frightening. We were at sea in the middle of a storm we had absolutely no power to stop. Maybe Mr Beck would come back. Maybe Julia would come back. Since Mania's death, I had never felt so alone and so helpless. And crazy as it sounded, I wished she were here because she was the one person who could muster up the courage for us all. She wouldn't be afraid to talk about what had happened. Instead, she would have badgered my father and mother until they came up with a solution to our problem. But I wasn't my sister. I was ashamed at how I felt: powerless and with no will to fight.

All I could do was express my helplessness. I spoke as quietly as I could. 'Mama, everything is out of our hands. When Mr Beck's sister-in-law wants to get married to a Ukrainian, it's our problem. When he drinks and plays cards with the Gestapo, we're worried. When he's drunk at work, we're panicked. He has fights with his boss, we're desperate... But no matter what happens he thinks everything will work out all right... But this romance with Klara? Do you think Julia will leave him? Do you think he'll leave Julia? What are we going to do, Mama? Is this it? All the suffering to end up like this?'

'I don't know.'

'What do you think Julia will do?'

'God doesn't even know.'

This was how my mother told me to stop asking questions. If God didn't know, how could I possibly presume that she would have an answer?

It was our third sleepless night since the fight. We had run out of food and water. We sat in such lethargy that despite the heat we barely remembered to fan ourselves. Barely a word had been spoken since Ala and Julia had left. As much as I wanted to, I couldn't ask Mama or my father the horrible question: 'What happens to us if the Becks don't come back?' I knew it was the question on everyone's mind. But to ask it would make the terror even more real. So even though 18 people were living on top of each other, in our most desperate moments we were often alone. We were silent because we were afraid words would give voice to our panic and could very well lead to frantic, impetuous actions. Mania had run away during the fire. The Steckels had their vials of poison. There was even a five-litre can of petrol buried in the bunker. We were prepared and the grown-ups had already vowed that the Nazis would never take us alive. I prayed that the Becks would remember we were here. Yom Kippur was coming and we didn't even know if we would have a chance to atone for our sins. But atonement wasn't on my mind. When someone has a pillow over your face and is smothering you to death, all you're asking God for is one more breath.

The sound of the front door opening hit us like a bolt of electricity. I hoped it was Mr and Mrs Beck; that somehow they had found each other and were coming home together. But I only heard Mr Beck's heavy drunken footsteps, and he wasn't alone. He was with Sergeant Krueger of the SS, his best friend, drinking companion, gambling associate and partner in several black market enterprises, of which every one of us downstairs knew all the details. Only Julia and Ala were in the dark.

Beck was drunker than usual. Only when he was close to oblivion was his speech slurred.

I wondered if he had finally gone off the deep end. When I prayed, I always prayed for him... I prayed for his health; I prayed that all his schemes would work; I prayed that he wouldn't get caught. And I prayed that he would stay lucky. My father said sometimes it was better to be lucky than to be smart. Beck's luck was our luck.

He called out for Julia and then for Ala, over and over. He searched the house, going from room to room. We heard the doors open and then slam shut. Finally, he collapsed into a chair. 'To hell with them. C'mon, Krueger, sit down already, you're making me nervous standing around. I'll get us a drink.'

'Not tonight. I just wanted to make sure you got home in one piece.'

'We can play some cards. Listen to the news from London.'

'London?'

'C'mon, Krueger... don't tell me you don't listen to Radio Free Poland. It's your job.'

We couldn't believe that Beck had just admitted to a sergeant in the SS that he had an illegal shortwave radio. It was a hanging offence.

'It's not your job, Beck. And I don't want to know everything that goes on in this house.'

Beck laughed and we heard him scrambling around for a bottle and glasses, which he then proceeded to slam on the table for emphasis.

'Well, at least have one goddamned drink before you shoot me. But then again you won't shoot me. I'm the only damn friend you have in this goddamn town. I love you and you love me. You're the only Kraut that has a goddamned sense of humour. Really, I don't see how you stand those other bastards. I don't understand how you don't blow their brains out just for being so fucking dull. Especially Von Pappen. I'll shit on his mother if he gives me any more trouble.'

'Go to bed, Beck... before you say something really stupid.'

Beck laughed. 'Get the hell out then.'

I knew my mother wanted to cover my ears to such language. For a change, she had something normal for a mother to worry about instead of our impending slaughter. When

Mania was alive, after the others went to bed she would keep me up discussing the conversations over and over, taking every word, every phrase apart and getting such a kick out of doing it. Mania lived for eavesdropping.

We sighed in relief as we heard Sergeant Krueger cross the floor and the door slam behind him. A moment later, Beck banged on the hatch. Patrontasch crawled over to open it. Light poured in the bunker. Beck was too drunk to even kneel; he lay on the floor and stuck his head in the hatch.

'Where the hell is my wife?'

Patrontasch was nearest Beck, so he answered. 'I don't know. She and Ala left three days ago, just after you.'

Beck reached into his pocket and pulled out a piece of paper. We could see that it was crumpled from being in his pocket for a long time. 'Then give this to your sister.'

He handed Patrontasch the note.

'And tell her I want an answer right away.'

Beck staggered up and we heard his body fall into the bed. Patrontasch gave Klara the note. She waited for a moment before reading it, but she knew it was too important to put off. Every eye was on her, even the children. She read the letter and then slowly put it down.

In a voice that was flat, even for Klara, she said to no one in particular, 'He wants me to run away with him. He wants to save me.'

It was her older brother, Patrontasch, who asked the question for us all. 'What will you do?' It was hard to believe how normal his voice sounded, as if he wanted to know whether she wanted lemon or milk in her tea.

'You don't think I know what it would mean if I left this hell-hole? I'll give him the good news.'

I didn't know how to read what was in her voice. I didn't

know what was real or what I was making up or what I wanted to hear. I heard sadness and regret; bitterness and shame; resignation and triumph and revenge. I heard how much she missed her daughter Luncia and how much she loved her dead husband. And I heard how little the affair meant because her very life meant so little to her. She crawled to the opening and climbed upstairs. Her brother gave her a gentlemanly hand up. We waited for them to say something to each other. There was silence and then Beck turned on the radio to some very pleasant dance music. We could hear the murmur of a conversation but no words.

My mother turned to my father. 'If I had known...'

'Known what?'

'Would we have done anything different?'

'Don't kill yourself with this kind of thinking.'

I knew they were talking about Mania.

Mama went on: 'I don't know... I just remember the day when the Russians came and took my mother and sent her to Kazakhstan. You said not to feel sorry for her... that some day you might envy her. How did you know?'

'I didn't know anything. What could I have possibly known?'

'I couldn't believe they sent her away, even though Papa died in their prison while waiting for his pardon to come through. So many things, Meir, so many crazy things... Mama gets sent away with my brother... we were so upset and then so happy for them when the Nazis invaded because they were safe. Then we get a letter... first day on his job, his apron gets caught in a machine. And then Mania... It seems no matter what we do... we're in God's hands and He doesn't even know we're there.'

Klara's legs slipped down into the bunker. She didn't say a word. She crawled to her pallet and faced the wall. Upstairs, Beck roared. I didn't know what there could possibly be left up there for him to break, but we could hear furniture crashing and splintering against the wall. I was thankful that all the houses around us had burned to the ground and hadn't been rebuilt because otherwise the police would almost certainly be banging down our doors with so many outbursts and so much screaming and noise. Then there was silence and the crash of Beck's body on the bedsprings and the unmistakable sound of sobbing. I couldn't believe I felt sorry for Beck, but I did.

Patrontasch crawled over to Klara. 'What the hell did you tell him?'

Klara didn't face her brother or us. 'Does it sound like I said I'd run away with him?'

The next morning Beck disappeared and we were alone again. Again our terror started eating at us in our silence. Maybe this time Beck wouldn't come back. We hadn't heard a word from Julia or Ala. We were used to Beck's uproars and outbursts, but we counted on Julia. She was our rock. Beck had made decision after decision to keep us alive after every close call. But it was Julia who, day in and day out, shopped, cooked and kept us alive.

A wall of the bunker collapsed and the men spent the day shoring it up with wooden slats, perhaps grateful to have a task to keep their mind off our predicament. Then the door opened and Julia and Ala walked in. Our smiles were silent cheers. Julia went straight to the hatch and called for Patrontasch to open it. She had brought back a bag of apples and as she passed them out it was as if she had only been gone a few minutes. She was smiling and happy and it seemed like nothing had happened to upset her. The apples gave everyone diarrhoea. In the late afternoon, Julia invited Lola and me, her two confidantes, upstairs to talk. I don't know why Julia chose us, but I was grateful for any chance to get out of the bunker. The pleasure of sitting in a chair with several feet of ceiling above my head and a window to look at, even though the curtains were drawn, was enough to pretend for a moment that my life was normal. Of course, I was dreading if Julia asked for my advice. I was 16, an innocent, naive 16. I was a girl who had never even held a boy's hand in earnest.

Julia poured us tea and gave us some rolls to help with the diarrhoea. Julia sat down at the kitchen table with us. 'It's not just Klara, you know.' Lola and I looked at each other. I could tell that Julia had wanted to get this off her chest for a long time. I could hear how casual she was trying to make it sound, as if she'd been rehearsing in front of the now broken mirror for days on end.

'What do you mean?'

'It's his sister-in-law. The one he ridicules because she puts on airs of being from Polish aristocracy. Oh well, I knew what I was getting into. He was like this when I met him and he won't change until I bury him, which I will, you know. I'll miss the bastard.' Both Lola and I had lots of questions, but we heard the key in the lock. Beck walked in, staggering drunk. He carried lilies in one hand and a fur coat in the other. Lola and I started to get up.

Beck motioned for us to sit. 'No, no. Stay… I might need some protection.'

'That depends on who the lilies are for.'

Beck handed Julia the flowers and kissed her on the cheek. His breath and skin reeked of alcohol. He held up the fur coat and spread the fur out across the table. 'What do you think? You need a fur coat. I always wanted to get you a fur so you can be like all those other rich bitches who look down their noses at us all the time.'

'I don't need a fur coat. Beck, where'd you get the money for it?'

'I used some of the dollars I got from the druggist.'

'Dollars? Why don't you just tell the SS we're hiding Jews?'

'Who do you think I bought the damn thing from?'

'Krueger?'

'Of course, Krueger. He said he'd take all the dollars I could get my hands on. He's convinced it's just a matter of time, which should make you two young ladies pleased as punch, if even the SS is convinced it's a matter of time.'

He held up the coat again in an effort to have Julia admire it. It really was a very smart fur. Lola grabbed the lining and looked at the stitching admiringly. 'Look, it's made from single pelts and not pieced together from scraps. I can tell it was made by one of our better furriers.' Beck was pleased. But then something caught his attention. He looked at the coat a bit more closely. He held it up to the light and stuck two of his big, callused fingers through two small holes. He wiggled them. Then he threw the coat down.

'That bastard! I told him it was a gift for you. You think I'd give you a coat with bullet holes? You don't think I know how they got there?'

'Please, Beck. Just go to sleep. The coat is beautiful.' Julia got up and tried to lead him to the bedroom. 'Lola can sew it. It will look like new. Krueger's your friend. He probably didn't even know the holes were there.'

Beck struggled against her. 'He knew! That bastard!' He staggered to the front door.

Julia grabbed hold of him. 'Clara, Lola help me.'

We grabbed on to Mr Beck and tried to pull him away from the door. Normally, this would have been an impossible task because he was extremely strong. You wouldn't think so just looking at him because he was as skinny as a fence post. But underneath he was all steel. Everybody in Zolkiew said that nobody could work like Beck, whether he was sober or drunk.

'Quick! The bathroom!' It was the only door with a lock. Julia started to push him to the bathroom. Beck resisted but he was so drunk he could hardly stand. Without too much trouble, we got him into the bathroom and closed the door. Julia grabbed a chair and positioned it under the doorknob so he couldn't open it.

Beck banged on the door. 'See what she does to me? Can you blame me for what I do? I bring her a fur… a famous Zolkiew fur; made by the best Jew furrier in this godforsaken place… His sons are all furriers in Paris!'

'Go to sleep. You can sleep in the bathtub. You've done it before.'

'I'm not stupid enough to scream bloody murder… Julia, open the door. Open the goddamn door.'

'Please, Valentin, please just go to sleep.'

We waited for more protests, but Beck had either given up or passed out. Lola embraced Julia, who told us, 'Go ahead, ladies. Try and get some sleep in this insane asylum. I'll be all right.'

I did my best to avoid looking at Julia's hands as she helped me down into the bunker. The joints in her fingers were swollen and arthritic, probably from all the cleaning and scrubbing of other people's houses, wringing the water out of their clothes as she did the laundry on the washboard. I had never thought much about those things, but now I thought about them all the time. A share of the money Julia earned on her hands and knees, scrubbing German officers' floors and doing their laundry, was going to feed three Jewish families who had employed her as a servant. Yes, we had been kind to her and good employers. Would we have risked our lives for her and Mr Beck? I don't know. I would like to think so. When Mr Beck came down to the bunker to drink and smoke and talk with the men and the rest of us, Julia remained upstairs, sitting on the bed listening to the party, if you could call it that, going on beneath her. The arthritis in her knees and hips prevented her from coming down into the bunker except on very special occasions, which usually had somehow to do with saving our lives. She was a woman with little joy in her life, but with an immaculate sense of duty. She was religious, but I didn't know if that was where she got this sense of duty from. The Catholic Church around here wasn't exactly in love with Jews. She called herself a peasant with a certain amount of pride. Her parents were typical Polish farmers: uneducated, superstitious, fright-ened and deferential towards any and all kinds of authority. Mr Beck believed in his own luck and was driven by his enormous contempt for any and all in positions of authority. But it was Julia Beck, plain, homely, arthritic almost to the point of defor-mity, old beyond her years, and scorned by her own husband, who was the strongest of us all.

If Beck had been married to another woman, we would have been dead a long time ago. Julia was a saint. Our saint. The Patron Saint of the Long-Suffering Jews and drunken and unfaithful husbands. Since I was a child, I'd been told the stories about the 36 righteous for whose sake God didn't destroy the universe. I liked to think that Mr and Mrs Beck were two of them. God knows they didn't look like the long-bearded wise rabbis I thought these *tzadekim* looked like in the picture books. But as much as I believed we wouldn't live through the war, and that my mother was right to insist I write a record of our time in the bunker so people after us would know what happened to the Jews of Zolkiew, on nights like this I was convinced that we would survive.

Lola understood what I meant, but when I tried to explain

this to my mother she said I was as crazy as the Becks. I knew Mania would understand, and I realized that as much as I wrote at my mother's insistence, I was now also writing my diary for Mania. She would have given anything to be alive to see the Becks fight about the beautiful Zolkiew fur coat with the bullet holes. She would have loved to put her fingers in the holes.

Chapter 10

DAYS OF AWE AND ATONEMENT

September 1943

Thursday, September 23rd. The Germans admitted themselves that they gave up Poltava. So something is going on after all. Maybe we will be able to leave this hole soon. God! If Mania would be alive! She was so happy with any bit of good news! She was clinging to life so much! And died so young. It's thanks to her that we went into hiding. She was begging from the day the Germans came 'let's go into hiding'. I want to live. Mama didn't want to go because of her asthma but she went on Mania's insistence. I remember distinctly her words, 'I want to live and you have to live for me.'

*

Zosia was asleep with her head on my lap and although I wanted to write, I didn't want to wake her up. It was still very early, but the heat was already oppressive in the bunker. The faces and arms of the others were coated with sweat, even the children's. Yom Kippur was in three days and it was to be our first *Kol Nidre* without Mania. Zygush and Zosia now slept either side of me. We told them Mania went to hide some place else and, though I could see Zygush didn't believe us, he didn't say anything. I was afraid of Mama's reaction during the memorial service that is part of Yom Kippur even more than I was afraid of my own reaction. The tension was building but none of us dared mention it. This holy day had taken on a special meaning because all of us had lost so many people that I couldn't even write all the names in my diary. There had to be hundreds and hundreds. We were asking God to forgive us for our sins and asking God for help to forgive those who had sinned against us, but how could we possibly be asking God to forgive the SS? How could this be? How could I say such prayers with sincerity and how could I pray for them without being the worst liar in the world? How could God ask us to do this? How could this not be a mockery of everything we thought holy?

I could hear and feel something moving against the sticky shift I slept in. We hadn't had much of a mouse or rat problem down here because we fought them for every crumb and scrap of food and we always won. Even the potato peels went into the soup and were devoured. In the millions of years of their existence, I'm sure the vermin had never seen people so crazy for food. I couldn't possibly imagine what might be crawling behind me.

I turned around and couldn't believe what I saw. A frog had jumped on to Zosia's chest and was resting there. The frog must have come in through the air vent we opened at night. Zosia opened her eyes to discover the frog staring at her. I would have expected Zosia to jump through the roof, but she just stared at the frog, fascinated. Neither Zosia nor I moved. Zygush opened his eyes, saw the frog and smiled. As I put a finger to his lips, the frog jumped on to my chest. The frog rose and fell with each breath. I couldn't imagine what the frog was thinking, but I knew what Zygush was thinking. If I told him not to catch the frog, it would be the first thing he would try to do. I could see his little boy devil of a mind at work. He had already made up his mind that this new pet of his was the best thing that had happened to him since he came to the bunker. In his head, he was building the little cage and teaching it frog tricks and giving it a name that would be an insult to somebody down here, most likely Klarunia, whom he tormented every chance he got. When reprimanded, he'd pretend he didn't know what anyone was talking about. Looking at him, I knew he couldn't resist the temptation a second longer, no matter what I said or did. He went for the frog, which leapt away and scrambled across the bunker, from body to body, waking everyone. Zygush followed the frog deep into the bunker where it disappeared.

I picked up my diary and started to write. Sometimes I wrote to shut out the world; sometimes to escape the boredom or to ignore an argument; or as a way of reminding myself what the Becks were doing for us. But that day I wanted to write because something wonderful was happening. We had a frog. But soon enough my blue pencil fell from my hand as I joined the others in watching the comedy of Zygush and the Frog, even as they tried to hold on to their dignity while he crawled all over them. At least, today, for a few minutes, there would be something to smile about. When Zygush emerged from the bowels of the bunker, he was covered in dirt. Only his teeth were white.

The frog made me think that the coming of this little boy into the bunker was as much a miracle for us as for him. Any time that we could forget, even for a moment, where we were and why we were here nourished us more than food, and it was Zygush more than anyone else in the bunker who gave all of us this relief. Even when sitting still as a stone, his eyes were still alive with mischief. As the days passed one into another, he turned from a boy who couldn't read a word into a boy who devoured books. He would have started school last year and learned to read. Compared to the death of his mother and everything else that had happened in his short life, educational deprivation might seem insignificant. But we had to take our triumphs in small places and this was one of them, especially for me because I had the joy of teaching him. Even here, at my father's urging, learning happened. If Zygush's outer world was circumscribed by dirt walls, his inner world was expanding into the past; into faraway lands; into adventures that even he couldn't imagine. Hearts of stone could be softened watching Zygush and the others as we taught them. Time and boredom were our enemies too and Zygush more than anyone else in the bunker was our champion. Time and time again, he would rescue one or another of us from our torment. Mrs Melman was next.

As every morning, the first thing Mrs Melman did was examine her precious water pitcher. She turned it over. It was bone dry. She was satisfied that at long last she had the irrefutable proof that someone was stealing her water in the night. She held the pitcher up for all to see.

'See, I told you. There's a thief in here! We're dying of thirst and someone's stealing my water.' Zygush, fresh from his frog hunt, sat next to Mrs Melman. He looked at the ground where the pitcher was sitting. He noticed something and felt the dirt. It was damp. He put his nose to the dirt and, like a little terrier dog, sniffed. Mrs Melman watched in silence as he took the vessel from her hand. He turned it over and looked at the bottom very carefully.

He pointed at the ground. 'Mrs Melman… Mrs Melman. Look, the dirt is wet right where the pitcher is! There's a crack. No one's stealing your water. Look at the crack. It goes all the way through!' He held up the pitcher for everyone to see as Patrontasch turned on the light. Zygush had just uncovered one of the mysteries of our universe and solved the alleged crime, which, if it didn't drive us apart, was driving us crazy. Nobody wanted to believe there was a thief of water in our midst and, as annoying as Mrs Melman was, the theft of water was a serious accusation.

Mr Melman looked at the pitcher and saw that in the bottom there was a faint crack. Mrs Melman felt the wet ground and looked away. She couldn't face anybody and I could see in her eyes that she wanted to smash the pitcher. Instead, she took it and put it on one of the shelves. My mother leaned close to me and whispered, 'Looks like she needs another pitcher. Maybe she'll get the next one from a museum.' I know my mother. If I had said such a thing, I would want to take it back. But I knew my mother's only regret would be her cowardice at not saying it louder.

I looked around and could see how relieved we all were about the outcome of the mystery of the pitcher. There were unwritten commandments in the bunker. No bad tempers. No yelling. No arguments. We were not three families used to keeping things in. At least now we wouldn't have to listen to Mrs Melman's daily carping any more. More importantly, poor Mrs Melman wouldn't have to be suspicious that we, her friends and family for more years than anyone could remember, were stealing her water. She had been eating her guts out over it. Now she was merely embarrassed and she would surely get over that quickly enough. But most relieved had to be Mr Melman as he wouldn't have to ask forgiveness for his wife any longer. He never apologized with words. Just his eyes. Mrs Melman never thanked Zygush for removing this burden from her soul.

The next morning it was as if the thought of anyone stealing water from her never occurred to Mrs Melman. The mood in the bunker became solemn and holy as we started our preparations for Yom Kippur, now only two days away. The air was thick with emotion and unspoken grief; the bunker became crowded with the ghosts of our lost loved ones, their faces hidden in the darkest corners and their voices whispering to us the sweetest things they ever said, which countered every small and petty moment that transpired between us; their souls filled us up with love. It was life's final irony that death is the flint and spark that ignites the eternal flame of a loved one's spirit, which lives forever within the breast. And it was not lost on us that in this year's Day of Atonement we would be praying to be inscribed in the book of life as we had never prayed before. I cannot say that these prayers in past years were without meaning or without the deepest sincerity, but I can say they were offered up to the Almighty in the knowledge that chances were we supplicants would be around to say the same prayers next year. Now we knew that chances were this might be our last Yom Kippur. And our last chance to pray for atonement in this lifetime.

The women were cleaning the bunker as best they could. The men were dividing up the service. My father was going to be both rabbi and cantor. There was some discussion about bringing the Torah that had been in the Schwarz family for 250 years down from its hiding place in the attic. To read from this Torah would give us, we all knew, a deep connection to all that was holy. Each letter in each word of the Five Books of Moses was written in kosher ink made from the crushed outer bark of a wasp's nest; written with a quill made from a turkey or goose feather; and written on parchment made from a calf killed for food as scribes had done for thousands of years. Our Torah took a year to complete, as does every Torah. Not even one mistake is permitted and each Torah is read again and again after comple-tion. The men were worried that the moisture and mould in our bunker might harm the Torah, so they decided to leave it in the attic where it was safe and dry. We would read the Torah passage from the *Humash*, which was the Torah in book form.

I had eaten a few more of the apples Julia brought back from Lvov and was now facing the consequences. I knew there were other people who needed it, but I was squatting over the bucket and couldn't move. My mother came over to see if I was all right. 'You know you can only eat potatoes, Clarutchka.' Believe me, *this* I already knew. She went back to cleaning and from where I was sitting I could see the men huddled around the map and a German newspaper Beck had slipped down into the bunker. There were lines and dates marking the Russian advance. Preparations for the holy day were momentarily suspended and the mood broken by Mr Melman announcing, 'We've stalled outside Zhitomir.' We weren't quite dead yet, and as long as we had breath we would argue. I could sense a heated discussion coming on.

Mr Patrontasch, who acted as if he and Melman were in charge of the Russian troops, voiced his frustration. 'Back and forth, back and forth, we've taken and lost Zhitomir half a dozen times. The whole war is being fought at Zhitomir! We'll never get out of here.'

Melman: 'We could always just hang ourselves, but we couldn't do that to the Becks.'

My father gave Melman a look I've only seen once or twice in my life. 'I don't want to hear talk like that! Especially around the children.'

Melman was the kind of man who would sacrifice anyone and anything for the sake of a joke. He had a good sense of timing and so waited until he had everyone's attention to deliver his punch line. 'I mean, how would they get rid of the bodies?'

Mrs Melman was shaking a potato peeler at no one in particular and didn't even look up from her work. 'This is the sense of humour I've had to live with. I thank God for one thing. Now you all know what I've had to put up with all these years.' This kind of remark was the last thing you would expect from Mrs Melman. I laughed and groaned at the same time.

Later, Julia came to collect the money to go shopping for our

meal to break the Yom Kippur fast. I was weak from the diarrhoea and from where I was lying on my pallet writing about my
episode on the pail, I could see Julia's legs behind her husband,
who was standing half in the bunker and half out. Professor
Steckel was squatting uncomfortably in front of Mr Beck,
handing him some bills.

Steckel was giving orders as usual. 'I want a nice chicken.'

I could hear Julia's patient voice: 'I'll do the best I can.' I
knew she was wearing her usual placid expression.

Steckel was about to say something, but Mr Beck looked him
straight in the eye. I felt Mr Beck was ready to explode. So did
Professor Steckel.

'We all know how much the professor loves his *pupik*, obviously for its medicinal qualities. We all know that a chicken's ass
is a delicacy.'

Everyone was laughing to themselves except Zygush, who
turned to me. 'Will we have chicken?' My father overheard and
kissed Zygush on the head. 'Some other time.'

Zygush knew enough not to argue or beg or complain. The
resignation was almost as hard to bear as the fear and the grief.
I prayed we'd get out of here before the boy's spirit was broken.
He was small for his age, just as Uchka had been small, and he
had a little man's face that seemed to age every day. My mother
whispered to my father: 'Have we asked them for one thing in
half a year? You'd think the holiest day of the year they could
spare a few zloty for the children.'

My father whispered back: 'They don't have children, they
don't understand.'

'They don't understand because they don't have a heart.'

This was what I loved about my mother.

*

The holiest night of the year. It was a hot, hot September night. The men, still dressed in their underwear, carefully unwrapped their tallith from their tallith bags and tins, and kissing them, middle, left and right, put them on. By now, I was used to the sight of the men and their skinny legs and black socks. They had been living in their underwear for months and so there was no longer any discussion whether it would be appropriate to pray in underwear. Still, I wondered how I would feel about it. Before the war, the idea of men in underwear on the high holy days would have sent me and Mania into shrieks of laughter. It wasn't that I was used to the sight of skinny legs that made it seem normal for me. It was the sense that this Yom Kippur had enormous significance. Would it be my and our last? We would be praying for Mania. My emotions were at a fever pitch. I felt like I was going to pray, really pray, at Yom Kippur for the first time. There was so much I wanted to ask God.

The women instinctively, solemnly gathered on one side of the bunker, all clutching their prayer books. My father, prayer book in hand, stood bent over, his skinny, long, stork-like legs and his back hunched over like a flamingo's neck. He kept checking his watch. Zygush and I were at the tiny window, looking out at the dying light of the day. A sliver of light from the setting sun reflected off the window of our house across the street.

Professor Steckel looked at his watch then cleared his throat. It was important to start at the exact moment of one hour before sundown. This had been our tradition for thousands of years. The German papers kindly published times of sunrise and sunset for military purposes. But Herr Doktor Professor Steckel was his usual impatient self. 'Mr Beck went to a great deal of trouble to find out the exact time of sunset today.'

Sunset is sunset, but my father didn't want to use the time announced in a German-controlled newspaper. Of course, he hadn't bothered to tell Steckel he would be using the Talmudic agricultural method, which calculates sunset the moment when the sun goes down over the horizon. The horizon in this case was our house on the other side of the street.

'I'm aware of that, Professor Steckel... I'm sure it will be just another moment.'

I was staring out of the vent through a veil of flowers and greenery. The last rays of the sun hit the house and then dropped down and faded. I climbed down and nodded at my father, who turned to us. I could see the sorrow hiding behind his little smile.

Our rabbi always started the service with a little story, something to humanize the grandeur and solemnity of the event. Even though we were a few Jews in a bunker in the dirt, I felt as holy as I did when there were so many Jews at the Sobieski Schul we couldn't all fit in. We Jews had been praying in hiding, in caves, in cellars, for our entire history, so the setting didn't feel inappropriate.

My father cleared his throat. 'Before we begin, I'm reminded of a little question our beloved rabbi used to ask his students.'

My father had undoubtedly been thinking about how to start the service for months. If he had not become a merchant he would have certainly become a rabbi like his brother. Everybody said so. He knew the Torah and Talmud backwards and forwards and spent hours of his free time reading late into the night. I knew what he was going to say and couldn't help smiling. He asked: 'Why is the Day of Atonement called, in Hebrew, a day like Purim?'

He looked around the bunker. Of course, there were no hands raised to answer.

'No answers? So I'll tell you. On both days it is customary for us Jews to masquerade. On Purim, Jews masquerade and adorn themselves in the costumes of non-Jews. On Yom Kippur, we Jews masquerade as pious Jews.'

He looked around for his words to sink in, looked at everybody, but made a point not to look at the Steckels, and then he began to chant almost in a whisper. I knew the words were coming from his heart even before they reach his voice: the opening prayer of the *Kol Nidre*.

'*Kol Nidre, Vi Et Areh, Vi Char Ra Me...*'

The entire prayer goes: 'All vows, obligations, oaths or anathemas, pledges of all names, which we have vowed, sworn, devoted or bound ourselves to, from this day of atonement, until the next day of atonement (whose arrival we hope for in happiness), we repent, beforehand, of them all, they shall all be deemed absolved, forgiven, annulled, void and made of no effect; they shall not be binding, nor have any power; the vows shall not be reckoned as vows, the obligations shall not be obligatory, nor the oaths considered as oaths.'

When I was little I didn't understand this prayer. How could the most holy prayer of our religion absolve of us all sins in advance? It was just crazy. Sometimes I would listen to the discussions about this. Some of the men would say this prayer was a reason for so much anti-Semitism because it allowed the gentiles to think it was all right for Jews to break their promises and agreements in every way possible and their God said it was okay. My father explained that this prayer is between man and God, not between man and man, and it demonstrated the great and overwhelming sense of God's understanding of human frailty and His capacity for compassion and forgiveness. My father said we started the service with the *Kol Nidre* to inspire us to be more like God. He told me that the prayer was written in the early Middle Ages when under threats and torture many Jews had to give up their religion or convert. Since we Jews take our vows so seriously, God doesn't want us to feel bound by vows that would cost our lives. I had never thought so much about the meaning of *Kol Nidre* before tonight.

As we beseeched God to forgive our sins and write us in the book of life for the coming year, I thought about the meaning of the words in our prayers. When you're 13 years old and the worst thing that has ever happened to you is getting the measles or a broken arm from ice-skating, you think you'll live for ever. Now I didn't know if we would live another day. And I couldn't stop thinking about Mania. I was angry at God. I didn't know how our God could exist and allow all this to happen to us, his supposed chosen people. The murder and suffering and grief were enormous, more than I or we could bear. It was too much for the human heart to take. I knew my mother's heart was about to explode, but it continued to beat, as did mine and those of the others. I didn't know how such a thing was possible. I didn't know how I could be so furious with God and yet find so much consolation in our prayers.

We didn't talk much after the evening service was done. I went to bed, holding the children close. The little ones didn't have to fast and we had some bread for them. Fasting for the rest of us was nothing. It was a way of life. Never has fasting been so easy for me.

It was hard for me to pay attention to the service the next day. I was filled with dread at the thought of the upcoming Yizkor service, where we would commemorate all those who had died the year before. I knew the service almost by heart. We supplicated ourselves in every way to God's power and forgiveness. The words resonated with new meaning and a new force, humbling me, frightening me. One of the most powerful prayers was a simple enumeration of any and all kinds of sins which man might possibly commit against himself, his family, his fellow man and ultimately God. We beat our chests as we enunciated each prayer.

'... nothing is hidden from You. You search our innermost thoughts and our hearts... And so may it be Your will to have mercy on us and forgive us our sins, grant us atonement...

'For the sin we have committed before You of hard-heartedness... of immorality... a gathering of lewdness... by deceiving a fellow man... by insincere confession... by eating or drinking... by committing usury... by casting out the yoke of heaven... with proud looks... by a grudging eye... knowing or unknowing... by causeless hatred... For all these, God of pardon, pardon us, forgive us, atone for us... I am dust in my life... may it be my will, Lord my God and God of my fathers, that I shall sin no more and the sins which I have committed before You, erase them in Your abounding mercies...' We were asking for forgiveness for our sins, but what about the sins of the Fascists and the Nazis and the SS and the Gestapo and the Ukrainians and Tilzer and Schitling? When did they atone? And what for? Did they even think they were sinning in this upside-down world?

My father turned around. It was now time for the Yizkor service. It was and is our custom that those with parents still among the living leave for this part of the service. Mr Melman sent me, Igo and Klarunia into the passageway near the latrines. We were the only ones who had parents living. Zygush and Zosia waited in the main part of the bunker, watching while I and the others crawled into the passageway.

My father waited until everyone was in the passageway and then chanted the opening prayer of the Yizkor service: *God, What is Man...?* I have always thought it was one of our most beautiful. I knew from my father that our prayers were not only the work of rabbis but that many had been written by rabbi/poets in Spain in the Middle Ages.

Lord, what is Man that You recognize him?
The son of a frail human that you reckon with him?

Man is like a breath; his days are like a fleeting shadow.
In the morning it blossoms and is rejuvenated,
by evening it is cut down and brittle.

According to the count of our days, so may You teach us;
then we shall acquire a heart of wisdom.

Safeguard the perfect and watch the upright,
for the destiny of that man is peace.

But God will redeem my soul from the grip of the lower world,
for He will take me, Selah!

My flesh and my heart yearn –
Rock of my heart, and my portion is God, for ever.

Then the dust returns to the ground, as it was,
and the spirit returns to God Who gave it.

I was listening to the prayer and thinking about Mania and looking at little Zygush. I could see in his face that he was slowly realizing that his mother, Uchka, was dead. Zygush was smart enough to know that my father would never have made a mistake about such a thing. He started to cry softly. He simply looked at his little sister, who knew the words and recited them without knowing what they really meant. He took Zosia's tiny hand and held it, then brought it to his lips and kissed it. She smiled at her older brother, but she didn't understand that he was crying because he knew that their mother was dead.

Everyone was now looking at Zygush, realizing our horrible mistake and the burden we had put on his shoulders. The bunker had become holier than any synagogue.

My father also knew, but continued: 'May the all merciful Father who dwells in the supernal heights, in His profound compassion, remember with mercy the pious, the upright and the perfect ones.' We gave the response: 'He who makes peace in His heavens, may He make peace for us and for all Israel. Amen. Next year in Jerusalem.'

The families hugged and embraced each other, drying their tears. I crawled to Zygush and Zosia and embraced them. I saw my mother, standing alone as my father closed and gathered the prayer books. I saw Mania's name on my mother's lips. I went to my mother and we embraced, locked to one another, afraid of ever letting go.

There was a knock on the hatch. Patrontasch opened it and we saw Mrs and Mr Beck framed in the hatchway above us, our two angels in the heaven of their bedroom. They handed down the trays with the post-fast meals. The Melmans, Steckels, the Patrontasches, all had trays with the small roasted chickens. Zygush and Zosia watched the food go by. My mother couldn't help herself. She looked at the food and the children with bitterness in her heart, although I knew the Melmans and the Patrontasches would share on this day.

Then Julia, arthritis and all, climbed down into the bunker. She turned and reached for two potholders and brought down a big pot of chicken soup, filled with noodles and pirogies. 'Mr and Mrs Schwarz, this is for you.'

For once, my mother was almost speechless. All she could get out was: 'But we—'

Beck smiled. 'Don't but us...'

And Julia blushed and said with a huge smile, 'I even got you a rooster. I remembered the custom. I knew you needed a rooster.'

My mother embraced Julia and then Beck and then we were all embracing each other. Zygush was crying now, for he did allow himself tears of joy. My mother immediately started pulling out the best pieces of meat to put in the children's bowls. Nobody was talking now as they ate in satisfied silence, grateful for just a few minutes.

I couldn't help thinking about Mania. Her presence in the room was stronger than ever. I remembered the last Yom Kippur before the occupation. The night before the night of Yom Kippur, we were gathered in our backyard as was our tradition. My family, all my aunts and uncles and cousins, more than 20 of us. Uchka called for Zygush, who was in the walnut tree, and he flew down like a little monkey and ran to where Mama had gathered all the children in a circle. We put our arms round each other. My father had a live rooster in his hands. He held it by the feet and swung it around the heads of the children and he started to pray. 'May You bless and protect these children and may their sins all be taken on by this rooster which we sacrifice in Your name.' When the prayer was ended, he would give the rooster to Mama, who would take it to the *schochet*, ritual slaughterer.

The electric light flickered, went out, flickered, came on again... then went out. We were left in darkness.

Chapter 11

A YEAR UNDERGROUND

November 1943 to New Year 1944

Monday, 22 November. The policeman left in the morning but came with another one for dinner and they invited themselves to sleep over again. God! When will they leave already! Today there was no electricity again. We had three candles burning because today is the anniversary of the 'November Akcja' where Melman and Lola lost their family. My God! Last year, after the carnage, we came out of the bunker and thanked God for saving us from death. We didn't expect to live another year in these circumstances. I don't know where does one find the will to live! You lose your loved ones and you still want to live…

It's 11 pm now. The Germans didn't come yet. Maybe they are not coming. It's bad enough to sit tense all day. It's worse when one cannot sleep.

*

We were sleeping more and more. The Nazis had started rationing the electricity and thrown the entire town into the dark. We now only had light for a few hours in the evening or a few hours in the morning. We never knew when. There was little for us to do in the dark and cold, so we slept to keep warm.

Zygush always kept a book within reach and the moment the light came on he would grab it. Since he had learned to read Zygush would spend hours with his books. He would quietly read to himself, or else, in a soft and tiny voice, to Zosia, his mouth only a breath away from hers. Even in the dim light, I could see the spark in her eyes when her big brother read to her. I loved that they loved books like I did.

Since we would only be in the bunker for a 'few weeks', I had only brought a few of my precious books with me. I don't know why. Maybe I thought it would be unlucky. Here I was in the bunker alone, and on my shelves in our house were my beauties. Historical novels were my favourites. Big fat novels with stories that went on for ever. Dumas, Dickens, Hugo. I read everything they wrote. And when I think of some of the titles: *Les Miserables*, *Bleak House*, *Great Expectations*, *The Hunchback of Notre Dame*, *The Man in the Iron Mask* ... And the plots! *The Count of Monte Cristo*, *A Tale of Two Cities*, *David Copperfield*... Prisons, dungeons, wars, revolutions, false imprisonment, traitors, murderous corrupt power-hungry leaders, betrayal, greed, heroes, impersonations, phony trials, torture! When I was reading them, in the fright of my most gruesome nightmares I never imagined my life would resemble these books in any way. I also loved the Warsaw stories of IB Singer, but I was considered too young to read IJ Peretz, even though there was a portrait of him, done completely with tiny letters, on the wall of our living room.

I also loved the Polish historical-novel writer Henryk Sienkiewicz, who wrote such titles as *With Fire and Sword*, *The Deluge* and *Fire in the Steppe*. Sienkiewicz, who won the Nobel Prize for Literature, also wrote *Quo Vadis,* which had spawned three movies and an opera. But you must remember, I was only a young teenage girl, and I always found the time for the new

Kurzmahler book. In her stories, orphan girls always turned into princesses and the only endings were happy ones.

Now my reading depended on whatever Mr Beck could scavenge from the hundreds and hundreds of books abandoned in the streets, looted from the homes of deported and murdered Jews. These books apparently held little interest for the German troops or the Poles and Ukrainians. Even if we had the money, Beck couldn't buy even one book without raising suspicions. He had a reputation for many things, none of them having anything to do with books. I was grateful for anything; I could hardly ask him to get on his hands and knees and browse through the ashes for my favourite writers. There was a book, I can't remember the title, which Artek, Lola and all the grown-ups were passing around like dessert. I wanted to read it, but my mother said it was risqué and inappropriate for someone of my age. 'Salka,' Artek said. 'It's a book! Who knows if any of us get out of here? And you don't want her to read a book because it might be bad for her?' We had to laugh.

Zygush wasn't the only puppet in this child's closet. As soon as the door opened and light shone in, we all came alive. Cleaning. Peeling potatoes. Boiling water. Washing our faces. Rolling up our pallets. Slicing the stale bread, which at least was easy to cut. If the light stayed on for a while, I would teach the children their lessons, or even now and then we would share a few moments of play, of making dolls. If only the Fascists knew that Jews were darning their socks! Thank God Lola was here to teach us all these things. We tried to make money any way we could, but with no electricity, we were making even less than before.

We were always on the brink of starvation, yet somehow we managed to get by. Every decent thing we owned had been sold long ago. My very last dress had brought us 200 zloty and 5 kilograms of flour. Beck had sold some of Papa's underwear for 110 zloty and given us 120. God bless him. But now there was truly nothing left for us to sell.

Papa was not a forgetful man. He remembered every birthday of everyone in our big family. He knew the Talmud and Torah by heart. He was the holder of our collective memory. Mama had been rummaging through the very back of our makeshift shelves recessed into the wall in a last attempt to find something when she stumbled upon a large package in twine. None of us knew what it was. We had wrapped everything in newspaper in a futile attempt to keep the mould at bay. When my Mama held up Papa's beautiful charcoal grey coat, she shook her head in surprise. 'Oy, my *aiver butelt* husband!'

Mama had had the coat made right before the war. The wool was imported from England, had an Afghan lambskin collar and was worth a fortune. Now it brought us only 600 zloty. But it was enough to eat for a week. Even Mama, who had been breaking down, with constant headaches from worry and grief, started to look like her old self again. Every time she'd look at Papa for the next few days, she'd just shake her head and smile. At least we were safe. While we hungered, or sat crouched in the dark, others were being killed or deported.

The news from the outside world hadn't been good. In fact, there was no news at all. For what seemed like weeks, nothing was happening. At last the BBC announced that the Russians had taken Zhitomir and Kiev. It was the first significant Russian advance in months. Mr Patrontasch took out his map and marked the new front. But only a few days later, the Nazis took back both cities. When Mr Patrontasch erased the advance on his map, I felt like he was erasing our hope as well. They fought on the Eastern Front. They fought on the Western Front. They conferred in Moscow. They conferred in London. But it was all moving with the pace of a tortoise.

We had been in this tiny hole for one entire year, surviving by the generosity of the Becks and sheer luck, almost in equal measure. Despite the fact that time seemed to stand still in the bunker, a whole year had gone by. On 22 November, the anniversary of the first *akcja*, we lit three candles in memory of the Jews murdered. If we had lit a candle for each person who had died, our bunker would have shined brighter than the brightest star. It was almost unfathomable to think back to when we had first arrived. Back then we had thought we would be stuck in this hole for a couple of weeks at most, but now with the game of chess Russia and Nazi Germany were playing it could go on for ever. Out of nowhere Beck had said that he thought we might be in here until next November. Another year! I couldn't imagine it. I don't think Beck understood how much we depended on his every word for our sense of what was real and what was imagined. I didn't think it would be possible for us to hold out for another year. There were so many close calls, and Beck's drinking caused him to be very unreliable, and now Julia and Ala seemed to be torn between saving us and protecting themselves from further hurt and humiliation.

Over the past several weeks, the two of them had moved in and out half a dozen times. Julia didn't even knock on the trap-door to announce her plans any more. And when she was at home, she would leave her suitcase at the door as a reminder to Beck. Beck was now having regular 'dinners' at the sister-in-law's house. A couple of weeks ago Beck had told us that this sister-in-law was romancing a Ukrainian policeman. As she had known about us since last Christmas, their pillow talk could spell disaster. But Beck had told us not to worry. 'I'll talk her out of it. She's a reasonable woman.' And he had gone off to her house just outside of town. Now it was clear that he was doing more than just talking. Was this Beck's way of keeping her quiet?

We didn't even know this woman's given name and Julia didn't tell us. She only referred to her as the 'sister-in-law'. Not referring to your sister-in-law by name was as good as a slap across the face. It was that big an insult, and was all that Julia could do in revenge. Julia didn't let us see how hurt she was. Until he straightened himself out, she would only come home at night when Beck was at work. She would have left him altogether if it wasn't for us.

We were horrified for Julia, but there was nothing to do. Our lives were in his hands. We couldn't risk his anger, even though this new affair was endangering Julia and Ala as much as us. There was no understanding Beck. Anyone who would dare to hide 18 Jews had to be crazy, defiant, arrogant and confident. I couldn't even be angry with him. None of us could. We'd just sit in silence and deal with this one added threat to our survival and go on.

Adding to the problem was Ala's new boyfriend, the Nazi pilot. Adolph had been flying fighter planes on the Russian front for over two years. Beck had immediately told us that he was a good man and had confided in Beck that he despised Hitler. But even someone who despised Hitler could betray us. But Ala was in love and so Adolph came to the house often. He would come in the afternoon, sometimes unannounced, spreading panic in the bunker. Or he would come for dinner, bearing flowers and little gifts, staying late and sometimes even staying over. Beck liked him, so he would even come when Julia and Ala were away at Julia's sister's house. Our narrow window of freedoms had been slammed shut. We couldn't move, cook, talk, or even go the bathroom when Adolph was here. The card table was in the Beck's bedroom, right above where our pails were. Adolph and Ala would play cards, chat and listen to music for hours and hours. They'd dance right over our heads. Or if it wasn't them,

Beck would be entertaining his card buddies or others in there. It seemed like there were people upstairs more often than not in the evenings. While these visits might help defy the rumours and accusations that the Becks were harbouring Jews, it sentenced us to long stretches of silence in which we could not move or speak. Even my own breathing had become shallow. Our lives were miserable. Finally Patrontasch asked Beck to move the card table to the living room so that we could at least relieve ourselves without fear of being overheard.

While the progress between the Russians and the Allies seemed hopelessly stalled, the news from our little town was more than grim. It seemed like every day, either Beck or Julia was forced to be the unfortunate messenger of bad news. I mourned the growing list of lost friends.

When Beck returned from the Janowska work camp in Lvov, where he would go and gather news for us from stolen conversations at the barbed-wire fence, he had to announce the final extermination of the inmates there. We had already known that Hermann had perished during the summer, but there was no more protecting Lola from the truth. She had lost everyone now. When Julia returned from Zaleszcryki, a nearby town, she said that partisans had been hanged like Christmas ornaments from the trees. They had deported old Mrs Twordyewicz. She was stooped over, practically blind and deaf, just a wisp of a woman. Not to mention that she had converted to Catholicism as a little girl and had gone to mass every day of her life. But they deported her just the same. Another friend of ours, Misko Segal, had been found and murdered. Sometimes the details were hazy. They had found another Jew in hiding. His name might have been Springer. Beck wasn't sure. It hardly seemed to matter what his name was. Beck had announced that the man had at least had the time to hang himself and cheat the Nazis of the pleasure of killing him. Would we be brought to that? It seemed inconceivable that that idea would be a solace at such a time. But so much of what we were hearing and living seemed inconceivable. Beck was most shook up by what happened to Mr Chachkes, a well-known lawyer in Zolkiew. Beck had heard that he and his sister-in-law had been captured in a small village outside of town. Beck didn't know Chachkes at all, but he and Julia were both frantic because the police had found papers on Chachkes that incriminated the peasants who had hidden them. Both Jews and their saviours had been taken away in chains to Lvov.

There had been a new round of rumours that the Becks might be harbouring Jews. Beck's boss at the alcohol depot, Meyer, apparently thought Beck was leading a life 'too rich' and 'too good' for his salary. He informed none other than SS Obersturmführer Von Pappen, the SS officer who organized the deportations and liquidations in Zolkiew, of his concerns. Even two of Beck's diehard Polish card buddies, Eisenbard and Dr Lucynski, who didn't mind playing with Krueger, Schmidt and the other Nazis, were terrified of Von Pappen and no longer dared to come over to play cards. Eisenbard had told Beck he had heard his house was 'unclean'. If Beck's best friend was saying that, what would the rest of the town be thinking?

Beck was right to be worried. The man was ruthless. It was common knowledge that Von Pappen had had a talented Jewish carpenter working for him by the name of Hiam Schott. Von Pappen liked him and had protected him. There had been orders that no one was to bother Schott. So he had been spared the deportations and the *akcja*. When Schott had cut part of a finger off, Von Pappen had personally driven him to the hospital to have the wound taken care of. But as they walked out of the hospital together, Von Pappen had nonchalantly pulled out his side arm and shot Mr Schott in the head. God knew what would happen if Von Pappen or any other quisling found out that Beck once stole his Christmas carp to celebrate with the Jews he was hiding downstairs!

Beck had already just been sent to Von Pappen because his rifle had been stolen. This was enough of an offence for Beck to be shot or hanged. Beck had fallen asleep on the job and the rifle had been stolen by a Ukrainian Blue Coat. Beck had had the *chutzpah* to inform Von Pappen that he had been pretending to be asleep. He had claimed that all the Ukrainians were thieving bastards and that he had wanted to catch one of them in the act. Von Pappen had said he would have to think about what measures to take and had sent Beck home.

The litany of deaths, the rumours and Beck's own provocative behaviour convinced the men in the bunker that something must be done. This grave offence would not go unpunished. After much discussion they had come up with a possible solution. Mr Patrontasch would have to convince Beck to apologize to Von Pappen.

Mr Patrontasch knocked on the trapdoor and, a few minutes later, Beck opened it.

'A word, if you have a minute,' was all Mr Patrontasch said.

Our lives were at stake and we were sending him on a mission that was as perilous as an escape from the ghetto or high-level diplomacy between Roosevelt and Stalin. Convincing Beck, who was as stubborn as any human being could be, to apologize to a man he thought a murderer would be a difficult feat. But just a few minutes later, Patrontasch returned, pen and paper in hand. Beck wanted Patrontasch to write a letter to 'soften up' Von Pappen. Even though Beck was a *Volksdeutscher*, he had very little German. Patrontasch started to write in his elegant German script how honoured Beck was to be able to serve the Reich in whatever capacity he might best be used. He wrote that it had always been a dream of his that Germany would return to Poland and fulfill its destiny of eastward expansion, bringing culture and civilization to the Slavic masses. He wrote how much he admired Von Pappen personally and how pleased he was to have the privilege to serve under such a German patriot. The lies flowed effortlessly. 'Beck' begged Von Pappen to understand that his personal failings in no way detracted from his loyalty to the Fatherland.

When Beck came back a few hours later after delivering the letter, with vodka and tobacco as a reward, he bragged that Von Pappen had been eating out of his hand. The crisis had been averted and the men shared an uncomfortable laugh with Beck. If only Von Pappen had known that a Jew had penned the eloquent ode to the Fatherland. But the relief was short-lived.

That same night we were awakened by Julia screaming and knocking on the trapdoor. 'It's the Ukranian police!' It had to be three o'clock in the morning. Mama was so upset she fainted and the children started crying, but by this time they knew how to cry silently. The rest of us started praying. Beck must have been reported by one of his many enemies. It could have been the rifle. It could have been anything. The 'why' didn't make any difference. The police were at the door and we would know soon enough. We listened as they informed Julia that they needed to bring Beck in. The commandant of the Ukrainian police wanted to interrogate him. As calmly as she could, Julia asked what he had done. The policemen didn't have the entire story, but they said that Beck had been as 'drunk as a Polack' and that he had said 'something' to the chief of their Blue Coats. We had heard Beck at his worst so we knew it could easily have been any one of a hundred horrific things. Beck had just escaped Von

Pappen and now the Ukrainians were after him, and in the middle of the night. These men had grudges that went back years and years and now they were looking to settle old scores.

Beck must have passed out because otherwise he would surely have been yelling at the Blue Coats to 'shit on their mothers'. It was Beck's standard expression when he was cursing. The first time Beck had used it, poor Mama had looked shocked and had immediately shot Mania and me one of her looks that said, 'You better not have heard that and if you did, you better forget you did.' But by now, she was thankful this was the only curse in his arsenal. He usually said it to Julia.

One of the policemen found Beck and grumbled to his colleagues that if they wanted to bring him in, they would have to carry him. The commotion must have woken Beck up, because we heard another one say, 'Go to bed, Valentin. We'll just say we didn't find you at home.' The same policemen whom Beck had accused of stealing his rifle were now protecting him. They left shortly thereafter.

While Julia was still trying to find out from Beck what exactly he had said and when to warrant an interrogation, Beck, in his drunken stupor, decided he had to go to the police station, confront his accusers and get to the bottom of 'this travesty of justice'. Julia stalled him while Ala went and hid his bicycle, hoping that if Beck insisted on going, the walk might at least sober him up on the way. I heard Julia scream, 'I can't take it any longer!' and slam the door shut after her and Ala. Beck continued to curse and throw furniture around the place while trying to find his bicycle. Then a door was smashed in. It sounded like the bathroom door. Why was he looking in the bathroom for his bicycle? He must have been beyond drunk. Beck cursed Julia, calling her an idiot. 'I shit on your mother!' I didn't know if he even realized that his wife and daughter had left. We heard the outside door slam again and then there was silence. The idea of what a drunk Beck would say to this Ukrainian police chief who hated him and was looking for any reason to see him shot was terrifying. There was no hope of sleep now as we waited for either Beck or the police to come back.

When Beck came back in the morning, he refused to tell us what happened and, to make things worse, he was too sick to go to work that night. We were living below a live volcano that could erupt at any moment. Julia only came home for a few minutes to tell us she was going to Lvov to buy tobacco, and Ala left for work. As soon as we heard the bus for Lvov leave from the stop across the street, Beck knocked on the trapdoor. 'The house is filthy. I want you to come up and clean it.' Lola and I crawled to the trapdoor because usually we do the cleaning. But Beck said, 'Klara, why don't you give me a hand?' We watched Beck's hand come down through the hatch, chivalrous and gallant, to help Klara upstairs.

The men watched and discussed the war between the Allies and the Axis powers with Talmudic fury. But it was the war between the Becks that had the most relevance to our lives. Italy, Germany, England, these were places in the novels I read. It was impossible to connect the conferences and battles to the battle-ground on the floor above. One wrong word and we were dead. It was that simple. There was a world war. It was taking place upstairs.

And now the war had spread into the bunker between the families over a piece of wood five centimetres wide. It had been brewing for months and months, ever since Zygush and Zosia came to live with us and Mania died a few days later. It was almost too horrible to talk about. Because of Mania's death we were too grief-stricken to ask for more sleeping space for the two children. It was the furthest thing from our minds. My parents had been religious about never mentioning her name. They told not one story about her to make them feel better. They didn't exchange one memory. We didn't have one picture of my sister. We were each alone with our grief. Zygush and Zosia learned never to mention her name. Our very silence was our song of mourning. But with the arrival of the two children, there was not room enough for the five of us. It was hard enough to sleep as it was and with Zygush and Zosia it was almost impossible. I didn't know why we endured the additional discomfort for so long. Perhaps it was because the two children had taken Mania's place on our pallets and even after she had been dead for eight months to say the words out loud would evoke her memory in too painful a way.

I knew we couldn't go on being polite and considerate with each other for ever. The resentment on our side about the space and the three families' resentment about the Steckels' hard hearts was like a leak in a gas main. All we needed was one spark. The men had been whispering from time to time about asking the Steckels for help, at least for the four children. But they never did. My father was afraid to offend the Steckels, because he knew the Becks depended on their money and he didn't want Beck mad at us. I knew these men were brought up not to ask for anything, just as Mania and I were. It wasn't a matter of pride. It was just in the Jewish world of Zolkiew, no one ever had to ask for help. It was always given without a word. It was a sin to humiliate a man by calling attention to his poverty. The Steckels had perfect vision and could calculate to the gram the weight of any piece of bread, lard, meat, potato, onions or anything else. Yet they were blind when it came to seeing that the children's legs looked like clubs, all bone with the knob of a knee in the middle. They could see their big eyes when the food passed by their faces. I know the children just liked to look at the food and smell it because they couldn't help themselves and it was better than nothing. Zygush's little face was looking like an old man's from hunger. Sometimes all I dreamed about was the day I would be alone with a loaf of bread and a knife and I could cut myself a slice as big as I wanted.

The two children in eight months had never once asked why the Steckels didn't share their food with us and not once did they ask them for even a crumb. There had to be a word for people incapable of feeling shame. To me, the Steckels were as bad as the Fascists. I felt there were only two kinds of people in the world. Those who wanted to save us and those who wanted to kill us. Even in times like these, a person couldn't be only for himself. Poor Mania endured torture to save us all, including the Steckels. Yet they dared hoard their money as if they didn't even know Mania's name. They owed Mania their lives and did they ever offer their condolences? No! Did they offer to share what they had even for the children in her memory? No! I tried not to hate the Steckels as I hated the Fascists. They were after all hiding from the Nazis just as I was. They were fellow Jews. But to them, my sister's death only meant a few more centimetres of sleeping space.

My father said almost too softly to hear, 'I've been meaning to mention it. Since the children came to live with us... we don't have as much sleeping room...' The spark. We were now five people and had only sleeping room for four. When the children first arrived, we were so happy they were there and grateful they were allowed to stay that we didn't dare ask for extra space to accommodate them. It meant that not one of us could sleep on their back or stomach. It meant we could not turn in our sleep.

The words came out of nowhere. I know he must have been thinking about saying it for months and months. I was hoping that the others would be ashamed for not thinking about it themselves and just agree. But as soon as I saw the expression on all the faces, especially the Steckels, I knew it was not to be. Not one of us asked for one extra anything in over a year. Not one. Not a cup of water. Not a potato peel. Not a drop of oil when we had it. Mama looked up from peeling the potatoes. There was no reaction at first as everyone was looking around the room for someone to say something. Mrs Melman started to say, 'The children…' She didn't have to finish the sentence. I could read her mind. 'The children could get us all killed! We didn't want them. Beck shoved them down our throats and now you want us to give up our room? *Genug is genug*, enough is enough, already!'

'Every family, everybody, has more room than us. You think that's right?'

'We do you a favour and this is what we get? A lot of *tsuris*, trouble!' Mrs Melman continued.

'Look at you and look at what we've got!' Mama was pointing at our sleeping area. 'How dare you! Who are you anyway to come in here all high and mighty?'

'You lower your voice!' Mr Steckel actually hissed.

'I beg your pardon?' said Mama.

'You heard me. *Shatt! Shatt!*'

Mr Melman tried to be a peacemaker, but it was too late. We were pushy, bossy, picky; we were taking advantage. We were risking everybody's life. Including their children's!

I was shaking and the children were crying. They understood no one wanted them there. I couldn't believe that the other three families were ganging up on us. What had we done? All we had done was lost my sister. I was afraid Mr Beck would hear upstairs and get angry. I had never seen Papa so angry. And then I started screaming. 'Quiet! Everybody be quiet!'

My father turned to me and, before I knew it, he slapped me hard across the face. He had never raised a hand to anyone in our family. Ever. He looked at me like he wanted to hit me again. His eyes, so black and drained with exhaustion, had a look I had never seen. Hot and brutal. Furious with contempt. I wanted to die. From shame. From hurt. From hurting him. From feeling how hurt he was. But then he realized what he had done. All the warmth returned to his eyes. My father had come back. I had never seen such a look on his face except for at Mania's death. Everyone in the room was stunned. I had succeeded. The bunker was silent.

All Mama said was, 'Meir.' Then Papa was holding and kissing me and begging me to forgive him. There was nothing to forgive. He was exhausted. He was not able to mourn Mania. He felt responsible for her death and nothing would ever take that ache away. He would mourn her all his life. Mania's death, a silent accusation, would stand between him and Mama to the end of their days.

Mr Patrontasch took out his measuring tape and crawled across to us. He excused himself and measured how much room we shared. Then he measured every other family's sleeping space in the main bunker. He opened his little notebook, licked his pencil and made some calculations while we all watched.

'What's fair is fair,' he announced. 'Everybody gets 35 centimetres in which to sleep.' He grabbed a slat or two from each of the other three families and put them next to ours. Nobody said a word. When we went to sleep that night, it didn't seem like we had any more room. Mania would have thought it hilarious.

The Becks called a truce for Christmas. We were all lying on our pallets listening to the party upstairs. The radio was on and everyone was dancing. It seemed all of Zolkiew was above our heads. Beck's family as well as Julia's. Adolph. Krueger and Beck's other police cronies. Professor Lang and Eisenbard. I couldn't tell if there was another soul asleep; I assumed we were all awake. The pounding from the dancing feet seemed like it was inside my head. Earlier in the day I had been crying out of love and thankfulness for the Becks. But now the tears were falling because these people were happy celebrating while so many thousands were dead and dying. I heard Mr Beck's feet crossing right above us to the radio. He turned the radio off and almost one by one the feet stopped dancing. Mr Beck said, 'Listen.' In the distance, I heard carol singing. I could picture them walking up through the snow, all bundled up against the cold, holding candles to light their way. From the sound of their voices I knew they were not far from the church where Mania had been captured. Her memory intruded on almost all my thoughts. As the carol-singers got closer and closer, I was able to recognize the song. It was *Przybiezeli do Betlejem*. It was one of the most beautiful of all Polish carols and one that Mania and I had sung together just one year before.

By now I could make out the words of the carol-singers. But it wasn't the Christmas songs we knew. And even worse, we could hear the Becks and Ala and all their guests laughing along with carol-singers as they sang in exaggerated, mocking Yiddish accents, laughing so hard at their joke that they could hardly get the revised lyrics out...

> *Joy to the world, the Yids are dead*
> *Hung by their necks, shot through their heads*
> *Joy to the world, the earth is red with their blood*
> *It started as a trickle and now it's a flood...*

Beck was howling with devilish laughter. Zosia and Zygush huddled in my arms, too frightened to talk. The Becks' laughter only magnified our terror. I whispered in the children's ears that it was all okay, but I didn't believe it for one second. It was like one of those devil's masses old peasant women loved to scare the local children with.

> *Joy to the world, a present from our Lord, Jesus,*
> *I found under the tree...*
> *The dead bodies of a Yid family... mother, father, daughter,*
>   *son...*
> *Killing them was so much... fun...*

We knew there would be no rest until the last bottle had been drained, the last toast drunk and the last dance finished. One by one the guests wandered off into the clean, fresh, winter night. Adolph lingered and lingered. After we had heard the door close for a final time, Beck sent Ala downstairs to bring us all up. He apologized profusely for having gone along with the singing. It had been an act. All the Becks were ashamed. That after all they had done for us, they would even worry about such a thing was a testament to their goodness. Mr Beck cried and apologized and kissed each of the children.

The tree, with its boughs so fresh, filled the room with the fragrance of pines. The hundred candles resting on the branches were a choir of light. The children stared and stared. How dare this world be so different from ours in the bunker? Ala and the Becks had little bags of sweets for the children. The children forgot everything as each went through their bags piece by piece, making sure that no one else had one sweet extra. God bless the Becks to remember the children.

The Becks' truce continued through New Year, when they came down with vodka for the men and cookies for the children. Julia had good news. She had finally sold some of the sweaters I had knitted and had come to give my father the money. Mama beamed at me, and Papa simply nodded in approval. I wasn't just his little girl any more. I felt so proud that I was able to help in a tangible way. Even Zygush thanked me. If only the day could have ended there.

I couldn't have dreamed what Beck would tell us next. After refilling the vodka glasses yet again, he cleared his throat. 'The Germans have requisitioned one of our rooms. They assigned two trainmen to live with us.' Adding almost as an apology: 'We didn't have much choice. But don't think this is so bad. We'll be safer. Who would ever think you'd be here with trainmen living right upstairs! This is good. Really.' Only Beck could be such an optimist and even I knew he couldn't believe what he was telling us. We didn't know if these trainmen who'd be our upstairs neighbours were the very trainmen who took our friends and families to the camps. Papa asked, 'How long?'

Beck shrugged. 'Who knows. A few weeks. A few months. I just don't know.' That was it. He had told us what he had had to say. There wasn't anything left to add. Even the vodka couldn't soften the blow. He left us the bottle and retreated upstairs.

Mr Patrontasch's voice broke the silence. 'Perhaps the time has come for us to consider the other option.' I had never heard such bland statement in my life. His voice was emotionless. It was as if he were asking someone to pass him the bread. This was to be an adult-only conversation and I was asked to take the children to the furthest corner of the bunker.

While Zygush started to read aloud from his book, I strained to hear the others. But it was impossible to make out more than a few things here and there. 'We have no choice...' 'There's no way we will survive this.' 'There's still the can of petrol.' 'But we should spare the children as much as we can.'

I saw Mrs Steckel's hand grasp the vial of poison she wore round her neck. My mind was racing. Could Papa actually be asking for the poison for the children? After everything we've been through, after Mania and all she sacrificed for us, after all of this, could this be it? Was this the moment when the 'if' had turned into a 'when'? Was there no remnant of hope left? Beck had sounded so optimistic. They couldn't stop trusting him now. He had pulled us through so much before, he would get us through this too. I wasn't ready to stop fighting. If Mania were here, she wouldn't let this happen. How could my parents agree to this? Thoughts of suicide had passed through my mind, but now that it was being discussed openly, I wanted to scream NO! I wanted to scream it at the top of my lungs. But nothing came out.

There was such pain in Mama's eyes. She looked like she had when Mania had died. After that I couldn't hear a thing. It wasn't until Mr Melman was right next to us that I heard him say, 'Clarutchka, we're done.'

I couldn't bear to look at the others. I didn't want to see the truth of it. I just held Zosia and Zygush close to me and listened to the end of their story.

Mania and I in our sailor suit school uniform, aged 5 and 6

With my father and Mania, 1938

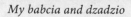

My babcia and dzadzio

The photos my friends and
I took when we didn't know
if we would survive the war,
1942. Above: I am with Genya
Astman (left). Below: Mania

*From left to right:
My mother Salka, (in
front) Julia Beck, Fanka
Melman, and (behind)
an unknown friend*

Lola Elefant

*Klara Patrontasch
and her brother
Artek in the 1930s*

Mr Valentine Beck,
after the war

Ala Beck

Myself with Mr
Beck and Mr
Melman, 1946

My diary

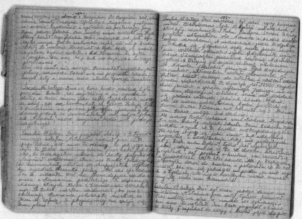

The Melman's house

Mr Patrontasch's carefully crafted hatch in the floor, still there today

The bunker as it looked on our last trip

In Montreal with Ala and Lola, early 1970s

At home with Sol, Zygush and Zosia in 2007

Chapter 12

VALENTINE'S DAY

January to February 1944

Thursday, 1 February. Mr Beck was in the bunker today. He says he heard on the radio that there are conferences in London. They want to end the war in the middle of March in order to save the remainder of the Jews… Sorry, it's too late, there will be very few Jews remaining when this is over. I can't imagine there are more people like the Becks who save 18 Jews.

Today is the first of the month. We have to pay. Everybody paid. Mr Patrontasch paid half, and mother gave her wedding ring. We didn't sell it until now. Daddy thought Mr Beck will not like it, but his generosity has no bounds. He didn't say anything. Please God, bless him because a single human cannot thank him enough.

*

How many times in the past year had I had to face the moment of my imminent death? Five? Ten? Twenty? Certainly more often than the times my belly was full. When I had to prepare, to picture the bullet and the flash of muzzle, or the axe or whatever weapon was at hand. To imagine the pain, the hell of being dragged through the streets and thrown on a train going to a camp. I had seen it with my own eyes. I was not a morbid girl, obsessed with her own death, but I was a witness. It was all there, more indelible than if it was etched by lightning in marble. And I had to weigh every second of life against every second of suffering. I knew there was no equation to give me an answer. I knew most of the suicides I had heard about were desperate reactions to imminent situations. Men and women running to the wire instead of to the marsh. Throwing a noose round the neck as the SS broke down the door. Taking poison in a cattle car already littered with corpses. Someone would have to inform the Becks. Someone had to convince the Steckels to give the poison to the children. It was one thing to contemplate taking one's own life, but once it was decided, the how and when became matters of practical concern. We had no time. Mr Melman dragged the five-litre can of petrol out of its grave in the far bunker and left it there. But nobody was moving. Nobody was saying anything. The can was mocking us.

We knew what would happen. Our suicide would murder the Becks. That was something we would never do. There was nothing to do but face the arrival of our new guests and go on.

As much as I tried to prepare myself for the arrival of the trainmen in the next few hours, I realized there was nothing I could do. I was already practised in the ways of hunger, thirst and silence. I had trained my digestive system to wait long periods of time before relief. I was able to sit without moving for hours and to sleep with pain. I could endure maddening rashes and prickly heat without scratching. If more of these qualities were required, I prayed I would find the will to continue. I could even control my fear to a certain degree. But what the trainmen were bringing was an unabated and continual terror of being discovered and eventual but certain death. Under such circumstances, would I, and we, be able to fight to the end, bitter or sweet? Even as we thought about ending it all, if we didn't act as if we were going to survive, there was no chance at all.

We were all waiting with desperate apprehension. It was as if the men were already here. Nobody was taking advantage of the last minutes of freedom; we were frozen. Then there was a knock at the door. We listened as Mr Beck invited the two strange voices and footsteps into the house. If there was any tension upstairs, we couldn't feel it. It seemed like a social call, with the requisite exchange of niceties and social decorum, rather than the Nazi imposition it really was. Beck had the vodka out and Julia offered the traditional bread and salt. I recognized the flirtation in Ala's voice as she told them a little about Zolkiew. I could tell that there was a huge gap in their ages. One seemed like a young man, almost a teenager, while the other's voice was much more manly.

As they chatted, I could tell that Beck had a plan behind his gracious welcome. He was fishing for information about these men's schedules to minimize surprises. He commiserated with them about their long workdays and their extended trips. Their schedule was erratic. We heard that sometimes they'd be working a few days; sometimes just overnight. And then there was a little laugh at the expense of German efficiency. Sometimes, they wouldn't be going anywhere for days. I was listening with big ears. We all were. What would we do if they stayed at home for days? It was already hard enough to keep still and avoid detection when Adolph stayed overnight, or during those endless parties. But days on end? I didn't see how we would manage to cook; to empty the pails; to get our food from Julia; to do all the meagre but essential things our lives had been reduced to.

They never volunteered to the Becks any details about their jobs. I didn't know if they were merely being cagey or if there was something in particular they were hiding from the Becks. All we knew was that they were trainmen. In times of war, a title was all you got, details were hushed over whenever possible. Everything I knew about the Nazis, and especially the trains, filled me with dread. There had been all those broken bones and the gunshot wounds of the jumpers. And then there was the terrible story that Beck had told us. Apparently the Polish trainmen working on the deportation trains and the trains that went to Belzec and Auschwitz would get off several miles before the camps. The Nazi trainmen would then take over for the final miles. I didn't want the men upstairs to be 'those' Germans. I wished they might be simple workers, mechanics or oilers, anything but the men who drove my people to their deaths. I didn't know what the others were thinking as these men made themselves comfortable and I heard their heavy bodies (they had to be heavy from the way the bedsprings creaked) flop down on the bed. But as their big hobnailed boots hit the floor, I wondered if these pleasant gruff voices indeed belonged to the men who drove the trains to Belzec and Auschwitz. And if they did, how could they laugh and groan with such contentment on the Becks' freshly washed sheets?

We did our best to organize our lives around the schedule of the trainmen. When they left the house, Beck would watch them walk down the street until they were out of sight. Then he'd knock on the door and, like our own little army, we'd charge into action. Patrontasch would rush upstairs to empty the buckets. Julia would hand us down the food and Mama would start cooking. Julia could only take our food orders in the rare moments when they weren't here, so we had to cut our rations to almost nothing. A cup of 'coffee' and a slice of bread in the morning. Watery soup for lunch. And one potato, the size of a walnut, for supper.

Like everything else I thought we couldn't adjust to, we somehow adjusted to life with the trainmen. I couldn't call it will or even resistance. We somehow just managed to do what was needed at any given moment. Stay still when the men were upstairs, and concentrate any necessary movements into the hours they were away. Despite my unbearable terror, knowing those Nazis to be upstairs, I'd eat my beloved potatoes and continue to breathe the fetid air. I had read the word 'fetid' in I don't know how many novels, and I could now proudly say I finally understood the concept in all its foul glory. We'd live on, from meal to meal and day to day, until we were either liberated or killed. A few weeks ago the others had discussed taking our own lives, but now, after hearing the fits and starts of the Soviet advance, we had begun to hope that there would be a life for us after the war.

But most of all, we were hungry for news from Beck. If the Russians advanced a few kilometres or had just taken Szeptowka, a town on the way to Lvov, there was enough hope to keep me going for a few more days. And when the German press reported that the Russians were making a push from Rovno in the direction of Lvov – God! What joy! Lvov! To hear the name of Lvov mentioned on the radio made the idea of our liberation a reality. And when Beck told us that ten German divisions, all of 200,000 men, were surrounded near the Dnieper river and were doomed, I prayed with all my heart and soul for the very Russians who had killed my grandfather.

In Zolkiew, the news was also encouraging. Julia told us that Pan Domrecki, who was notorious for being one of the nastiest collaborators, was getting ready to leave. Domrecki had sold out, for zloty and vodka, dozens of Jews and the Poles who had protected them. He and his thug friends would patrol the railroad tracks looking for jumpers. When they found a Jew, they would pretend to offer help. Instead, they'd bring them straight to the SS. They would show up later at the alcohol depot where Beck worked, exchanging their chits for blood vodka. I felt as if I could cut every Nazi henchman and collaborator to pieces.

Beck said he knew who every one of these bastards was. If Domrecki and those other bastards were running, it surely meant the Russians were winning the war. The hope egged us on. We had been subsisting on so little, but now the good signs were close. But all in all they didn't change anything in our lives. We couldn't look to the future with longing because we needed every fibre of will and concentration to be focused on whatever task lay at hand.

The deportations and the deaths continued. It was no wonder we were all going crazy. We were on a seesaw of emotions. Mama fainted almost every time there was a knock at the door. She would faint every time Beck or Julia told us of the brutal end of yet another friend. When she had come to again, Mama would say, 'Write, Clarutchka, write.' If every Jew in Zolkiew was destroyed, there would at least be my diary to tell the story. Mama made Beck promise that nothing would ever happen to the diary. She didn't have to add, 'If we died.' We all understood.

From time to time, Mr Patrontasch would grab a piece of paper and write down all sorts of equations and columns of numbers. When he was done, he'd tell us that we had been down in the bunker for 31,536,000 seconds. He'd have this satisfied expression on his face as if he had just discovered the meaning of life. And then he'd record the number in a little book. Lola wrote from time to time, but didn't show us what she was writing. Of course, we didn't ask. And the women, especially when there wasn't a crumb for a cockroach to eat on the dirt floor, would start exchanging recipes. They'd argue about whether black or golden raisins were better for noodle puddings. Or how to make the lightest sponge cake. And how much honey to put in the chewy raisin cookies I adored. It was the *meshuggenah* driving the rest of *meshugge*.

Finally Papa couldn't take it any more. 'If you *balabustas*, good homemakers, are such geniuses in front of the stove, why don't you bake us a honey cake out of potato peels?'

All this absurdity meant one thing. We were still alive.

I kept on reminding myself of our good fortune, even when it had been 20 below zero outside for weeks and the trainmen hadn't budged from their chairs in all that time. They would just sit and sit and sit, reading the newspaper and listening to the radio. Every second of their relaxation equalled agony for us. Sometimes I thought I could even hear the pages rustling when they turned them.

Mr Patrontasch couldn't risk going upstairs to empty the pails when the trainmen were at home. But if we didn't get rid of them regularly, the stench would give us away. On several occasions, Beck had to send Ala in to entertain the trainmen in their room and keep them occupied. After Ala turned up the music, Beck would knock on the trapdoor and keep guard while, Patrontasch, barefoot, sneaked up the corridor to the bathroom to empty the pails. Nobody would breathe during those moments. It only took a few minutes, but it felt endless.

I had nothing to do except to sit and stare in a state of constant expectation and dread at everyone all day long. There was nothing worse than sitting and sitting, hour after hour, day after day, only interrupted by sleep. We had become animals. Our skin was beyond pale. It was grey, the colour of dirty sheets, and our hollowed-out eyes, even the children's, were ringed with the darkest of circles. We were *dybbuks*, spirits of the dead, while the trainmen lazed about with their newspapers. I knew they were ignorant of their effect on us, and on the Becks, but I hated them for it. The only silver lining to their presence was that the Becks were compelled to act as if everything was wonderful in their marriage. At least that brought some peace into the house.

*

When the weather warmed up a little, the trainmen were finally assigned a job and left for a couple of days. After they had gone, I felt as if I had exhaled for the first time in weeks. Beck came home from work at six in the morning and knocked on the trapdoor. I was desperate for any task that would take me upstairs. He told Papa and Artek to go to the cellar to cut wood for the oven and asked Lola and me to clean his room. We followed the men upstairs and started cleaning. After weeks and weeks downstairs, the sight of sunlight coming through the curtains, a clean polished floor and the smell of fresh air were enough to make me drunk. Beck too seemed to be affected. He ordered us to load the stove with wood. Wood was so scarce that the house was always cold, but now he wanted heat! Beck brought some plants the sister-in-law had given him back into his room. Julia had moved them from their room to the pantry in the hope the cold air would kill them.

While the men were in the cellar cutting the wood, Klara went to the trapdoor and asked Beck for a pot of water. Water was as precious as food or money. Water was our lifeline. We used it to cook the potatoes into a soup and the water we washed our hair in was reused to soak our clothes. Not a drop was wasted. Ever. Klara was our biggest user of water and was always borrowing from us or the Melmans. Her asking Mr Beck for an entire bucket of water was like asking for a million dollars. What got into Klara, to ask for water with Julia in the house, had to be a symptom of our collective insanity that day. Had I even heard her correctly? What could she have been thinking? This was surely going to produce a big fight, just now when things were somewhat peaceful between the Becks. I didn't want to look away from my loading of the stove, but I couldn't help myself. I saw Beck fetch the pail of water.

As if on cue, Julia walked in and saw the bucket of water pass between their hands. She must have also seen that Beck had moved the plants back to the room because she started to scream: 'Don't put that wood in the stove! Stop it! You think I'll waste wood on that whore's flowers! Not one log in that oven!'

Beck yelled at us to ignore her.

Julia repeated: 'Not one log! You hear!'

Lola and I looked at each other, not knowing what to do or whom to listen to. Then Julia picked up some dishes and started throwing them against the walls and floors. 'Not one log! Not one log!' Over and over again. The pain in her voice seemed to come right from her heart. She was helpless to change him. It seemed like this was to be their end. As frightened as we were, my heart was breaking for this poor woman's pain. Beck didn't say a word in his own defence. Julia picked up the flowerpots and threw them to the floor.

'MY FLOWERS!' Beck yelled, as his open hand smashed Julia in the face.

Blood was streaming from her lips. 'I'll never go near that trapdoor again! She can starve for all I care. They can all starve!'

We had all become the other woman in Julia's eyes. She ran into Ala's room and slammed the door shut behind her. We heard sobbing from within. Then the fall of the door knocker on wood. The trainmen had returned. Beck quickly gave us some potatoes, told us to get downstairs and closed the trapdoor. He left a few minutes after the trainmen settled in. He didn't come back at all that day or that night. We knew, as Julia must have known too, he would be at the sister-in-law's house.

Julia had been pushed and pushed like no other woman I'd ever met. Her strength of character and her generosity were boundless. I knew Mr Beck loved these qualities in her. He had told us so, many times. Whether he ever told Julia or not, I didn't know. But, of course, in the face of his love affairs such words would be more slaps in her face. But the truth is, he did love her. And she loved him.

The next morning, Julia knocked on the trapdoor to give us some water with which to cook the potatoes. She took our orders for food. She wouldn't look at Klara. I didn't know what we had done to be worthy of her generosity. I prayed to God to somehow reward this woman who suffered so much for us. We didn't know what had brought on this change of heart. Had she made up with Beck, or he with her? I did know for certain that if we weren't here, she would leave him. But as long as we were here, she was trapped.

Something must have happened between them, because not long thereafter Julia decided to throw her husband a large Valentine's party in honour of his name day. The night of the party, I heard the trainmen, Dr Lucynski, Lang, Schmidt, Krueger, Hans the policeman (who harboured affection for Ala) and a few voices I didn't recognize, all congratulating Beck as they walked in. The vodka was being passed around and the music was playing. There was nothing for us to do but sit in silence and listen. Usually during these parties the children sat close to me. But this time they had been playing with Klarunia when the first guests arrived and so they were on the other side of the bunker near the Patrontasches. As long as there were strangers upstairs, none of us moved. We became frozen. Little underground statues.

The dancing had slowed down and I could hear the conversation in every detail. Lang was talking. 'God help us when the war is over and the Jews take their revenge.' I couldn't believe that he was even worried about such a thing. At least he had a conscience.

One of the trainmen laughed. 'Not if we get them first.'

Something in this man's laughter frightened Zosia. She started to weep and then to cry. And then to actually wail. For all these months she had been trained to speak only when absolutely necessary. She had learned to be the most silent of all of us. For days on end, we would never hear her say a word. Not to ask for food or water or to go to the bathroom. Nothing. But now she was screaming the way only a terrified four-year-old could scream. I tried to shush her by putting a finger to my lips. All of us were doing the same thing. I was too afraid to go over to her to hold her. I was too frightened even to whisper something reassuring. It was too dangerous to add another sound to hers. I watched, paralyzed and scared stiff. Julia's footsteps rushed to the trapdoor and she knocked softly above us. Her voice was a whisper: 'I can hear her.' Something had to be done or the guests would surely discover us. Mr Patrontasch grabbed a pillow and put it over her face. Zosia struggled, scratching and clawing at Patrontasch's hands, but at least the sound was muffled.

Upstairs, there was casual talk about the war. The conversation varied from the weather conditions – Was the slight thaw good or bad? Would it help the Russians? Or the Germans? – to the trainload of German refugees who had come from the east and been stalled at the station. Beck was saying that the people had been starving, but that the SS hadn't let them off the train. All the while Zosia was still crying underneath the pillow. The conversation had moved on to the governor of Lvov who had been assassinated. Beck was saying that it had been the handiwork of Jewish partisans. Hans joked: 'It had to be the Yids. There are no Polish or *Volksdeutsche* partisans, hey, Beck?' A roar of laughter erupted.

Then Dr Lucynski added, 'Maybe the Jews Valentin is hiding are partisans!' A long silence followed. I was waiting for Dr Lucynski to tell everyone it was a joke. But he didn't. I imagined how Beck must have looked as he tried to gauge the trainmen's reaction without being obvious. The trainmen didn't laugh or acknowledge that the remark had to be a joke. Not a laugh. Not a chuckle. Just silence. I couldn't believe that Dr Lucynski, Beck's supposed friend, would make such an incriminating joke. I didn't know if Dr Lucynski actually knew about us. I couldn't imagine Beck would tell him, or anyone.

Suddenly, as if the wind shifted, they started to debate whether to believe the Russian or German propaganda. Did the Russians take back Leningrad? What about Churchill's speech in which he said the bombing of Germany would intensify for the possible invasion of Europe's Atlantic coast? The only thing the men agreed on was that all the politicians and generals were liars. Another good laugh ensued. Thank God. Lucysnki's remark had no traction. I prayed the trainmen just thought it a bad joke that had deserved only polite silence.

Mr Melman grabbed a piece of hard candy and stuck it under the pillow. Zosia's legs and arms were now still. I breathed easier. She had stopped struggling and just lay on Patrontasch's lap as still as if she were in a deep and peaceful sleep. The candy had worked. Patrontasch took the pillow away from her face. Even in the dim light I could see her face was blue. Her eyes were closed and her chest wasn't moving up and down with each breath.

Mama crawled across to Zosia and started rubbing her chest. She rubbed it hard. It seemed like Mama was rubbing her chest for ever. She put her fingers to Zosia's lips and pulled them apart. 'Zosia, Zosia, open your eyes.' Zosia obeyed Mama. She looked up at Mama and whispered, 'Can I eat the candy?' The hard candy was in her palm. Mama gathered her in her arms and helped her open the candy wrapper. Patrontasch had almost killed Zosia, but who could blame him? I was just so thankful that Zosia had pulled through. I had been petrified; I couldn't move a muscle. I would never leave them alone again.

It was a freezing night, and even down here, I could hear the wind whipping against the windows upstairs. There was no reason for the guests to brave the elements when there was still vodka. Around dawn the house became silent. I was exhausted. I was hoping I would sleep well past noon, as we had all been trying to do since the trainmen were living above us. Then there was an unexpected knock on the trapdoor. Mr Patrontasch turned on the light. It was Beck. He climbed down into the bunker. Beck said he needed to talk. He had brought a bottle of vodka with him. He seemed troubled. He had woken us up before, but usually it was good news on the radio. This time it seemed he had something weighing on his mind.

He poured vodka for the men. It was such a ritual. He told us that Dr Lucynski had taken him aside during the party and told him that he had spoken with some of the refugees on the trains. The reason they hadn't been let off the trains was that the Nazis didn't want the refugees to tell anyone what they had seen. The advancing Russians were murdering any *Volksdeutsche* and Poles who had collaborated with the Nazis. Dr Lucynski had been convinced that once the war was over, the Jews would murder as many Poles as they could in revenge for the mothers, fathers and children who had been slaughtered. Beck was frightened. Papa and the other men tried to reassure him that they would make sure he wasn't harmed. In turn, Beck wanted us to know that he would never abandon us. We shouldn't worry. He would stay with us until the end. I understood that he had never thought about the consequences our survival might have for him. Nobody had. We had only thought of ourselves. Of course the Russians would slaughter the *Volksdeutsche* and any collaborators. We had already seen what they had done to my family. He left the bottle for the men and crawled back to the trapdoor. Before he went upstairs, he said, 'I don't want to trouble you, but I was hoping you might do something for me.' I knew we would do anything he asked. But the way he asked was so courtly. His voice sounded gentle. Papa said, 'Anything.'

'There are bands of partisans, deserting SS, marauders, breaking into houses... I worry what could happen to Julia and Ala. When the trainmen aren't here, would you be kind enough to leave the trapdoor open at night when I'm at work?' They say there are no angels here on earth. But they didn't know Beck. As much as his face could be ravaged by drink and exhaustion, there was a purity and goodness in his eyes. He said, 'I just can't be part of people dying.'

It was a simple declaration. Those words kept us alive. They kept him going when his courage failed and his faith was tested. With the war raging outside and millions compromising everything they believed to stay alive, how many were like Beck? He held our lives in his hands and there was now no one on this earth I would have trusted with them more. It was in moments like these that I felt most strongly that we would survive. I had never met anyone like Beck before. My father was a good man. So were all the men in the bunker. But I didn't know if they had what Beck had. I didn't know if Papa would risk my life to save a stranger. We had been strangers to Beck and now it felt like we were his family. I had gone through four notebooks and the blue pencil that Beck had given me was down to a nub. Every time he gave me a new notebook, he said the same thing, 'Clarutchka, I hope you say nice things about me.' I prayed that I would live so the world would know his courage and his great love.

As soon as the trainmen went out for lunch the next day, the men started talking. We were all out of money and food. All the families were, except the Steckels. I couldn't keep it in any longer. I asked Papa again, 'Why don't we ask them?'

'We can't. It's not our way.'

They decided they would ask Beck to help them, and they

would make him a 25 per cent partner in their business. Mr Patrontasch drew up the contract in his beautiful handwriting.

When Beck came home later and opened the trapdoor to have me come up and weigh the potatoes, the men asked to have a word. Mr Patrontasch explained that they were out of money and couldn't pay him for their food any longer. They wanted to make him their partner. Of all the *meshuggenah* conversations I had heard in the bunker, this was perhaps the craziest. Who knew if we would survive? Who knew if there would be a business left after the war? Who knew if the factory wouldn't be bombed or every piece of machinery packed on a train and sent west or east depending who won the war? There was every possibility that the contract wasn't worth the ink it was written with. I knew that Beck was as aware as I was of the improbability of it all. But the offer pleased him immensely as he shook each of the three men's hands with vigour and strength. He went upstairs to get a bottle of vodka to toast the arrangement. We had heard the toasting going on during the party. All the traditional, ribald Polish toasts that the Poles were so fond of and that no festive occasion was complete without: 'I drink till I fall, fall till I rise, I rise to drink, I drink to be wise.' 'Every shot is a nail in my coffin – this will be a helluva coffin.' 'To the drunkard who lives half as long but sees everything twice.' 'To the health of our wives and lovers and may they never meet'… and so many more.

As he raised his glass, he gestured to us. *Sto lat.* 'A hundred years.' It was the toast traditionally made on a man's naming day. And then *na zdrowie.* 'To your health.' I had heard these toasts dozens of times. So often said sentimentally, said casually, said without thought. But Beck was wishing each of us health and a long life. I toasted him as well in the silence of my heart. Long life. A hundred years.

Chapter 13

THE SS MOVE IN

March to April 1944

Wednesday, 1 March. It's already March, the winter is over, but the winter didn't help us much. It's raining, it's thawing, it's impossible for the military to move. Nothing is happening at the front. Our situation is terrible. Our nerves are frazzled from these constant alarms. Any little sound made by somebody in the bunker sounds like thunder. One gets heart palpitations when one has to dish out the food on the table and to top it all is the fear of hunger. Almost nobody had any money for March. If we had more money, we wouldn't have to cook potatoes, we could eat bread.

*

As in everything else, Beck was true to his word. We had run out of money and he was providing our food now. He didn't tell us where or how he was getting the money. Or what kinds of risk he and Julia were taking. There was not a trace of pity in his voice, ever. When he came down to tell us that Finland had declared a ceasefire with Russia, he might as well have been in a tavern discussing the news of the day with his friends over schnapps. Or when he banged on the door a few hours later and told us about a misunderstanding between England and Turkey over something no one could quite figure out, he might have been giving us the update on the 1936 Olympics. He had not only taken on our physical survival but also, with his jokes, news, drinks and gossip, our moral and emotional survival as well. What was remarkable to me was that his effort was without effort. This avowed anti-Semite, misanthrope and despiser of all authority was the most naturally generous human being I had yet come to meet. And it came as naturally to him as pouring his next drink or sleeping with Klara or his brother's widow.

Papa, Mr Melman and Mr Patrontasch, all their lives, were givers. Charity had been a way of life for them. Nobody mentioned how much they had given to support the schools, the orphanages and the hungry in Zolkiew. Or how much money they had sent to Palestine. I knew that giving was as natural to them as breathing and that they felt, down to their very bones, that a man should take care of his family. Yet here we were. In this bunker, dependent for everything on the Becks. I was still a child, but every one of us, most especially the grown-ups, had become as children. Like all of us, Papa was a portion, a tithe, of the man he once was. His clothes hung off him like they once belonged to a robust businessman and he had found them, four sizes too big, in the trash and decided to wear them anyway. We struggled to keep as clean as we could, but now with the trainmen living like kings just above us, we couldn't even wash our clothes as often as we once used to. They were grey anyway from so many washings and now they were always soiled as well. And as much as Papa used to protest to Mama about how he didn't care about his clothes, I knew, even though he didn't have a vain bone in his body, that he loved the feel of a well-tailored suit jacket on his shoulders and a shirt that was starched just so. He and all the other men had made extra holes in their belts as regularly as they marked the days on Mr Patrontasch's calendar and their clothes were cinched and bunched around their waists. Where there were once answers in my father's eyes, now there were only questions. And Papa suffered more from the loss of dignity than he suffered from the lack of food. So much had been taken from us that there was very little of our past that was in our present.

We were fortunate that one of the reminders of our past was the Melmans' flush toilet. Plenty of envious jokes had made the rounds of the kitchens and back steps that the Melmans had given themselves *Tam Genadyn*... a taste of the Garden of Eden when they had it installed. Over the card games at the social club Mrs Melman was said to be the instigator. But however it had come about, we no longer cared. We were just grateful that Julia wasn't running to an outhouse in the yard with bucket after bucket of refuse, which would certainly have alerted the neighbourhood to our presence. While the Russians fought the Nazis in the mud and snow, inching towards Lvov, and the Allies were working their way up the Italian peninsula, our war became the emptying of our refuse. No spy operations were ever conducted with more military precision. However, when the trainmen didn't move from the house for days, we suffered. It was torture to hold in our bladders and bowels for hours and hours at a time. The children were allowed to go in the dirt and we buried it.

One day the trainmen had gone off to the movies and, as soon as it was safe, Beck knocked on the hatch so Patrontasch could run upstairs and empty the buckets. We were all waiting for Mr Patrontasch to come down with the empty buckets, when there would be a rush to use them again, children first. But something was wrong. Mr Patrontasch wasn't coming back. He'd been gone for half an hour, not the minutes we always counted until he was back with clean buckets. Then I saw his head in the hatch. 'There's something in the toilet. The *farshtinkener* thing is stuck. It won't go down. I stuck my hand down up to the elbow and it wouldn't budge!'

It was Mr Melman's toilet and, expert or not, he went up to help Mr Patrontasch. While the two were trying to figure out how to fix the toilet, Julia carried two heavy buckets out to the backyard. I knew she carried out plenty of night buckets in her time and I'm sure she didn't care about having to carry out our refuse as much as I did. It was one more way in which Julia had to take care of us. When she handed the buckets back down to us, her cheeks were flushed and her hands were raw from the cold. She had run out without a coat, but she still had a smile for us.

Mr Patrontasch and Mr Melman came down a few minutes later with unhappy faces. They concluded that the septic tank was full. Twenty-odd people using it over the past year had to be the cause. There would now be no other choice but for the Becks to empty our refuse into the outhouse. Julia told us not to worry. But with the trainmen living upstairs and the constant comings and goings of Beck's friends and Ala's boyfriend Adolph, who had just returned from leave, the buckets might be the death of us. If they weren't emptied, the odour would filter upstairs. Julia could smell when the buckets were full and came to collect them as soon as she could. But if she was seen by the trainmen, by the police or Blue Coats or any of the Poles who were making a living at the cost of Jewish lives, we were dead.

We had just got the buckets emptied and the trapdoor closed when there was a knock on the door. I thought it was the trainmen back from the movies. I knew I would hear them talking about the film with Beck, Julia and Ala and I was looking forward to the conversation. It was the closest I might ever get to a cinema. But I didn't hear their voices and their familiar heavy footsteps. I heard another voice, speaking a frantic, guttural and forceful German. I couldn't make out the words. I panicked. This was the search we had all been dreading. I started praying to the God who brought us Zygush and Zosia, not to the God who allowed all the Jews in Zolkiew to be murdered. I held the children's hands. I was looking up at the ceiling of the bunker as if it was heaven itself and God was going to tell me if I was going to live or die. No matter how many times I thought I was facing death, the terror never lessened. It only got worse, because I knew our luck couldn't go on day after day after day until the end of the war with so many forces conspiring against it. I counted six sets of boots and heard Beck telling them they would have to sleep with the trainmen. I heard them bring in their things. I knew they were soldiers. They left after a few minutes and Beck knocked on the trapdoor.

This was a face I had never seen on Beck before. These six men weren't soldiers. He told us: 'They're SS and I don't know how long they'll be here. They told me their car broke down and they have to wait for parts.' As much as I tried to turn my will to steel with which to face each new terror, I knew this was the end. Beck looked like he knew it as well. Not one of us said a word. We would have to accept the arrival of the SS inches above our heads as just one more of life's horrible mortal ironies. There was nothing for us to do. Not one solitary thing to help ourselves survive except carry on as we had been living while we waited to die.

But Beck had more to say. Five peasants had been murdered in the forest where all of Zolkiew's Jews were shot and buried a year ago. One peasant survived, and he said that Jews had been the killers. Misters Hecht, Hochner, Klein and Fern. I knew that the Fern family had escaped to Russia . As much as I feared the repercussions, I wished this were true. I wished for any Jew to be alive. It didn't matter to me how many collaborators they killed, if it was they who did the killing. The deaths of the men they killed wouldn't avenge what had been done to us, not even in the smallest way.

Beck also told us there was more panic about the Russian advance and that Jewish partisans had been fighting with the Russians when they took Dubno, which was only a few hundred kilometres away near Brody. He said anyone who had given a German a glass of water was terrified of the Russians. Papa again assured Beck that we would never let anything happen to him or his family if and when we were liberated. But Beck knew that Papa's words were only a sentiment, a hope. If the Russians wanted to shoot the Becks, no matter how we begged and pleaded for their lives, they would shoot them, and then move on to the next *Volksdeutsche* and collaborators they could get their hands on.

Papa and the men talked with Beck about the logistics of the new regime upstairs. He gave us a third bucket, which meant that the buckets would only have to be emptied once a day. The problem was how and when to empty the buckets. I knew that if the SS saw Julia emptying a bucket, they would know Jews were hidden in the house. Melman had to try again to fix the toilet upstairs. Beck would keep watch for the trainmen and the SS.

I had prayed for so many things. For our lives. For Uchka. For Mama when she was taking care of Uchka. For Zygush and Zosia. And for my beloved sister. And now I was asking God to fix our toilet. While Melman was upstairs working, Julia came back with 200 grams of lard and bread. Mama had given her some of our bedding to sell since the weather had become a little warmer. Lard! Fat! I didn't know where she got it, but she had such a smile on her face as she handed it down to us. Even with the SS about to come back over our heads, all I could think of was fat. Mama started cutting up potatoes to boil. We were going to have mashed potatoes! While the potatoes were boiling, Mr Melman came down with good news. He had fixed the toilet! It had been clogged. His wife actually kissed him. It was the first kiss I had seen in months. I then turned my attention to the lard, which I slathered on the bread and mashed potatoes. Zygush and Zosia couldn't get it down fast enough. It was better than any feast for any holiday I had had in my life.

While we ate, the men quickly decided that someone would always be on 'guard duty' in the part of the bunker that was under the bathroom. If someone upstairs was in there, they could almost hear us exhale below. The guard would alert the rest of us to be quiet. The person standing guard at night over the snorers also had to stand guard under the bathroom. I volunteered. During the evening, as we enjoyed our mashed potatoes, I thought I had lost all reason. I had begun to think having the SS over our heads was turning out to be a good thing. With the three Becks, the two trainmen, the six SS and Ala's boyfriend Adolph, there would be such a commotion that no one could possibly hear us. And while Julia was out buying us lard, Beck had found us a trove of books in the trash somewhere. He was always on the lookout for presents for us. Lola, Artek and I were the big readers. We couldn't finish them fast enough. We gave each other books the way people give each other colds. Maybe God did work in strange ways. I felt like I was more relaxed than I had been in months with my potatoes and my book.

But then I noticed the straw bedding and realized we'd soon

have new guests. Millions of them. Unless we changed the straw before the weather was warmer, all the dormant flea eggs would hatch. On the other hand, I hoped we'd live long enough to be tormented by the fleas, and their comrades, the bed bugs.

It was a strange and lonely feeling to be sitting up in the dark, trying to stay awake. I'd listen to the breathing of everyone in the bunker. Kuba Patrontasch was the worst snorer. Every time I had guard duty, I'd have to wake him up. I didn't know how he got any sleep at all. But of all the sleepers, I liked to listen to Zygush and Zosia the most. In the dark the quiet, small, quick breath of the children was somehow reassuring. With Uchka dead and Mama drifting into God knows where from time to time, I felt like their mother, and it was with a mother's ears that I listened to them sleep. I liked guard duty. I liked watching over the sleeping children. Any small thing that helped us survive made me stronger, no matter how it exhausted me.

Poor Zosia. She made more noise sleeping than she did when she was awake. After the episode with the pillow, she was frightened of saying even one word. Of even whispering. She was most terrified of the noise she made when she went to the bathroom. She would put her tiny hands between her legs and hold herself rather than make that noise into the bucket. I now asked every night before she went to bed, 'Do you have to go?' She'd move her face next to my ear and whisper, 'Maybe.' And then I'd say, 'Why don't you try? Why don't we go together?' Then I'd take her hand and we'd crawl together to the area we jokingly referred to as the 'park', where we had the pails. I would go first so she would know it was okay.

The entire house was quiet now except for the Becks. I could hear the trainmen and the SS snoring. I could even hear them breathing. It was a miracle that no one had heard us down here in all these months. Beck was whispering to Julia: 'There are no more Jews left in Germany. Adolph told me. He said the Nazis are planning to send all the *Volksdeutsche* back to Germany to work... whether we like it or not.' I couldn't hear what Julia said in response. Then there was silence. If the Nazis sent the Becks back, we were dead.

When Mama and Papa got up in the morning, I had to tell them. Mama took a deep breath and fainted. I got a damp cloth to revive her with. When her eyes opened she always looked so startled, as if she were surprised to have come to in this bunker. And then she would look ashamed, as if the woman who fainted was not Mama but an annoying relative who came to stay a night in our house and never left. When the SS and the trainmen went out that day, Beck didn't relate any of his conversation with Julia about the repatriation of the *Volksdeutsche*. But he said he had a disturbing conversation with Adolph, who was now convinced that our SS guests were deserters. The idea that SS marauders and murderers were sleeping in the room next to his wife and child terrified him. I had never seen Beck as frightened as we were. I hated that I was powerless to help him in any of the ways he had helped us. He begged the men to watch out for Ala and Julia if the SS tried anything when he was at work. The men said that they would, of course. They'd already promised to keep an eye on Ala and Julia when Beck and the trainmen were out. But what could they possibly do now that the SS were there, except die with Ala and Julia? Beck somehow seemed reassured and told us he was going to get a rifle from the partisans for us. We knew he had some connections with the partisans. He never told us what they were or what his involvement was. But I had a suspicion they were significant. He had access to so much information that would be useful.

Almost as an afterthought, he gave us some good news. The Russians were only 25 kilometres from Zbaraz, which was in

Galicia. Our Galicia. Patrontasch took out his map, where he marked each Russian advance, and each of us was granted a look to lift our spirits. It was on the map so it had to be real.

Zbaraz was less than 150 kilometres from Zolkiew. I loved Zbaraz. My favourite Sienkiewicz book, *With Fire and Sword*, was set there and its castle was one of the most famous in Galicia. Sienkiewicz had written the book to inspire the Polish people after our failed January uprising against the Tsar in 1863. To this day, it was a rallying cry for all Poles to fight for their liberty. I had been inspired by the book and it had made me so proud to be a Polish girl. But I wasn't thrilled now because of any literary nostalgia. Zbaraz was on the road to Tarnopol, which was only 125 kilometres from Lvov. Mr Patrontasch pointed to a semicircle he had drawn round Lvov on the map and said that when the Russians were 35 kilometres away we would be able to hear the music of their artillery.

I wanted to examine the map more closely, but the SS were just arriving home and Beck slipped back upstairs. We celebrated in silence, each of us now with more hope than we'd had in months. As long as I was one breath short of starving to death when we were liberated, I knew I wouldn't care. I knew each of us was thinking the same thing at the same moment. Tarnopol!

The SS didn't slaughter anyone in their sleep and stayed with us for six days. On the seventh, they left, just after the Russians had taken Tarnopol. The part arrived for their car and after goodbyes to the Becks, they were gone.

The SS might have gone, but the trainmen seemed to be growing roots in their beds. There hadn't been any work for them for days and days. They hardly ever went out now and kept to themselves. The only time Mr Patrontasch could empty the buckets was when they were asleep. Julia would wait up, as late as humanly possible, until long after she was sure the trainmen were asleep. Or if, as they did last night, they stayed up almost all night drinking, she'd get up early when she knew the trainmen would still be asleep.

We all had been up early, waiting for her. No one could sleep because of stomach cramps. I heard her slippered feet on the floor above us, although she had learned to walk with barely a sound. There was her quiet tap on the hatch... Patrontasch opened it with the care of a surgeon. Poor Julia had to lie down on the floor to talk to us because it was painful to kneel and almost impossible for her to crawl in because of her arthritis. Her voice was a frightened whisper: 'They're all asleep.' I watched Julia as she struggled to her feet and Patrontasch slipped upstairs in his socks, which had been darned and redarned by Lola and looked like a patchwork quilt. Melman had one of the buckets in his hand, ready to hand it up. Patrontasch took it.

Melman was watching Patrontasch wait for the signal. Julia had walked to her bedroom door and opened it. She looked out and then nodded back at Patrontasch. He walked quickly out of the bedroom and down the hall to the bathroom. We heard a flush and then a moment later he walked quickly into the bedroom and gave me the empty bucket and took the other full bucket from Melman. Julia, watching at the door, gestured for him with the crook of an arthritic finger. He slipped into the hall and, after the flush, walked back into the bedroom. In his haste and relief he forgot to close the bedroom door after him.

The flushing apparently reminded one of the still drunk trainmen that he had to use the bathroom as well. He walked past the bedroom on his way to the bathroom. He stared right at Patrontasch, who was standing with a bucket in his hand right next to the hatch, which was protected from view by the bed. The trainman looked at Patrontasch with curiosity then continued down to the bathroom. Why he just continued past without inquiring about the stranger, I didn't know.

Patrontasch jumped quickly down into the bunker and closed the hatch. He turned to us all. 'One of the trainmen, he saw me.' The children were asleep, but the rest of us were united by a bolt of electricity that ran through us all. This is how our world would end. After all the close calls and dumb luck and the deaths and the sorrow and the suffering and the hunger: our lives would now be forfeit by our own refuse.

Upstairs it was happening already. It seemed dozens of feet were scurrying back and forth above us, scouring every inch of the house. All around the bunker families were embracing, yet careful not to disturb the sleeping children. Artek grabbed Lola. Even Steckel grabbed his wife's hand. My poor father held my mama as we heard above us, like it was all happening in our own minds, the trainman screaming and pointing to the spot where Patrontasch had been standing. 'I swear I saw him! Right in the bedroom!'

My father was mouthing words in the darkness lit by a single candle over and over until I could hear the words in their silence. 'Just say it was a visitor. Just say it was a visitor. A visitor. A visitor...'

Julia said, 'A thief – it must have been a thief.' A thief! Why did she say a thief? I knew that the trainman would run to the police station and they would be tearing the house apart in a matter of minutes. I could hear Julia's feet running over to the closet.

She pulled open the closet door. I had heard that closet creak open and shut I don't know how many times a day, but today it was louder than any bomb. We heard Julia pushing aside her clothes and then the tumble of boxes on the floor right above our head.

Julia was near hysterics. 'I had some silver candlesticks. From my dowry. I kept them hidden in the closet for safe keeping.' The other trainman was now in the room and we heard him tumble to the floor and heard the sarcasm in his voice: 'Of course thieves. But there's no one under the bed.' I could tell from his footsteps that Julia hadn't put the rug back to cover the hatch. I could hear him right above me. His body had to be covering the hatch as he looked right under the bed!

The first trainman must still have been pointing to the spot right above the hatch where he saw Patrontasch. 'I swear I saw him! Standing right there. He was short. Dark hair. Dark eyes. Wearing just an undershirt.'

I looked at Patrontasch. We all did. The trainman was describing him exactly. I heard the men move to the closet and then out of the room, searching everywhere. I heard doors being opened and closed. And cabinets being opened and closed. Julia and Ala followed them around as they asked if anything else had been stolen. We also followed their progress with our eyes on the ceiling above us. Zygush woke up and started to say something, but the look in my eyes quietened him right down. He saw we were all frightened to death. He was stoic as usual. Zosia woke up now, but was quiet.

Julia had changed tactics. 'Maybe it was a partisan.'

The trainman replied, 'Whoever was here he's not here now.'

Julia was doing her very best. 'The window was open. He probably saw you and jumped out the window.'

All I could think was: *Fifteen months in this hole. To die now with the Russians in Tarnopol!*

Ala, dear clever Ala, laughed: 'Mama, I'm sure if we're really nice to Papa, he might buy us another pair of silver candlesticks.

He knows how much you loved them. Mama's a little crazy about those candlesticks. She doesn't ever use them.'

The two trainmen laughed at her joke but one of them still went out to fetch the police. We waited and waited. In silence. I wanted to say goodbye to Mama and Papa. I knew this might be the last time I might say anything to them or tell them how much I loved them. I wanted to tell the children we would all be with Uchka soon. I couldn't say goodbyes to anyone. When the trainman came back it was with several other policemen, all of whom knew the Becks. Ever since the trainmen heard Lucynski voice his suspicions about Jews being in the house to Beck several weeks ago, I felt they suspected something, despite that not one thing was changed in their behaviour or conversation. I wasn't able to control the fear that tore through my mind, sending every thought to the desperate conclusions that only permanent terror can bring. As they looked through the house, I thanked God they were talking about thieves and not Jews, and then the conversation turned to something innocuous. I heard one of the trainmen laughing. 'Even if I had a gun, I wouldn't have shot the thief, even if he was a Jew.' And though I wasn't able to join them, for a moment I was grateful at the apparent decency of this one man whose face I had never seen. All the policemen laughed. Ala asked them to stay for tea, but after a few minutes they left.

And we were left, alive, one more time. Again, Beck was right. His friendship with the German police was paying dividends in the days and weeks and months added to our lives. The trainmen went out and we were able to cook our potatoes and empty the buckets. I even had a chance to help the children with their lessons. When Beck came home later, the trainmen were still out and he knocked on the hatch. Instead of panicking and worrying about his own survival, he said, 'You shouldn't worry about those two. They're all right.' And instead of reproaching Patrontasch for forgetting to close the bedroom door, he promised: 'You know I'll never leave you. I'll die with you. Your fate is my fate. And let me tell you what Ala did.' His eyes grew bright when he talked about her. 'She called Hans from work – you know, the policeman who is besotted with her – and told him about the robbery and how the trainmen suspected Jews were in the house. Can you believe it? How smart she is. And you know what Hans said? This is the best!' We waited for the punchline. '"Jews in your house?" he told Ala. "Those trainmen are out of their minds. Jews at the Becks! I live with you practically. Acch! Some people see Jews everywhere."'

This was Hans, who bragged about how many Jews he had killed. I didn't know how Ala and Beck did it. In almost 15 months, they didn't lose their heads with the Germans. Not once.

Then he said to us, 'You know you shouldn't worry. Beck is lucky. Beck is always lucky.' He whistled a few bars of 'All's Well That Ends Well' to prove it.

Perhaps Beck was right. Perhaps 'All's Well That Ends Well'. Because the next thing he came down to tell us was that the Russians were 80 kilometres away from Lvov. Two hours in a car, that's all! We were jubilant, hugging, embracing each other; the end was near. His piercing blue eyes had always betrayed his feelings even before he had said a word. Either they had the warmth of a summer sky or they were cold like ice, looking inwards. Today I could see that the commitment he had made to us was ripping him apart. He admitted that Ala had been transferred to Krakow and Julia wanted to go with her.

Papa and Mr Patrontasch did everything they could to convince him that it was going to be okay. They even told him that all of us would give our lives for him and his family in a heartbeat. It was true. I knew I would. Beck didn't say anything for a long time. That he didn't laugh in our faces was just one more example of his decency. He just looked around the bunker at his sorry excuse for an army. 'You think you could fight the Russians? To hell with the Russians. Even the Ukrainian bastards would rip you apart.' Of course he was right. It was a crazy idea. I didn't have a gun. I had a spoon, a fork and an enamel plate. I couldn't have weighed more than 40 kilograms. The last time I had been upstairs cleaning, I had caught sight of myself in the mirror. Although I didn't look as bad as some of the others, I knew I shared equals odds as a rabbit against a bloodthirsty Ukrainian.

Papa said, 'You could hide down here with us.'

Beck simply shook his head and went upstairs to talk it over with Julia. He came down a few minutes later and told us that it was final. Julia was still frightened and would leave with Ala on Monday. I was counting the hours to Monday. With Julia and Ala gone, even if Beck remained behind, how long could he stay with us? Surely he would have to follow them sooner rather than later. Maybe he would even leave with them on Monday, or a couple of days later. He'd leave us with food for a few days and join his family. Every time he came back from town, he'd tell us about one family or another who had already fled. It felt like he was preparing us for the possibility that he would also leave. Again and again he would assure us that he'd never abandon us, but his promises weren't enough. I was afraid he would have no choice. I understood, but I dreaded his leaving more than anything else. Everything about his presence was reassuring, from his voice to his familiar footfall and whistle above us. One day he would simply walk out of the door and disappear. There would be nothing we could do.

We all waited in terror for Monday. I was awakened by the sound of Ala weeping. She must have been saying goodbye to her father. I hoped she would come down to say goodbye. I wanted to thank her for everything she had done for us. We wouldn't be alive were it not for her. There was a knock on the trapdoor. It groaned and squeaked as Patrontasch opened it. It was well made, but with the warm air above and the dank humid air in the bunker, the wood had swelled almost overnight. There would be no more sneaking buckets when the trainmen were at home. I expected Ala, but it was Beck. I could hear Ala was still weeping.

'The trains aren't coming. They can't leave. The trainmen aren't here, but we don't have much time.'

I didn't know what he meant. It was only when I saw Julia handing down bread and potatoes that I understood that Julia and Ala were going to hide down here with us if they needed to. Beck brought down 18 loaves of bread, 60 kilograms of potatoes and a bag of salt. Salt! It was more precious than gold. I hadn't seen so much food in over three years. Beck didn't tell us where he had got it all. I couldn't imagine, first, all the money it cost, and then where to buy so much even if he had the money. He went back upstairs and a few minutes later handed Julia's sewing machine to Papa and Mr Melman. They put it in the back bunker on the other side of the 'park'. It was Julia's most valuable possession. For a moment I thought the food would be just for Julia and Ala, but Beck quickly told us it was for everyone.

Beck had no sooner gone up through the trapdoor when I heard him mutter something about the sister-in-law, at which Julia let out a scream as if scalding water had been thrown in her face. 'In my house? In my house? You and your whore can go to hell!'

'How can we say no! She's blood!'

'Not mine! And not yours! Are you crazy? She's seeing a Blue Coat. A Ukrainian. A policeman! And you trust her to keep her mouth shut? Mine and your daughter's lives in the hands of your whore? You care more for her than your own daughter? I know how much you care about me, but your own daughter, for crying out loud!'

Beck was calm. He simply asked, 'You'd rather see her dead?'

'Let the Blue Coat take care of her! She's descended from Polish aristocracy! He probably believes her. The liar.'

'She was married to my brother!'

'She might as well have been married to you! I've had enough! ENOUGH! You hear me!'

Julia ran to Ala's room and slammed the door shut. How could Beck have thought Julia would agree to letting the sister-in-law stay in the bunker? Julia, Klara and the sister-in-law in the same bunker. With Beck as well? There wasn't a bunker big enough for the four of them. I had never read any novel with situations like the ones we faced day in and day out.

Beck stuck his head in the bunker and said to Mr Patrontasch, 'Help me. You have to convince her. You're the only one she'll listen to.' Mr Patrontasch knew he couldn't argue with Beck.

'Come up here. Talk to her; I'll watch out for the trainmen.'

Patrontasch's wife leaned in to ask, 'What are you going to say to her? What are you going to do?'

'Beg. Beg and then beg some more.'

He climbed up the hatch after Beck.

With the trainmen still out, we had to take advantage of the time to cook some potatoes and empty the pails. So we went about our tasks while our ambassador went off to negotiate a peace treaty. Zygush took out his little penknife and threw it again and again into the dirt of the bunker. I knew it annoyed everyone, but it was the only toy he had and nobody had the heart to ask him to stop. He knew when it was safe to play with the knife. And the other children knew not to ask to play with it.

The potatoes had been boiled and eaten and still Mr Patrontasch hadn't come back. When Beck was upset, he paced back and forth. He hadn't stopped since Patrontasch had gone to speak with Julia. The floor creaked in the exact same place every time. It was like a waltz. One two creak. One two creak. One two creak. Between Beck walking back and forth and Zygush throwing the knife in the ground, I thought the bunker would explode. Patrontasch didn't come down until an hour later.

He had been successful and Beck showed his gratitude with vodka. When Lola asked how he had convinced Julia, Mr Patrontasch said that he had at first tried to be reasonable, saying that it would be safer for everyone if the sister-in-law were in the bunker with them. He had argued that Beck's sister-in-law might become angry if they didn't let her in, in which case there would be a greater chance of her saying something to her policeman lover. He said Julia hadn't seemed to care what happened to her, to Beck, to us, to anybody. But then Patrontasch told her, 'We've had our lives. But think of the children.' He told us that he didn't think Julia could take much more. Up until now she had been our well that never ran dry. There weren't enough words to describe her goodness. I loved Beck; he was our saint. But he wasn't a saint for his wife. What she endured from Beck, nobody ever went through.

I didn't know if Julia's argument with Beck had any effect on Klara. Or if it made Julia feel differently about Klara. All I knew was that a miracle happened. Klara had been standing up through the trapdoor asking Beck for something. Julia must have seen them and asked if she could speak to her. Her voice was calm and pleasant. Usually the sight of the two of them in conversation would send her off into a rage. Beck didn't know what to do. He just left the women together and walked out of the room. I couldn't hear what they were saying. But I had never seen so many eyes and so many ears trained at the floor above us. Even if the SS had been upstairs, nobody could have been more still.

I knew our survival hinged on the relationship between these women. We never knew which way the door would slam. But I had to admit that really I just wanted to know what the two women were saying to each other. I was nosy. We all were. The affair had carried on, it had lasted for over 14 months by now. We never could talk about it openly. All I had got on the subject was a few words from Lola over a year ago: 'Thank God he didn't choose me.' And that was it. We had chopped, boiled, eaten and digested every metre of ground taken or lost in the war. But the war between these two women had been fought in silence. Not a word had been said by the two former best friends. Before the war, a sin of this magnitude would have meant shunning and banishment. Now the final battle was taking place upstairs. I didn't know what to expect. Julia's fury had been directed for the most part at Beck. But I think she felt more injured by Klara. Beck's infidelity was expected by Julia, if not tolerated. It was like the arthritis that had deformed her hands. It was inevitable and had to be endured. But Klara had been a friend. As close as a sister. There was supposed to be a code between sisters. Something that went far beyond 'for better or for worse'. Far beyond the mysterious yearnings of men and women that I did not understand. This was the code my grand-father talked about when he admonished Josek not to 'send a girl up the chimney'. Julia's life, I had learned, was built on a foundation of faith and loyalty. In all the times Julia was kind enough to invite me up to her kitchen table, she had never once spoken with me about her religion. She never said one word about her faith or told me she was saving us because she wanted to be a good Catholic. Such a thought, no matter how sincere, would never have occurred to Julia in a million years. The deepest precepts of her faith, kindness, charity, sacrifice, were so ingrained in her character that even the fears and anxieties which turned friends into enemies and neighbours into traitors couldn't turn Julia against us. Every day I could feel the anxiety coming off her like sweat, and yet she never wavered. She would have sacrificed her life for Klara and the rest of us. She had demonstrated that every day for the last 15 months.

Klara's legs dropped through the hatch. Her brother was there to help her down. She wiped tears from her face. Although none of us could be called radiant, for those first few moments her face looked like that of a young girl's. Free of worry. She moved to her spot and sat with her legs lined out in front of her and her back against the wall. She didn't say a word about what she and Julia had talked about. And not one of us asked her. Everything we needed to know was written in her face.

Later, Mr Beck put his head down into the bunker and called Zosia to come up. She looked at Mama and me for help. I had heard the sister-in-law come in and I wondered what Beck was up to. But we both nodded for her to go up. Beck had always been like the uncle that spoiled her, calling her pet names, stroking her blond curls with his rough hands, always an extra piece of candy for her. Zosia had learned two lessons in the bunker: the virtue of silence and the virtue of Beck. Mr Beck picked her up from Patrontasch. 'C'mon, Zoskia, I have somebody for you to meet.'

We could hear Beck say, 'Zoskia, this is my sister-in-law. Her name is Mania and she might come and stay with you downstairs for a while.' We had never known what her name was. That she shared the same name as my sister seemed unfair. I refused to think of her as a Mania. In deference to Julia, I promised only to call her the sister-in-law. Beck went on, 'Out of all of you downstairs, I thought she would like to meet you the most.'

The sister-in-law's voice, which I had come to think of as brassy, suddenly went soft. 'It's so nice to meet you. What a pretty girl you are.'

Beck quietly said, 'Zoskia, can you tell Mania how you came to live downstairs?'

When I heard the question, everything stopped. Zygush's brown eyes were focused on the spot underneath his feet. He had vowed to protect his little sister and I knew he wanted to be upstairs with her. I was frightened for Zosia and angry at Beck. How could he make her remember? She was quiet for a while. I had heard some of the story from Zygush. And Beck had pieced together the remaining sequence of the last days of the ghetto, Uchka's death and the little ones' odyssey. But never had I heard any of it from Zosia's voice.

Beck's voice was even softer. 'It's all right, dear, go ahead.' She had barely said anything in the last year and the little she did say was hardly more than a syllable. More often than not, she simply nodded her head, yes or no. I had forgotten how melodious her voice was. Hearing it again called me back in time to the days when she had been just learning to talk. I'd walk into her house without knocking and little Zosia would call my name over and over in delight: 'Clarutchka, Clarutchka.' Then she'd jump in my arms.

She started, 'Mama was crying and smiling and she picked me up. She said we were going to stay somewhere else for a while. She carried me next door and up the stairs to the attic.

She told us it would be better and safer for us. She gave me a piece of bread. Then she said she'd come back soon. She kissed me all over and told Zygush that he was the man now and to take care of me. She said she'd be back soon and kissed me all over again. Then she went away. But she didn't come back like she promised. I cried. I cried so much...'

Mama couldn't stand it. Her face was buried in her hands and Zygush was crying. So was I. Her voice filled the bunker with memories of Uchka, who was so alive in her daughter's mind.

But Mama didn't come back. We waited days and she still didn't come for us. Zygush told me not to cry, but I couldn't stop. I missed her. I was so scared. I heard guns all the time and people screaming and I was afraid it was Mama. I was afraid she'd be shot like everybody else. Then Uncle Dudio came. He said Mama was here and for Zygush to take me. Dudio said there would be lots of friends to watch out for us and not to be scared. Zygush wouldn't leave the attic until he wrapped all the underwear around him. That made Uncle Dudio laugh. We walked by the big church and heard the singing. Then we came here. But Mama wasn't here. Clarutchka told me that Mama was with Auntie Rosa and that I'd see her soon. I really want to see my mama.' I heard her voice catch and I knew her cheeks would be wet when she came downstairs.

The sister-in-law said, 'A brave girl. I don't think I've ever met such a nice and brave girl.' I now understood why Beck had brought Zosia upstairs. He wanted the sister-in-law to know exactly whom she would be betraying if she informed on us. He didn't trust her entirely and had wanted to ignite her conscience before allowing her to live with us. Zosia was the match. He gave Zosia a piece of candy and lifted her down to me. As I helped her back down into the bunker, Zosia said the lady was nice.

The memory of her mother was still in her eyes. I could see Uchka there.

The weather had got suddenly warm and with the warmth came the expected invasion of fleas. When there was light, at least we could pick the fleas off each other. The children excelled at this task. Zygush and Zosia would be kept busy for hours, their eyes squinting, almost cross-eyed in concentration. I could tell by the way that Lola and Artek picked the fleas from each other that there was growing affection between them. I didn't know if I was the only one to have noticed what was happening between them, but I did know that Lola would never allow herself or Artek to be compromised in any way in our tiny society. They had found each other, and I was glad for them. Lola had become a kind of surrogate sister to me. Any happiness she could find made me happy too.

At the beginning of April, bringing down some food Beck informed us that Von Pappen had ordered all the *Volksdeutsche* to leave. They were needed in Germany to work. He said Beck and Ala were exempted because of their work at the alcohol depot and the post office. But Von Pappen had told him that if they wanted to, they could go. Over the past month, we had heard Beck tell us that almost every family, every friend, every acquaintance the Becks had were on one train or another. But still the Becks stayed. And even though Ala was not leaving on the train, she still went to the station every time to watch it head west. If she went to see it off, I knew how much she wanted to be on it.

The war would end in a matter of months. We knew that. We didn't know if we would be discovered or liberated first. It was a race to freedom or death. And as the pressure built on the Becks with the news of every Russian advance and German retreat,

Ala knew time was running out for her as well. She was free, young, beautiful. While we were trapped, she had no reason except her goodness to keep her in Zolkiew. As Beck went upstairs, I sat with the knowledge that as much as the Becks had our lives in their hands, they had put their lives in ours. I didn't even know if I could look Ala in the eye now.

The trainmen had gone out and we heard a knock on the trap-door. When Patrontasch opened the hatch, we were surprised to see that it was Julia. In her hands were two trays. Potatoes of course. And then we recognized the smell of meat. Somewhere she had found a piece of veal and had roasted it. I was starving. I wanted the veal, but I knew I would pay for it worse than I had with the apples last year. Potatoes. Potatoes and bread. It was all my stomach could tolerate. I was tempted by the delicious aroma of roasted meat with the slightly crusted edges, but it would be insanity for any of us to eat it. Eighteen people with diarrhoea – which would inevitably result – in a house full of Nazis and only sporadic times when we could empty the pails.

On the other tray was a small roasted chicken neck, a bowl of salt water, some bitter herbs and a tiny bowl of apple mixed up with crushed walnuts. All the ingredients for a Seder. Where she had found them was a mystery. We had known that it was Passover. Papa kept the calendar with religious commitment. But Julia had remembered for us too, and for that we were grateful.

The other tray held food. Now there was a plateful on my lap but I could hardly eat it, even though I knew I needed to. Every day I thought of my sister. Every time I looked at Zygush and Zosia, I thought of Uchka. But on this holiday, their spirits were more present and palpable than I could bear. It was like one of those dreams that felt so real. It was alluring and terrifying all at once. Yet I craved the presence of their ghosts, despite the cost in grief.

We ate our meal and didn't even explain to the children the meaning of the bitter herbs and the Haroseth and the other things on the Seder plate.

The next morning, we woke up to the roar of airplanes and the ground shaking from explosions. The Russians were bombing Lvov. I had no idea that the explosions could be powerful enough to shake the ground where we lay. Almost immediately the electricity went out. They must have hit the electric works. We should have been elated, but like everything else, this victory had a double edge. They were bombing Lvov, but we would be in the dark and without food.

Beck returned home from an Easter visit to the sister-in-law shortly after the bombing ended and came into the bunker to show us a rifle he had got for protection. This was the second rifle he had acquired. I knew it wouldn't guarantee our safety, but I hoped it would give Beck the confidence to stay with us. I was wrong. He looked over at Klara and said, 'I've been thinking it over. I can't take it. Those Ukrainians are bastards. I've got to join the partisans before they kill every Polack left in Zolkiew. I'd be a coward if I didn't. I can't even look myself in the mirror. But don't worry, Julia's sister Maria will take care of you.' I knew Maria couldn't cope with a tenth of what the Becks did for us. I was sure she would disappear at the first sign of trouble. I no longer felt like a real person. I was a reflection of Beck. If he was depressed, I was depressed. If he was confident, I was confident. If he wanted to kill the Ukrainians, so did I. If Beck had hope, I had hope. If he had none, I was also hopeless. I felt if I looked in the mirror I would see his reflection looking back at me.

The next time the trainmen left the house, Papa, Mr Melman and Mr Patrontasch crawled into the far bunker where the

Steckels were living. They had finally decided to ask Mr Steckel for money. Beck had run out of zloty. There was nothing left to sell in the black market and nobody left to buy it. A loaf of bread was so expensive not even Steckel could afford it. I couldn't understand why, when we were starving, the men didn't just take the money from Mr Steckel. I couldn't imagine anyone not sharing their money. I knew Mr Steckel was paying the Becks 'rent', as we had when we had the money. Even Beck, who deserved it for risking his life for the Steckels, didn't ask him for a zloty more. They were all too *bababatish*, too 'fine' for their own good.

If it was up to me, I would take their money in about two minutes. At the point of Beck's gun if I had to. Each of the three families had small children who were starving. But still the men hadn't asked before now.

Papa came back a few minutes later. At first Mr Steckel had outright refused, but finally he had given them a shiny gold English pound sterling. It might have been a rock or a lump of coal. To try and use this gold coin to buy anything would send every policeman, Blue Coat and Gestapo agent left in Zolkiew to this house. Any meal bought with the coin would have been the last supper. But the men looked at it like an answered prayer. When Beck came down and they showed it to him, he refused to buy anything with it. Nobody would touch it. Before the war and up to a few months ago, a pound sterling would have fetched much more in zloty than its value. But now, fear had overcome even greed. Papa told Beck not to worry about trying to sell it. That as long as he stayed with us, we could endure the hunger. Beck didn't say a word. We didn't know what to think of it. How could a useless one-pound sterling piece keep the Becks with us? I feared the Becks leaving even more than I feared the Nazis. As long as they were here, we still had a chance. He finally took the pound sterling from Papa's hand and said he would try to find someone he could trust to exchange it for zloty.

On the eve of 18 April, the day Mania had been murdered, I went to sleep knowing what we would be facing the next day. It was hot at night now and the fleas were relentless, but I had still managed to find some sleep every night. But that night there was very little sleep. I knew Mama and Papa were lying in silence, awake, next to me. The next morning, we said *yahrzeit*, the mourner's prayer, and as we lit one of the few candles we had for her memory, I wondered if perhaps my beloved sister wasn't the lucky one. Her suffering had been shorter than ours. But I also knew that Mania would have fought for every second of her life. I owed it to her to survive. To fight for every second as she would. That to give in now would desecrate her memory. I would live for both of us.

There was another knock on the door. I heard four soldiers informing Beck he had new tenants. They walked through the house, from one room to another, pausing before moving on. They stopped in the room right above the hatch. One was standing on the hatch itself and said, 'This room will do.' If the soldiers took this room, we might as well use the can of petrol. But Julia in her sweet and honest voice asked, 'Please, sirs, if my husband and I could keep this room, we would be very grateful.' There was a moment of silence and then a kind voice, that I would come to know as Norbert, said, 'We don't want to put you out. Stick us anywhere. We'll be fine. And don't worry. We'll stay out of your hair. We'll be gone most of the day.' That's what they all said before they got used to the comforts and Beck's radio and card games that went on despite the fact that the card table was resting on quicksand and bullets were whistling past their ears.

Chapter 14

WE ARE JUST STARTING TO SUFFER

23 April to May 1944

Tuesday, 9 May. You could think that a person who looks into the eyes of death as many times as we do would get used to it. But it's the opposite with us. The more we are in danger of dying, the more we are frightened. One wants to live no matter what and no matter how. Every day we look death in the eyes and every day has its own history. If at least we had a verdict, a time, how long we will suffer. We are sitting here and we don't even know if it's for nothing.

*

Beck moved the soldiers into the room next to theirs, and Ala moved in with her parents. The soldiers would be sleeping right above the bunker where Lola, Gedalo, Kuba, Artek and the Steckels slept. Unlike the trainmen, whose names I hadn't discovered in the two months they'd been with us, within minutes I learned that the soldiers were Norbert, Dieter, Richard and Hans. With six Germans living above us, water, food, the pails would all be impossible. If the soldiers were here, the trainmen would be gone, and vice versa. It was like one of those theatrical farces where characters run in and out of doors, barely missing each other in a ridiculous chase, except the comedy going on above our head had lethal consequences.

As soon as Norbert's duffel landed on the floor, he fiddled with the radio until he'd found a station that played popular music and light opera. He started singing right away and suddenly reverberating through the floorboards was a clear and vibrant tenor. Most people when they sang to themselves, especially when others were around, were at least a little inhibited, even if they adored their own voices. But Norbert was singing to the audience in the balcony. He knew, it seemed, every song on the radio. My life couldn't have felt any stranger to me at that moment. I didn't know who Norbert was, what he looked like, where he came from, or whether he would turn out to be one of those Germans who'd regale the Becks with his proficiency in killing Jews. All I knew of him was that he had a voice that people would have paid money to hear and I had been moved by music in a way that had not happened since Mania sang at her concert three springs ago. I didn't want to love his voice. I didn't want to be moved by a man who had perhaps murdered Jews, but I was helpless. 'You're Mine Tonight', 'My Song Goes Round The World', You Are My Heart's Delight', 'Today I Feel So Happy' were popular German cabaret songs innocuous enough to survive the censors. I had heard them on the radio before the war and while we were in the bunker. Listening to the radio through the floorboards was one of our only respites and when there was music on, it was a diversion, fleeting as it might have been. But when Norbert sang, I had a box seat at a concert. I listened to Schubert's 'The Miller's Daughter' in both fear and rapture.

You have wept, too,
Your dear eyes are so wet,
A tear fell out of the window,
A rose grew there in the grass.

We all did. The song was about death and lost love and I fought the emotion it was bringing up in me. How dare a German have such a beautiful voice when his finger was on the trigger of a gun and there was a Jew in his sights.

Mama was so upset by the arrival of so many soldiers upstairs, she fainted. Yet neither I nor Papa dared move to help her because we were afraid of being heard, despite the noise upstairs. Life in the bunker had trained me to resist almost every natural impulse I had, so I watched the rise and fall of her chest as if she were in a pleasant sleep, and hoped she would come out of her faint without making any noise at all.

The second after all of them had gone out, Beck came down and said that God was sending an army to watch over us and keep suspicion far from our door. I didn't know how much longer I could believe in Beck's luck. I tried to see in the dim light if he believed his own words or was just encouraging us. But I couldn't see his eyes, and then there was a knock on the door, and Beck ran back up. The groaning trapdoor closing was covered by the sound of Beck's feet rushing to get the door. The hotel was full. I didn't see how they could fit anyone else. But it wasn't another guest. It was a Nazi policeman.

He was telling Beck to come with him to the chief of police. Immediately. Beck hadn't been ordered to the police station for months and months and this policeman was a stranger. Beck went away whistling, but we didn't believe it. One onerous reason after another swept through the bunker. He had been reported for hiding Jews; for dealing with the partisans; for selling English pounds on the black market; for stealing vodka, and any of the other treasonable sins. Otherwise we would have heard laughter, gossip, an easy-going greeting and the reason Beck had been called. I prayed for Beck the way I prayed for Uchka, for Mania, for Zygush and Zosia. I prayed for him in the way I prayed for my dearest loved ones.

Waiting for Beck and our fate in darkness would have been too frightening to bear. Since the initial bombing of Lvov last week, we never knew if we'd have electricity or not. I didn't know if Beck would come back unharmed, or the police would break down the door and kill us. Ever since Beck had been taken away, we had all been so on edge that I feared we were going insane. Mr Patrontasch was calculating seconds, minutes, hours and days in his book again. Gedalo was writing madly, but wouldn't show it to anyone. Lola had her hand to her mouth, suppressing her laughter. The more everyone looked at her, begging with their eyes for her to stop, the harder it was. She turned her face to the wall until she calmed down. It had to be hysteria because there was nothing funny going on this morning. The Steckels fingered the cyanide capsules around their necks as they always did when we were threatened. Zosia grabbed a pillow and put it over her own face and started to cry silently. And there was Mama in the dirt. At least we had light this morning.

When we were alone in the house again, I asked Lola to tell us why she had been laughing so hard.

'I was looking around the bunker and saw that everybody's hair had turned white or grey and so I didn't feel so bad about my hair.'

She was right. I hadn't noticed before. Mama, Papa, the Melmans, Artek, Gedalo, the Patrontasches all had grey hair now. Only the children and I had any colour at all. Some of us looked at Lola like she had snapped. But I understood. No one could control the crazy things that went in and out of our minds down here. Yet unless we were able to exert self-discipline and control our fears and our suspicions, the society we had built in the bunker would disintegrate. Lola's laughter was the kettle singing. It was a warning that her emotions were boiling over inside her. I knew how she felt. At times I thought I couldn't stand it one minute longer. If there were guests upstairs, I wanted to scream at the top of my lungs and bang my fists against the ceiling, just wanting it to be over. Beck had told us stories of Jews running to the wire in the camps and the ghettos. That might have been my fate if I was not in the bunker.

Beck must have run into the soldiers because he came back into the house with them. He was whistling 'All's Well...' At least we knew Beck was all right and we were not dead yet. I knew we'd have to wait until the soldiers and the trainmen next went out before we found out the reason Beck was called by the police chief.

When he was finally able to come down, he told us that they wanted him to stand guard at the train station in addition to his regular job. He was still a trusted *Volksdeutscher*, and a vital part of the local German war machine. He was given a new gun, and he said he would give one of his guns to us as soon as he had the chance. I didn't know if there was a man in our bunker who had actually fired a weapon. But Beck was relieved and so were we. He also told us that the soldiers promised him they wouldn't be a bother to the Becks because they would be spending most of their time at their jobs, which were preparing the German motor pool for retreat. As soon as I had heard what they'd be doing, I knew they'd be here until the bitter end. The arrival of these soldiers caused so many changes for us that I felt despite all the suffering of the past 17 months, in so many new ways our suffering had just begun.

A conspiracy of events had to occur to get us fed. There had to be electricity. The trainmen and the soldiers had to be out. And the Becks had to be able to find food for the 18 of us. So Beck instituted a ration system for all of us down here, even the Steckels. He said we'd each get one kilogram of potatoes and 300 grams of bread per day. And even though 300 grams of bread would barely keep us above starvation, bread was so scarce I doubted Beck would be able to find even that much.

There was always a trainman or soldier at home, so the pails became almost impossible to empty. The men were forced to dig a trench in the back of the bunker and cover it with a piece of wood. This was our new toilet. I knew the smell would give us away. It had to. Days, weeks, a month, who knew? The trench added one more level of inevitability to our capture, but we had no alternative. Since the middle of April, the bunker had become increasingly hot, dank and oppressively humid. We were now in our summer uniforms. Slips with the backs cut out for the women and cut off long johns or shorts for the men. It had become so hot that we spent all our time, hours and hours every day, except when we were eating and sleeping, fanning ourselves with pieces of cardboard until our hands and arms were cramped with pain. We'd start out fanning with the speed of hummingbird wings, but soon these pieces of cardboard, which couldn't have weighed more than a few grams, felt like sheets of iron. When the trainmen had been out, the Becks could open the trapdoor to give us a small break from the heat. But now there wouldn't even be those few brief moments of relief from the heat, which I had looked forward to, just as I looked forward to food and water. The heat was so oppressive it became hard to breathe.

The only momentary relief any of us had was the few hours in which we slept. But the soldiers robbed us of that also. We were so frightened that they might hear a snore, a cough, a sneeze while we slept that we were forced to change our sleeping arrangements. The Steckels, Gedalo, Kuba, Artek and Lola slept in the part of the bunker right underneath the room in which the soldiers slept. We hadn't removed the posts that supported the floor and it wasn't dug out as much as the main room. There was only enough room to lie down. Lola had started snoring and Kuba's asthma had got much worse as soon as the weather warmed up. He said it was the mildew. Whatever the cause, Kuba was coughing. Loudly. We were terrified that his cough would waken the soldiers. We decided that everyone who slept in that part of the bunker would sleep during the day and stay up at night. Awake, at least we had some control over our actions. At night, a snore, a sneeze, a cough could mean the end of us.

Mr Patrontasch conferred with Papa and they leaned over to me. Papa asked me to switch places with Kuba. I didn't snore, so it would be safer for us all if I slept where the soldiers were over-head. One of the few pleasures I had was to sleep with my arms around the little ones. But there was no question I would switch with Kuba. No one ever questioned anything that would help our survival. They needed someone slim and someone who didn't snore. They asked. I said yes. It was that simple. But since I didn't snore, I was at least permitted to sleep at night.

Within days of the soldiers' arrival, we started to deteriorate. I couldn't imagine that the few minutes the trapdoor had been opened a day had made such a difference. The prickly heat returned like a plague. Everyone was stricken by it. Mama had a bad case and so did I. But for some reason the prickly heat attacked the Patrontasch family with a viciousness that turned each of their backs into a carpet of raw, bright pink pustules. Not a centimetre of normal skin was visible. On all of us the back was most severely affected, and the pain meant we couldn't sleep on them. There was no room to sleep on our stomachs because no matter how hard you try, you have to stick out your arms a little bit at least. And once you choose to sleep on a side, there is no moving, and the pain in shoulders, hips and knees became a dull and constant ache all night. And we didn't dare scratch ourselves. If the pustules started to bleed, they would become dangerously infected because of the humidity and lack of sanitation.

But if the Becks left us, all the planning, all the sacrifices, everything we had endured would mean nothing. There was nothing left to us except to go on. Hunger, thirst and fear had become my life. It was so simple now. I was in a train station and everything depended upon which train came first. Freedom or death. The itching, the exhaustion, the pain in my arms from fanning were all irrelevant. They were just something to occupy myself and my mind while waiting to see which train I would board.

The soldiers and the trainmen had gone out to the German soldiers' club in the city. The Russian air force was bombing Lvov again and since no one was home, Beck let us come up a few at a time to see the lights and the explosions. The night sky was lit up like nothing I had ever seen before. Not even the fireworks the Russians set off every May came close to the bombardment that turned night to day. And when the bombing finally stopped and the windowpane I looked through stopped shaking, the dark sky returned, but the horizon was a rim of fire. I was looking at the end of the world through slightly parted damask curtains. Beck had brought us upstairs to give us hope. He was thoughtful that way. He wore the smile of a false god as he told us it couldn't be too much longer because the Russians had crossed the Dniester, the river of Galicia, which rose in the Carpathians south of Lvov.

Beck could lie to the Germans but he couldn't lie to us. I was attuned to his eyes and voice in the way a baby was attuned to a mother's face. I also knew that, with us, a lie was a piece of foul meat in Beck's mouth that he would be compelled to spit out no matter how much he wanted to keep it down. Back down in the bunker, by candlelight because the bombing had knocked out the electricity again, he told us that he had again run out of money and there would not even be the food ration he promised. He told us the Ukrainians had posted a new ultimatum. All the Poles had to leave Zolkiew by 1 May, which was just in a few days away, or be murdered.

As he talked he became more depressed than I had ever seen him. He told us, 'The bastards are still catching Jews. Mrs Bernstein and her three children. An informer told the Gestapo they were hiding in the Malachinski's barn.' Mama fainted. She was close friends with Mrs Bernstein. To find out in the same breath that she was alive and in hiding as we were for the past 17 months and then murdered as the Russians were approaching was too much. Beck told us how much Ala had been pressing him to leave. Ala, like our darling Mania, wanted to live. She had done so much, and how much more could we ask of her? She was a child, barely three years older than I was, and I didn't want her to die for me. I couldn't imagine the torment in Beck's heart as every day he had to choose between us, strangers, and his daughter who was the love of his life. It would take a miracle for Mr Beck not to go with his daughter even as he assured us he never would.

The next three days were hell. The eternal darkness in the bunker made every moment endless. With any light at all, even a candle, I could read, teach the children, sew, anything to keep my mind occupied. But now with no light except for the short time we lit the candles so we could eat and take care of our bodily functions, I had nothing to do, none of us did, except stare at the thin blade of light coming from the air opening and pray for a swift end to the war.

I spent all my time listening to the soldiers. Norbert's voice lost its charm. I heard them talk about their wives and girl-friends and children. I heard Richard's cynicism about the war. I heard Hans screaming, 'I'm fighting here and the Allies are bombing the hell out of my family!' His wife and children lived in Hamburg and he was furious at the reports of the Hamburg bombings he heard on the radio and in the news. Last year Hamburg had been firebombed by an allied armada of almost 800 planes. In the few weeks the soldiers had been here, Hamburg had been bombed three times. I hated Hans. Not only for his anti-Semitism but also because he was lazy. When he wasn't working, he spent most of his time in bed. When there was even one German in the house, we couldn't move, couldn't talk, couldn't cook, couldn't use the pail. And that German was usually Hans.

We were sitting in the dark listening to the card game go on for hours upstairs. It was a full house. Hans the policeman was drunk and happy. He had found a comrade in Hans the soldier as they swapped exploits and bragged about the number of Jews they had killed. Hans the policeman entertained the group by his most recent triumph: the Bernsteins. Mama had to listen as Hans, as loud and boisterous as a best man giving a toast at a wedding, recounted the Bernsteins begging him to spare their lives. They were refugees who lived not far from Aunt Rosa in western Poland and had come to Zolkiew in 1939. Mrs Bernstein was a relative of the Britwitzes, who had lived next door to the Melmans in one of the houses that burned down in the fire. Mrs Bernstein was born in Zolkiew and she knew Mama when they were both girls. Here the Russians were breathing down Hans's own neck and would, God willing, be here in a matter of weeks or months, and still he took joy in finding and slaughtering Jews.

Beck had to pretend to hear it all for the first time and we heard his hearty congratulations. His sincerity at Hans's good fortune was convincing. The soldier Hans was not to be outdone and recounted the murders of each of the 75 Jews he had personally killed. He had been keeping count. The extermination of a people had been reduced to entertainment over schnapps, sausage and Julia's pirogies. I was next to Zosia, holding her. She didn't cry any more as she listened to Hans's brutal laughter and backslapping joy at his accomplishment. All she knew of life was this persecution, of people trying to kill her, of vilifying her for being something she was far too young to even understand. Her Jewishness meant nothing to her. I wanted to write. I wanted to get every word down, but there was no light so I had to listen without my blue nub of a pencil in my hand. I listened in darkness and my face had the freedom to express its grief, if only silently, and its rage, if only mute. Beck had to sit across from both murderers, deal the cards, pour the drinks, serve the food and listen, laughing, looking both men in the eye while we remained hidden. For 17 months all we had to do was hide, yet day after day, moment by moment, the Becks, and especially Mr Beck, had to lead a double life, like the most brilliant spy in the most brilliant spy novel. How he withstood the pressure was beyond me. My courage was nothing compared to his.

As soon as the soldiers and the trainmen left for work the next day, Beck came down to the bunker. He had a bottle of vodka with him and poured drinks for the men. Beck didn't say anything for a long time. 'I'm sorry', he said. 'I'm sorry. Please. I hope you don't think I meant what I said last night. I hope you know I don't feel like that.' He was apologizing to us. He wanted us to know the words he spoke upstairs weren't his true self, which he only dared show us. I had so many questions to ask Beck. How was he able to keep up the front that he was a loyal *Volksdeutscher*? Where did he find the courage? How could he be so calm and natural with our enemies? I could tell he was very fond of Krueger and Schmidt. But the others? The two Hanses? Was Beck afraid? How could he control his fear? Did he have that much faith in God? Did he trust his own luck that much? But most of all, why? Why had he risked his life for us? He talked about honour sometimes. He ranted that the Ukrainians and the Germans had no right to kill Jews. But somewhere I felt there was another reason, hidden perhaps. And I hoped that some day we might have a chance to talk about it, if I ever got up enough courage to ask.

There was so much going on now I couldn't keep up with recording it all in my diary. Beck had given me the present of a new copybook and as I wrote the fresh pages were quickly covered in the sweat dripping off my face. My entries were smudged by the wet pages and it was almost impossible to write legibly. Compared to what was happening around us, a smudged page didn't seem much, but the copybook was now my most precious possession. And if we perished and if the diary was found, I didn't want one moment of the Becks' courage to go unknown.

I realized now we were in the same situation as the day of the fire. Even if there was another place to hide, we'd never make it. There had been a mob in the streets that was also filled with German soldiers, police and Blue Coats. If we had tried to flee we would have been caught in minutes. Now there were very few civilians. Soldiers were living in every house on the street. There were over 20 living in Papa's factory. And many more were camped near the cemetery, which since the fire was in direct view of the house. We were on the main road to Lvov so military patrols and traffic were constant. There were no Poles left, so there would be no place to hide and no one to hide us if we did try to leave the bunker.

Beck told us that the Ukrainian police were collecting arms, arresting and shooting anybody they wanted and stealing Polish homes and possessions at will. And since Ala's transfer to Krakow was certain again, Beck said he was going to the forest to join the partisans. Beck was a patriot and wanted to pick up a gun and fight his country's enemies. I understood that. I felt the same way. If he said come to the partisans with me, I would have gone. I also knew Beck was hoping one of us would say, 'Go. We'll be fine.' But no one said a word. Klara finally said, 'Go. Go ahead. But before you do, please take your rifle and shoot us. Kill us. Please.' We had all condemned Klara for her relationship with Beck, but it was only their love affair that allowed her to speak so bluntly to Beck. And it was keeping him here with us and protected. I didn't know if he was in love with her. I didn't know if he would abandon us, but he would never abandon her. There had to be a war raging inside him. He was loyal to us, his family and his country. But he couldn't protect us all and fight as well.

He agreed to stay. We were safe for now. Beck reassured us that he would go only if Von Pappen made him. He also told Mr Patrontasch that the Russians had taken Sevastopol, Odessa and had recaptured the rest of the Crimea. Now the Russians could turn their forces north and west. I had new hope. The Russians moving their main force towards Vinnytsia, and the bombing of Lvov, had to be a prelude to a major offensive in Galicia.

The next time the Becks and the soldiers went out, Mr Patrontasch took the buckets upstairs to empty them. When he came back down, I knew something was wrong. When he told us, every hope I had for survival vanished. Mr Patrontasch saw that the Becks had packed up all their belongings and lined them up in the hall. The man I had come to trust as much as my own father and in whom I vested all my hopes for survival had looked us straight in the eyes and lied to us. There was only one possible conclusion. They were going to leave and not tell us.

Chapter 15

I'M LOSING HOPE

10 May to 6 June 1944

Wednesday, 10 May. Trouble again. Lang who was always saying he is staying, decided to leave... Mr Beck says he is not leaving unless they force him, but we don't know if one day he will just leave without telling us. Pappen is coming back any day. What are we going to do if Mr Beck says Pappen gave an order to go?

*

It was decided that Mr Patrontasch would talk to Beck, as he always did.

'We were worried that you had changed your plans.'

Mr Patrontasch had a certain way with Beck. He was able to understate the most frightening things. Now he told Beck simply that we worried he might have changed his plans. Beck knew exactly what he meant and how terrified we all were.

He put our fears to rest immediately. 'If I told you I wasn't leaving, then I'm not leaving. We moved up some things from the cellar in case there's a fire, that's all. If they're bombing Lvov, they'll be here before we know it. No sense losing everything we own in a fire.'

Mr Patrontasch replied, 'Thank you for telling us. We knew there would be a reasonable explanation. You understand—'

Beck interrupted him: 'Don't give it another thought.' Then he went upstairs.

But his words did little to alleviate our fear. I trusted the Becks, but Mr Melman couldn't be convinced. I didn't know if Mr Melman's fears were real or influenced by the depression and despair that poured off us like sweat. We were all starting to disintegrate physically and mentally. Grey hair was trivial compared to Mr Melman's skin coming off like potato peel, the sores on Mama's breasts, teeth falling out, bleeding gums, rheumatism and the prickly heat that afflicted us like one of the ten plagues.

Almost every night we had guests until two or three in the morning and almost every afternoon we had a full house for lunch to listen to the radio. Beck had become very popular and all his Polish friends were asking his advice. As usual, the conversation turned to the killing of Jews. Hans the policeman said that he wished he were in Hungary because they were killing Jews there like they used to kill them here. He discussed murder as if it was a hobby, like skiing and searching for where the snow was the freshest. Soldier Hans conversed in some detail about his preferences for killing Jews and the various pleasures of the garrotte, gun and knife. Dieter chimed in that he could not kill an unarmed Jew, but would of course if they had a gun. Ala and Julia were serving food that the policemen brought home for them to prepare. Norbert said, 'Sometimes I think a bullet is too damn good for a Jew. Much better just to hack them to pieces.' I don't know how Julia and Ala didn't drop the trays of food. I was stunned to hear these words spring from Norbert's lips. I had earlier loved listening to him sing, but now his voice only brought forth images of a man hacking a Jew to death.

After Hans left, Norbert started prying. He asked Julia how long they had been living there. Julia blandly replied, 'Two years. Why?' 'I don't know. I was lying on my bed, when I thought I heard rustling, like straw being moved around. And then I swore I heard two glasses being clinked together under my feet. And I'd heard of Jews hiding in bunkers dug underneath houses with plenty of food.'

Julia laughed it off. 'Two years and I've never heard a thing.'

Hopefully that would be enough to convince him. If he suspected something he would tell Hans the policeman. I marvelled how the Becks could keep up their charade night after night, day after day. One misstep, one inadvertent word, one sour or shocked expression and we were all dead.

Julia left for Lvov to find some tobacco to sell. While she was gone, the ground started shaking and we heard the bombs exploding in Lvov. The electricity, which we had had for a few days, went off almost immediately. I began to pray that Julia hadn't been caught in the bombing. She came home in one piece, but couldn't come to the trapdoor to give us any food. Dieter was sick in bed and we spent the next two days sitting in the dark with no food and water. Poor Patrontasch. He started passing out from starvation. There wasn't even water to wet his lips. Papa whispered to Mama, 'If he dies we'll have to bury him down here.' I'd never heard Papa sound so cold about the health of a friend. There was nothing we could do about the lack of food. Compassion had become a luxury. If we had food we would give extra to Patrontasch, but there was no food.

What remained were the cold details of what we needed to do to survive. We couldn't empty the pails and the first trench was almost filled. The men would have to dig a new one as soon as we had light. The only place to put it was less than half a metre from Lola's pallet. She didn't complain at all when Papa told her where they'd have to dig. We'd have to be quick about it. Norbert had told Julia that he could smell sewage and that he'd be happy to take a look at it for her.

Ala came home laughing and happy. She rushed to Beck to tell him that she was going, finally, to Krakow. Beck was thrilled. It was wonderful news for Ala and for us. If she was safe, Beck would be more likely to stay with us. Beck was also in a good mood because the news on the radio said the Russian front was moving closer to us; the Allies had taken Monte Cassino just south of Rome, and Lvov had suffered yet another bombing raid.

Overnight it got hot in the bunker. We were rank with sweat and most of us were fanning ourselves as fast as we could. We looked like the violin section of an orchestra playing an allegro movement. The trainmen and the soldiers were out, as was Mr Beck. Julia was alone upstairs and had opened the trapdoor to let in some air when there was a knock on the door. The knocking turned into pounding. Now the knocking was accom-panied by repeated cries of 'JUDEN, JUDEN', 'Where are the Jews?' Fresh sweat broke out on all of us. Julia and Patrontasch rushed to get the trapdoor closed, mirroring each other through the floorboards in their rushed frenzy. Zygush, who had been playing with his paper-and-wax dolls, stopped in mid-attack. Everyone stopped everything but breathing. Hands stayed in mid-air. Only Lola kept sewing like nothing was going on at all. My poor Mama fainted and again there was nothing we could do. Zosia grabbed a pillow and put it over her own mouth as she now did every time she became frightened. She started to cry, not loudly, but in persistent choking sobs. The Steckels grabbed their poison and fingered it nervously. Through my fear, I felt anger rushing through my veins. They always thought of them-selves first. I hated them for doing this. Now that we had a gun, and bullets since Klara had begged Beck for them, Artek picked it up. Who would Artek use the bullets on? On them or on us? I didn't even know how many bullets there were. I'd rather be killed by Artek than be dragged out through the streets and tortured. But there was no time to tell anyone that now.

The Ukrainian police swarmed into the house, screaming. I don't know how many there were, but their boots shook dirt off the bunker walls. They were tearing through the rooms. I heard closets slammed open. I heard their fists banging everywhere looking for false walls; furniture moved looking for trapdoors. Several sets of footsteps descended into the cellar, where wood was kept. It was next to our bunker but we had never opened up a doorway into it. It seemed like there were thousands of them. All the time they were screaming at Julia: 'Where are they? Tell us and we won't kill you. You Polish bitch. Everybody knows they're here. We know how many! You've got 14 Jews! The whole town knows it!' I thought they would start beating her. I was afraid Julia would give us away, or worse, that they would kill her. But Julia was holding her own, screaming back, 'There are no Jews here! We have Nazis living here!'

A familiar voice joined the screaming. It was our anti-Semitic soldier Hans, yelling at the top of his huge lungs: 'SWINE! How do you dare search where German soldiers are living?'

The Ukrainian shouted, 'They're here! We have reports!'

Hans must have taken out his gun. 'You blue-coat, thieving sons of bitches, search, search all you want because there's no one here! But if I find one thing missing, I'll track you down and shoot you where you stand.' Caught up in his own arrogance, Hans had no idea how close he was to his own death. The Ukrainians were bloodthirsty. If they could get away with killing Hans, they would have done it in a minute.

'You'll see. What do you Germans know? Fucking Polacks lie every time they take a breath and they'll fuck your mother if you turn around. There's a bunker here and one in the Jew bastards' factory. And a tunnel that leads from one to the other.'

We had in fact wanted to build such a tunnel. But who could have possibly told the Ukrainians? The only ones we thought knew about that bunker were the ones in this room and a few close friends and family, most of whom were dead. We all looked at each other and wondered. Nobody had seen Beck's nephew Wladek for weeks. There was talk of him staying with us to avoid being drafted by the Nazis, who considered him a deserter when he didn't show up for his induction. He was in and out of the house hiding from the Gestapo and had known about us since that first Christmas Day. He was a nice boy, but we knew he wasn't strong enough to withstand an interrogation. But if it had been Wladek, the police would have been at the hatch in ten steps from the front door.

Hans followed the Ukrainians to the factory, where they found the first bunker we had built but never really used. It was empty and they came back to the house. Lola didn't miss a stitch the entire time. I think her calm infected us all. She continued sewing as if no one was there and her thread and needle and socks were the only things in the world. Patrontasch picked up his book and started calculating and recalculating how many minutes we had been in the bunker.

I kept on thinking about who had given us away. If I could unravel this mystery, maybe this nightmare would end. Could it have been that children playing in the factory might have found the bunker? Just yesterday, Mr Beck had told us that there were roaming bands of children hunting Jews. One of the boys had seen a suspicious opening in a wall: a crack through which a shaft of light or a breath of air might penetrate. The boys had called the police and had watched while they poured gasoline on the wall. As the fire spread, a group of Jews had emerged from a hidden doorway on fire. The Nazis hadn't wasted their bullets on them. They had watched them burn to death.

Finally, the Ukrainians left. Hans cursed their mothers in the crudest way possible. He told Julia to let him know if they came back again. He and the others would take care of them. I could feel the fury in his voice and I knew he wanted to kill someone. If it couldn't be Jews, then Ukrainians would have to do.

Hans had only come back to pick up something he had forgotten. Again, fate had intervened on our behalf. I didn't know what to make of it. We had cheated our deaths so many times. How many more times would we be saved? I felt like fate was taunting us. We sat in stunned silence as Hans left the house, whistling the tune he had picked up from Beck. Our secret code, 'All's Well That End's Well'. We would have to change our code.

Beck came home shortly thereafter. Julia hadn't even come to check on us yet. He must have been told about the search. Together with Julia they came down to the bunker. Even Julia came down. I thought they were going to tell us that this had been the last straw, that they would be leaving us. But they didn't say one reproachful word. Instead, they tried to calm us down and brought us bread. After all they had just gone through, they remembered to bring us bread. Sometimes, my mind did funny things. I whispered: 'Mama, if someone is bored with life, they could come and live with us. There's always plenty of excitement here.'

I thought back to our first Christmas here. If the Becks had known then what their future would hold, I could not imagine they or anyone else would have agreed to help us. Their spirit had been bent, but never broken. I thought of their tradition of setting an extra place for an uninvited guest at their beautiful

Christmas table. Not only did they have one extra. They had 18. When I was a child in our backyard watching Julia beat our rugs, I had no idea how strong her faith was. I didn't know if it gave her courage to save us or if it gave her the strength to resist her fear. What I witnessed every day in her was the remarkable sight of a woman doing what the saints and her saviour did without hesitation and without compromise. I knew that Julia would find her reward in heaven. I hoped she would also find it on this earth.

We were still in shock from the search, but the Becks were going ahead with a party for their 22nd wedding anniversary. I don't know how they managed to celebrate anything in these dismal times, but it was a relief to hear something else through the floorboards. The soldiers hadn't left the house for a day and now they were helping with the preparations.

The house filled up with guests. The music was loud and the floor pounded above our heads from the dancing. Beck sang several love songs to Julia, each receiving monstrous applause. Even Von Pappen showed up as a surprise guest and toasted Beck as a proud and loyal *Volksdeutscher*. To listen to the party, you would think there wasn't a war going on outside the doors of the house, in which the guests were playing leading roles.

The party lasted until three in the morning. Only then did the house become quiet. The soldiers and the trainmen left for work and Beck soon came down to the bunker. Something in his appearance startled me. I didn't know why I hadn't noticed it before, but he had aged almost as much as we had. His hair had turned grey and his face was drawn and had the haggard look of a lost soul. The soldiers had been living with us for five weeks now. I didn't know if it was their arrival that had aged Beck. He was in a dark mood.

Then Beck did something to convince me that he just wanted it to end, like any of the Jews that ran to the wire. Mr Steckel had given him 20 gold Austrian crowns to sell. Mr Steckel had calculated that it would allow the Becks to spend seven zloty a day, which he deemed enough to feed each of us for a month. I didn't know what had precipitated the pharmacist's change of heart nor what he had based his calculations on. Seven zloty wasn't enough to feed a pet dog given the skyrocketing prices of bread. But I was grateful nonetheless. Perhaps it was the sight of Patrontasch fainting and the children with the malnourished bodies and faces of the old weathered crones in the Grimm Brothers' fairy tale of our basement that caused him to develop a conscience after 12 months with us. Or perhaps he thought it was safer for him to keep us alive rather than have to deal with burying corpse after corpse down here.

Beck sold the crowns to the commandant of the Ukrainian militia, the very man who had practically torn down the house looking for us. Trading gold was punishable by death. The commandant could have shot Beck on the spot and then taken the house apart, board by board and brick by brick. It was common knowledge that Jews used to deal in Austrian crowns before the war. But Beck had his own strategy. 'Don't worry. Zavalinsky told me he would melt the gold for a ring.' There was no arguing with Beck. 'Are we alive or not alive? Has everything I've done to keep you alive worked or not worked?'

Sure enough, later that evening the commandant came over for drinks. And the next night and the next night. He and Hans, who a few days ago had almost shot each other, were now the best of friends, trading stories. Beck was right. With half a dozen Germans, a lieutenant in the German police and the commandant of the Blue Coats living or at least drinking and playing cards here every night, who could possibly think 18

Jews were hiding under the floor? Would Beck's and our insane good fortune hold out a little longer?

Norbert left us and was immediately replaced by an even more anti-Semitic soldier named Georg. He was rude and curt until Beck took him under his wing and threw another party, this one to welcome the new guest. A friend of the new soldier taught everyone to dance. For three hours, I thought the floor would cave in above our heads and it felt like we were sitting inside a bass drum.

It was the first of June and the heat had been becoming steadily more oppressive. Even at night it felt like it was over 30 degrees centigrade. Only in the early hours of the morning did a small amount of fresh air filter in through the brick-shaped opening and allow us a few hours' sleep. We could not survive another summer here. It was that simple. Some of us would die from starvation or cholera or typhus or some infection brought on by the combination of our raw and bleeding backs from prickly heat and the unsanitary conditions. Prickly heat! Before the war it had been no more dangerous than nappy rash. And now it could kill us.

The front had been stalled for weeks. The Allies had taken Rome, but that was all except for some advances into Romania. The men couldn't make sense of it. Why had the Russians, who had been tearing through the Germans at will, suddenly stopped? Every small advance was something to hang on to. Even if they took a town the size of Kulikow, which was just a church and a bakery, it was enough.

The dancing above our heads, which had penetrated the haze of my exhaustion and the blanket of heat that almost stopped my breathing, had become macabre. A dance of death, of madmen and women, of dancing simply because the world was ending and there was nothing to be done about it. When it finally stopped, the footsteps still pounded in my ears and the dancers, like *dybbuks*, had invaded every inch of me. As the sound gradually receded, I realized my heart was beating in near hysteria. There would be no end to this hell. As much as I wanted to weep, I kept my tears in. Somehow Zosia had fallen asleep on my lap despite the racket upstairs. As the others went to sleep, I decided to stay awake and watch Zosia. I didn't want her to wake up with a jolt and start to cry.

Hans the policeman stayed after the other guests had gone home and Beck warned us by joking, 'Hans, big strong guy like you afraid to walk home in the dark?' As long as Hans was here, any noise downstairs would raise a suspicion, and I was afraid that no matter how much he liked the Becks, his hatred of Jews would trump any feeling of decency. Hans was talking to Beck, and now that the house was quiet his voice sounded so close, like he was whispering into my ear and not Beck's. Then another fear crept into my mind. What if Hans suspected Beck? And what if he wanted to spend the night? But it wasn't us he was thinking about. It was Ala. She had been told she was going to Warsaw instead of Krakow and was scheduled to leave in a few days.

'Ala should stay here,' he said, sighing. 'Please think about it. As long as your family is in Zolkiew, I can take care of you. You'll be safe. Ala will be safe.'

Beck said he would, and they went to sleep. If the Becks were safe, then we would be safe. Our enemy, the same man who would root us out and take us to slaughter if he knew we existed, had an aching heart for a lovely blond girl with sparkling laughter. It didn't matter that she didn't love him and perhaps loved another. It was like Cyrano, a story of noble, unrequited, self-sacrificing love. I was determined to stay up until Hans left. I heard him stir above me around seven in the morning. He carried his boots to the door and didn't put them on until he was out of the house, considerate enough not to wake his hosts or Ala. When I heard his hobnailed boots on the cement of the walkway, I closed my eyes and fell asleep.

I awoke to banging on the hatch. It was so fierce that I panicked and opened my eyes to see Patrontasch opening it. Beck's face was leaning in. Julia's was behind his. I couldn't see their expressions. Patrontasch was in the way and my eyes hadn't adjusted to the light. Beck was almost screaming: 'The second front! It happened! In northern France. I heard it on the radio. Sixteen thousand planes. Hundreds of thousands of men! Four thousand ships!' Then he moved his head away and Patrontasch closed the door.

The second front. The delirium of our excitement and our renewed hope swept the bunker clean of despair for at least a few moments. But the coast of France was over 1,000 kilometres away. I couldn't see how our survival could depend on what Eisenhower could do in Western Europe. It depended on what Beck would do above our heads and how soon the Russian tanks would roll past our house. I wanted to be happy. I wanted to be sure we would survive. But I could not embrace this news as the others did, no matter how much I wanted to. I would believe in our survival the moment the Germans fled and we walked outside and saw the rough olive uniforms of Soviet soldiers. Until that moment, I could only pray.

Chapter 16

THE EXODUS

4 June to 24 July 1944

Wednesday, 28 June. I saw Hela Ornstein! I was cleaning upstairs and watching at the same time to check the soldiers are not returning. I was peeking out of the window. I saw two young girls walking, one of them was Hela. I admired how she walked so sure of herself, apparently she got used to her role as a gentile. Inside she is probably not so comfortable as she seems, she lost so tragically her father and sister.

Out there is beautiful, June, my heart aches when I see people walking, free, enjoying the beautiful weather, not afraid. We are vegetating here in fear.

*

I had been awakened by traffic in the middle of the night. Trucks and tanks drove by for hours and hours. When Beck came down in the morning, he said the radio didn't say anything about a Russian offensive, but something had to be happening. Maybe the Nazis were starting their own offensive. Something was hanging in the air. There was a thick mist, but we wouldn't know what was coming out of it until it was upon us. The idea that it might be the Russians didn't lessen our anxiety. It increased it. Imminent salvation always brought the corresponding thought of imminent death. The two went hand in hand, like twins, mocking us. And like the thunder of the dancing feet above our heads during the parties, it crowded out every other thought.

The soldiers and trainmen were out, so the bunker was frantic. We were cooking all the potatoes we had. Patrontasch was able to empty the buckets. And Artek figured out a new invention. He took out several bricks from the chimney, which was in the corridor. It was right across from the 'window'. We'd have to keep the bricks in during the day because if Julia was cooking the bunker would fill with smoke. But at night, we'd have cross ventilation! It was still going to be stifling hot, but even the smallest breeze was a triumph.

Ala left in the morning, but since the soldiers had been at home she couldn't come down to the bunker to say goodbye. Hans had driven her to the train station with the horse and buggy. I didn't know if I would ever see her again or have the chance to thank her for all she had done for us. But I was also filled with selfish thoughts. Without Ala distracting the soldiers, taking them for walks, entertaining them, it would make it that much harder for Julia to open the trapdoor to give us food and water.

Hans still kept coming to the Becks'. He and Georg had become fast friends. Their conversation always turned to the killing of Jews. Hans bragged that he personally was responsible for the 'relocation' of 32,000 Jews. I was familiar with what Hans was like, but the number still stunned me. If one man like Hans had killed so many, it seemed conceivable that no Jews be left in Europe. We might be the only ones. If there were 50 Jews left in Zolkiew it would be a miracle. Beck came home with another policeman and the Ukrainian commandant and joined the party. They sat drinking until two in the morning. Beck was usually as vocal as the others in expressing his hatred of Jews. But tonight he was telling these killers that God forbids killing. Richard, the youngest and nicest of the soldiers, who called the Becks 'Mother' and 'Father', answered that in war, killing was not only permitted, but necessary. He said he still believed that Germany would win the war. He told Beck that he would understand why if he listened to the news.

Beck turned on the radio and listened as the report stated the Nazis were bombing London with V2 rockets. Huge parts of the city had been destroyed and countless civilians had been killed. There hadn't been a word on the news about any movement close to us for weeks now. The Russians were attacking Finland and Romania. Mr Patrontasch took out his map and drew the new line of the Russian front. It had moved west of us. Where we were there was no movement at all. On the map, the front looked like a line with a big fat semi-circle in the middle. I had hoped that the military traffic that continued even now was a response to a Russian offensive. But with the rockets over London, this must be a Nazi counter-offensive. The soldiers responded to the news bulletin by singing Nazi songs and a rousing chorus of 'Deutschland Über Alles'.

There had been times when we thought we would be freed any day. There had been times when we had lost all hope. But never did I imagine we would be in this hole for 18 months. One way or another, I had thought it would be over by now. Still, the months went by quickly even if every day felt like an eternity. Now, with this news, it seemed certain that the war wouldn't be over soon. There was no one in the bunker who felt any different. The songs overhead seemed to echo the bombing of London. The news also said that the British sometimes had to spend up to three hours in their bomb shelters. I took out my notebook and calculated that we had been down here 13,000 hours. I had become as crazy as Mr Patrontasch.

After the others left, Richard stayed up late with Beck. They were whispering, so I couldn't hear the entire conversation. Richard was begging the Becks to go to Czestochowa, where the Nazis had sent Ala in the end. I heard him say that she would be safer with her parents. Who knew what would happen? They might not be able to find each other when the war was over. Or something worse might happen. No matter what occurred here, Ala was further west and it was safer there. Richard was a Nazi patriot and the most noble of the soldiers. He was in love with her and all he could think of was her safety, as well as that of the Becks. It didn't help our cause that the Becks hadn't heard from Ala for over a week. I knew that until they heard from her, the Becks would be on edge, wondering if they made the right decision to let her go alone. Beck knew that the Russians were slaughtering the *Volksdeutsche*, but Richard reinforced Beck's fears with numbers and towns. His young and earnest voice was full of care for Beck as he continued to urge him to save himself. Richard didn't know that right below him sat the reason why the Becks hadn't been on the first train west.

When Beck came down in the morning, we could all see the effect the conversation had on him. His depression was as oppressive as the heat. He gave us one piece of good news. The trainmen had left. But as happy as I was that there were two Nazis fewer over our heads, with housing so scarce, more Nazis might be assigned to the house. And if they were anything like the new SS man, it would be disastrous.

Without telling the Becks about his plan, Richard set about trying to contact Ala. The soldiers had a military phone in their room. They worked for the General Staff and so needed to be in contact at all times. I was sitting in the corridor near the 'window' because it was all of two degrees cooler when I heard the phone ring and Richard screaming, '*Mutter, Vater, Ala ist am Telefon!*' My heart started beating faster. Because Ala worked at the post office, Richard was able to place the call. After the call was over, I heard Julia weeping and calling Richard her son, over and over. I felt like I was hearing from my own sister and that the Becks were my own parents, my family.

The results of the phone call were a disaster. Julia decided to visit Ala. The trip alone would take three days there and three days back. For at least a week we would have only Beck to take care of us. Everything would be that much harder. There would be no Julia to cook for us. No Julia to bring the food down while Beck distracted the soldiers. When Beck came down to give us the news, he told us it would be all right and he would get Maria, Julia's sister, to cook for us. His words were reassuring, but he looked terrible. Every time he came down to the bunker, he seemed more depressed than the last time. His time was running out as much as ours, and the separation from his wife and daughter robbed him of his energy and his strength. Beck was not Beck without Julia and Ala. There was something mystical and invincible about the three of them when they were together that I only realized when they were apart.

Beck closed the hatch and went to work. While he was gone, Norbert came back. I heard the welcoming cries and laughter. On went the radio and the singing. My new fear was that between Norbert, Hans and Georg, they would start looking for Jews in the house. They no longer walked around the house in their boots, which allowed us to follow their movements and act with the appropriate discretion. For some reason, they all wore slippers and moved above our heads like ghosts. We never knew where they were. I listened to Georg on several occasions shut off the light and the radio and just stand in the middle of the floor right above our heads for minutes and minutes at a time. He had to be listening for us. We didn't breathe when Georg was above our heads. More than any of the others, Georg shot our nerves to pieces. His step, his silence, his voice, everything about him was suspicious and predatory. He seemed like he was stalking us, in the dark, with the patience of a hungry leopard waiting for his prey to give itself away with a breath, with a blink of an eye, with the rustle of a foot against a bush. He made me want to scream. Even the brutes, Hans and Norbert, were less of a threat. They were always vocal and obvious in everything they did.

The field phone rang and then the soldiers moved around above us like I had never heard them before. They were packing! They were shouting at each other about going to the front. Richard disconnected the field phone. I couldn't believe the moment had come! If they were leaving, the Russians must be coming. If we could have leapt into each other's arms, and shouted and danced with joy, we would have. Instead, we had to wait for them to leave the house. We waited and waited. They started pacing upstairs. Hours went by and still they were there. Richard was the first to leave. I was writing in the diary, with my hands slick with sweat, which also poured off my forehead and ran down my arms in streams. I was waiting for the moment, my hand poised to document their exodus. But Richard came back and I heard him tell the others that the order to leave had been rescinded. I knew nobody gave a damn about 18 Jews in a bunker and the generals in Berlin weren't considering us in their plans. But the persistent, fluctuating, desperate insanity of our situation made me think otherwise.

Beck was equally distraught. He couldn't get any hint of what was happening from any of the soldiers. They had suddenly become discreet about their plans. Even Richard wouldn't tell his 'father' what the Nazi army in Zolkiew was going to do.

Beck's response was to get drunk. The soldiers had gone out and Beck called Klara upstairs. We were eating our potatoes when Norbert strolled through the door. Klara ran down into the bunker and Patrontasch closed the hatch after her. Norbert had forgotten something and quickly left again. We waited, all of us, for the knock on the trapdoor to come again, but it never came. Klara started to worry whether Mr Beck was all right. He had been drinking and perhaps had just fallen asleep. We all went to bed with our tiny little window open. The flowers right outside the brick-sized opening were in full bloom and the night breeze drifted in with their scent. It was almost pleasant to lie with my eyes closed and my arms around little Zosia, smelling a sweet breeze. Of course my skin was on fire from bed-bug and flea bites, not to mention the prickly heat.

Around midnight, there was a knock at the door. Then again and again. The knocking turned to loud banging. We had all woken up but Beck wasn't answering the door. We heard the soldiers calling to let them in and still he didn't answer.

Klara whispered to me: 'He had a headache… a bad one. I thought it was just the vodka. Something must have happened to him. I know it!' The soldiers went round to the back of the house, knocking on all the windows and calling out his name, over and over. It was loud enough to wake the dead. But still he didn't answer.

Klara asked me to come up with her. I thought she was crazy.

'Even if they broke the bedroom window all they'd see would be him with two dark-haired women! They wouldn't dare disturb him.' After over a year of wondering what Klara's true feelings about Beck were, I saw now that they ran very deep. I agreed.

Papa intervened. 'No one's opening the hatch.'

'He could have had a stroke. Or he's lying in his own vomit! We have to go upstairs.'

Patrontasch said, 'No! Are you crazy, Klara?'

'They might want to shoot us. But they wouldn't shoot him. Not even Norbert and Hans.'

The banging and screaming got louder and louder. Loud enough to rouse him even if he were passed out.

We had to help him. He had risked his life for us every day. If he was dying and we did nothing to help him, we would be worse than cowards. The soldiers were banging now on the window right above the hatch. There was no way to open the hatch without being seen. It was too late. Patrontasch stood in Klara's way, blocking her. She looked at her brother, a flash of contempt in her eyes.

'Mother of Christ! Hold on!' It was Beck. We all said a little prayer of thanks. In the morning he told us that he had fallen asleep waiting for the news on the radio. He had been so exhausted he had thought the pounding on the door was coming from the radio. He also told us the soldiers would be leaving that day. We were cautious in our reaction. We couldn't bear being disappointed again.

As soon as Beck went back up, Mr Steckel said he had something important to tell us. I had never heard the pharmacist say more than two words to us, so I was curious and knew it had to be serious. He cleared his throat.

'My pallet is right under the soldiers' room... The first week they were here, Hans the policeman bragged to Norbert that he had killed 72 Jews with his own hands. The next day when Norbert came home he sang and whistled as usual until the Becks walked into his room to say hello. But Norbert was upset and he said to the Becks, "Papa, the bloody policeman Hans visited me in my office today. He shook my hand. I had to wash it ten times. I felt so dirty. Papa, I have had it good here. I don't want to know what is going on in your house. I don't see anything. I don't hear anything and the Jews in Brody I didn't betray either." He thought since Beck was a *Volksdeutscher*, he'd understand. But he didn't.'

Richard had also been in the room when Norbert had made this confession to Mr Beck. I wish I could say we were stunned by the news that the Nazi soldiers had known about us from the beginning. But we were so sick; so exhausted from hunger and thirst; so hot and so near the kind of mental and physical apathy that precedes giving up that we were numbed. We couldn't comprehend it. I understood their outrage when the Blue Coats were searching the house for us and Norbert had called them 'swine'. It was another incomprehensible miracle. Our lives were in the hands of these soldiers. They had been protecting us and we didn't even know it. We were so sure Norbert was the most foul of the Nazis and now we owed him our lives. I didn't know now if his anti-Semitism was just a ruse like that of Beck. But it couldn't have been the Becks they were protecting. They had only been here a week when the conversation had taken place.

I wasn't angry at Steckel for not telling us. He hadn't even told his wife. She seemed more surprised than any of us. We all knew instinctively that he had been trying to save our lives. If we had known and had let up our guard for one moment, it might have led to our deaths as well as that of the Becks. We were either vigilant all the time or not. To think that Mr Beck had heard yet hadn't understood this assurance from the Nazi soldiers was too much for our enfeebled minds to comprehend. I didn't know anyone who would have been so wise as Mr Steckel as not to report the conversation.

Even when the soldiers, having finally got their orders to go, said goodbye to Beck, they didn't tell him that they knew we were downstairs. Hans the policeman left in such a hurry, he didn't even stop to say goodbye to his dear friend Beck. He honked, waved goodbye from his car and was gone.

After they left, the house seemed oddly empty. We had survived for 18 months, survived the searches, the trainmen, the soldiers, the SS, the Blue Coats and so many close calls that recalling them was enough to make me wonder why we were still alive. I still found it hard to believe that we might one day walk out of the bunker. Even with the sound of artillery and the thunder of bombs in the distance heralding our impending freedom, I didn't believe in the inevitability of our survival. Even with the trapdoor open, and with Kuba and Artek cutting wood in the cellar without fear. Even with the radio on and Beck and Patrontasch giving us reports that the Russians were taking Minsk, Pinsk, Borosov, Wilno, Baronowice and Kowel, which was especially important because it was part of our front, I did not dare believe in our good fortune. Only when Julia arrived late at night, exhausted from her trip, after having got stuck in Lvov for over a day with no place to sleep, did the house become alive.

Julia called Lola and me upstairs to scrub away the stains of the Nazis, clean their rooms and strip their beds and boil away the imprints of their bodies on the sheets. Even though I was sitting with Julia in the kitchen with my hands around a tall glass of cool water that was replenished before the last sip was taken, I fought down my joy. It was 11 July: Mania's birthday. Two birthdays since she died. She would have been 15 years old. I had dreamed about her last night as I dreamed about her so many many nights. In my dreams, she was always alive. I always saw her in front of my eyes when I looked out of my little brick window. She was waiting for us. What right did I have to be alive when my sister was dead? I knew that if we lived, everything I enjoyed for the rest of my life would evoke her memory, her death, her courage and her absence. I vowed my life would be dedicated to her memory.

We finally went to bed that night with the hatch door open, letting the heat escape upwards instead of being trapped downstairs. The last thought I had before I drifted off was that it wasn't so bad down here. It was almost cool and, crazy as it was, I swore I could feel a breeze drifting through my hair.

I awoke to tanks and trucks rushing past the house and Beck staring into the hatch, whispering, 'The Nazis. They're back!' Patrontasch closed the trapdoor just as the banging on the front door started. Four soldiers told Beck they were moving in and began dragging in their gear. The bunker started heating up at once. It was certain now that there was a conspiracy in Berlin to torture us and taunt us with the expectation of freedom, only to rip it from our grasp. We were starving, sitting in the dark without electricity, hot as hell, waiting to die.

The Russians were bombing the nearby towns. When the SS went out, we rushed upstairs to help prepare the house in case of bombing: filling sandbags for the attic and the sides of the house; getting everything of value packed in case of fire; filling buckets and washbasins and tubs with water.

Mr Beck started organizing, giving orders, cursing as usual, the old Mr Beck, the boss, the man I loved like a father; even his curse I loved to hear: '*nasry matry*, I shit on your mother' I preferred to sweet talk.

The bombing was so close, the walls shook; the dishes fell off the shelves; timbers were shaking. My mother fainted and the Becks came down to hide with us. We didn't know what was happening. All through the bombing, we heard trucks and tanks rumbling down the streets.

In the morning after the bombing, we saw a bloody convoy of Nazi troops drive by. The house filled with soldiers fleeing from the front. They begged the Becks to leave. The Russians were only 11 kilometres from Zolkiew. We put on clothes, even in the heat, clothes we saved in case we would ever get out of this hellhole. The bombing continued. The soldiers were in the cellar where we kept the wood.

Julia was crying. She heard fleeing Nazis had found some Jews who had come out of hiding on Szeroka Street. They had shot them along with another family of Jews who were being hidden by a Polish peasant. The peasant had gone to complain that Ukrainians were stealing things (the possessions of the Jewish family in hiding). It was against the law. Under interrogation, the peasant confessed and was shot along with the Jews he had hidden for 18 months. We knew we were not safe.

The General Staff fleeing from the front had heard about Beck and his hospitality and moved in. We heard everything that was happening from the front. The Jews listening to Nazi HQ upstairs. If they only knew! The Nazi colonel was getting ready to run. We heard him tell the Becks the Russians would be here in the evening, or by the next morning at the latest.

I'm so mixed up, it's hard to concentrate. All kinds of thoughts are crossing my mind. I'm happy to be alive, but then I ask myself, am I happy to be alive?

We were still afraid to leave the bunker until the last German was gone from Zolkiew. The bombing and shelling started on Friday, 21 July and it went on for three days, only stopping for a few hours each night. Not too far from the house, the Germans had positioned some cannons, so Russian fire was directed right at us. One shell hit the house and half of one exterior wall was blown away. Another shell hit and part of the roof caved in. The Becks had gone to hide in a bunker the German soldiers had dug out in the backyard. With each shell we heard whistling overhead, we didn't know if it would be the one that hit the house. The ground was shaking with each hit and the dirt was flying off the walls. The floor above us and the support posts vibrated. Oh my God. The house was in danger of collapsing in right on top of us.

I held Zosia and Mama held Zygush for the whole of the three days. Once a day, Beck would run to the trapdoor and give us water. But it wasn't enough. The heat was brutal and I was becoming delirious from exhaustion and thirst. The small amount of water for each of us could not compensate for the sweat that poured off us in waves. The pallets, the straw, the bedding and even the dirt floor were soaked with our sweat. I wasn't able to sleep, but went into a stupor, not knowing day from night, only alleviated by a sip or two of water. Zosia's lips were as dry as cracked leather and she asked me if we were going to die. I told her we would be all right and asked God not to make me a liar. Despite the explosions that came as regularly as our breath, her eyes told me that she believed me. It became impossible for me to focus on any single thought as crazy, extraneous, irrelevant ideas flooded my mind without sense and without comprehension. I was happy to be alive. But happy? With the bombs bursting just metres away and my heart exploding inside my chest in terror? I was happy to be alive. But if we did survive, how could I face life without my sister? What right did I have? Why couldn't she have stayed with us? Trusted Papa and Mama's judgement? If she had been able to control her fear for just a few minutes, she would be here with me now, urging the Russians on and praying the last shell fired from the last cannon attacking Zolkiew didn't drop into our laps. I didn't know what kind of sense life would make without her. While we were in the bunker, we had all the time in the world to grieve, but because we were so contorted around our own efforts to survive, we hadn't even begun to truly mourn her. I wanted to record every moment, but I couldn't focus on any thought before another one pushed it away. It sounded like the end of the world out there and we were the only survivors.

And soon, I had only one thought. I wanted the bombing to be over. I didn't remember anything else until Mr Beck came banging on the hatch, screaming that the Russians were here.

*

One by one we crawled out of the bunker and walked outside. I felt afraid to go out. My mind was telling me it was all right. The Nazis were gone. We had survived, but there was so much fear in my body that it was an effort of will that took me out into the bright, overwhelming sunlight. We were all dazed and blinded by the light. There were spots in front of my eyes as I looked out at the surreal scene. The Poles were as dazed as we were, seeing the bombed-out street and the charred houses. Dead Nazi soldiers littered the road as Russian army vehicles and soldiers walked up the street. The men were haggard, rifles haphazard on their shoulders, smoking and laughing and waving.

We just hugged each other and continued to weep. We couldn't stop the tears. The relief! Mr Beck came along with two Jews he had found. The Bernstein brothers were alive! We embraced and wept. They had been hidden by the same Mrs Ornstein who had jumped from the train with her daughter, Hela. Hela, whom I had seen one day while cleaning upstairs. They could pass for Polish, and being from another town had been able to get papers. The Bernsteins had shown up on Mrs Orstein's doorstep. We shared the little we knew of the others. Mr Bernstein told us about a friend whose 15-year-old daughter had gone out to scrounge for food the week before. The Nazis had shot her. We wept at each story, each life lost. I wept anew for Mania and Uchka. Why wasn't Mania here with me? Why couldn't Uchka be a mother to her children? Somehow the reality of standing safely outside made their deaths seem all the more painful.

Zygush, Zosia, Igo and Klarunia tried to run after the soldiers who were passing out candy to the children. But they took a few steps and fell. Zygush helped the others up and they tried to run again, but their poor atrophied legs were useless. They looked at their legs, confused and crying, not knowing what was wrong with them.

I tried to run to Zygush but my own legs crumpled under me. I looked at our group of 18, our families; how many others were there like the Becks who saved 18 Jews? I was in a dream. I looked back at my mother and father, embracing each other, the Becks, the Patrontasches. Lola was embracing Artek, Kuba and Mrs Melman. In the bunker, they looked almost normal because that was what I was used to. But here in the sunlight and out in the open, I could see how close we all were to death. Our skin was translucent and hung off us like baggy clothes. We were sticks with lungs and hearts and not much else.

The Steckels stood alone and looked lost.

I got up and walked to Zygush and the other children, comforting them and telling them they would be able to run as much as they wanted very soon. Some Russian soldiers stopped and gave me and the children bread. We devoured it like little animals. The soldiers had to tell the children not to eat so fast, but their concern fell on deaf ears.

The soldiers asked over and over if we were Jews. We were afraid to say yes, until one with a kind face, no more than a boy himself, told us it was all right and we were safe now. I nodded. I heard a commotion and looked back at the house.

Mr Melman staggered out of the house, barely able to hold the Torah. He handed it to Papa. He stripped the wrappings off it, until the bright white of the satin covering, the gold and silver of the handle coverings and the golden thread dazzled in the sunlight.

I helped the children up and we walked over to Mr Melman. The men walked inside and came out with coverings for their heads. We started to say the prayers of thanksgiving.

I could see out of the corner of my eye, the spinster sisters walk across the street with our hand-carved wooden box of pictures, the only thing of ours they hadn't sold. But Mama embraced them and took the box of pictures. It was all we had of our old life, and of course Mania would be in there.

I passed out and when I woke up a few moments later, I was staring at the clouds floating overhead in a bright blue sky, a sight I thought I would never see again.

Chapter 17

ZOLKIEW WITHOUT MANIA

24 July to September 1944

*From 5,000 Jews only 50 are left. We're the only ones who have
parents. Whole families perished. There are only single people left.
Everyone is emaciated, we have nothing to wear, nowhere to sleep,
no money to buy food... We can hardly walk, our feet hurt, we are
not used to walking... But we are the lucky ones.*

*

The Russian soldiers gathered around us like little angels,
not knowing what to do with us, but afraid to leave us.
They shared their rations with us and supplied us with Soviet
army blankets.

Papa walked across the street and found a Polish couple
living in our house. We didn't know who they were. They asked
if they could leave the following morning and Papa agreed. The
three families decided to spend one final night in the bunker.
We didn't know quite what to do with ourselves. We didn't seem
to be able to make a decision about anything. The world above
ground was alien to us and like a family of trolls we retreated
into our dark and humid lair.

By the next morning, we had decided that we would move

back into our half of the house and Lola and Klara would move into my grandparents' half. Since their own house had been completely destroyed in the fire, the Patrontasches would move in with the Melmans. Our three families couldn't bear to be apart. Since Mr Patrontasch's sister and her family had died in the March 1943 *akcja,* their house on the other side of the factory stood empty. Instead of taking it for themselves, they gave it as a gift to the Becks. As for the Steckels, within hours of our liberation they disappeared. No goodbye. Nothing. It was as if they had never even existed.

The first night we spent back in our home wandering around from room to room, looking for things that were no longer there, looking out of windows, breathing fresh air, not knowing that our freedom was real. But most of all, feeling the emptiness of the house without my sister. All the rest that weren't there were things. None if it mattered except Mania. It was a shock to sleep in the same room that I had shared with my sister since the moment she moved out of her crib. The lace curtains were gone, as was every other thing that wasn't nailed down and many that were. It was like we had never lived there. But our presence, our memories, our conversations still hung in the air. They had somehow avoided the thieves and looters that had come through our house again and again like locusts. I didn't know whether they were in corners or closets or cracks in the wall. But they were all there was to welcome us back.

If I had thought in the confines of the bunker and with our attention so much focused on our survival that I understood what Mania's loss would mean, I only began to comprehend the bitter fact of her death with the first bite of the first meal we had in our own home. Looking across at Mama and Papa, I wanted to be Mania for my father. I was afraid for Papa. When she died, a part of him died with her and I knew he would never forgive himself. I wanted to be the daughter he had lost, but I wasn't my sister. Papa had fulfilled Mania's deepest and most frantic wish: that we would survive. And we only survived because of her courage. I dared not think what the Nazis did to her in her last hours, but I could not keep the thoughts of her face out of my mind. And as much as I wanted to enjoy the freedom and every tiny breath of air, they reminded me that my sister was no longer on this earth.

Over the first two days of our freedom, through the numbness of grief and our disorientation at living above ground, we slowly realized that we were human beings dressed in rags; that we had no shoes; that since the spinster sisters still looked Papa straight in the eye and told him everything we owned in the world had been stolen, we had nothing, nothing but some knives, forks, spoons and enamel plates, thin and worn towels and bedding. We wandered the city scavenging what we could. An old dress here or there. A coat there. A torn pair of shoes with hardly any sole left was a treasure. We went back into the bunker to see if there was anything of value. We found one thing. It was a shoe Rela left behind when she went back to the ghetto that first December to be with Josek. It was a half-heel patent-leather pump with a bow across the instep. It fit me. We took the one shoe to the shoemaker and asked him to make me its mate. He said he was sorry, but he had no patent leather. Patent leather! What would I need with patent leather? I just needed a shoe. He found a strong piece of leather with which he fashioned a shoe for me. When I picked up my new shoe, he found some shoe polish and gave it to me. I polished the new shoe relentlessly, but I could never get it as shiny as Rela's shoe.

Having survived on potatoes for 18 months, Mama had a severe gall bladder attack after three days of normal food. Artek and my father carried her through our backyard to the hospital, which was on the other side of the yard. The fruit trees were filled with ripening fruit and the walnut tree with nuts. Our grass was knee high and in horrible need of mowing.

Mama was emaciated and barely conscious and we didn't know until we got to the hospital that she was millimetres away from death.

Dr Lucynski was there when we brought her in and he broke into tears when he saw we were still alive. He was genuinely thrilled to see us. But as he took care of my mother, we could see the growing concern on his face. He told us there was nothing for him to do except give her morphine for the brutal pain she was in and fluids so she wouldn't be dehydrated. Mama's organs were shutting down. She weighed 40 kilos and there was only a slim chance that her system, given how weak it was, could recover from this. I cannot describe the grief mixed with fury that I felt on hearing those words. I looked at my father and saw that he had become old. I had no choice; I had to be strong for all of us.

We kept a vigil over my mother. Either Papa or I was always there, 24 hours a day. More often than not, we would both be there, while Mama lay unconscious. I had gathered the perennials from our weed-choked garden for a bouquet for Mama's room, but she barely noticed them, and when she did it was only to complain that the perfume made her nauseous.

Dr Lucynski came by and we walked out of the room to get his latest assessment. He wasn't hopeful and wanted us to be prepared.

We were so engrossed in the conversation that we didn't notice the priest walk into Mama's room as the nurse was changing her IV. The priest wore a black cassock and carried a purple scarf and the unguent in a jar used for last rites. But I didn't notice all this until a few moments later. We finished with Dr Lucynski, who again told us he was doing everything he could for Mama, and we walked into the room just as the priest was making the sign of the cross and placing the purple scarf across my mother's chest. Both my father and I were too stunned to speak.

The priest dipped his finger into the unguent and made a cross on my mother's forehead. My mother's eyes fluttered open, like a couple of butterflies whose wings were stuck in glue and couldn't get moving. The priest told her, 'My child, you're about to go on a long journey… we must be prepared.'

My Mama's eyes cleared and were open now and she said, without skipping the proverbial beat, 'Father, I'm not going on any journey. I just came back.'

The priest then recognized my mother and he began crying with joy. 'Mrs Schwarz, Mrs Schwarz, you're alive.'

Mama simply said, 'Until somebody tells me different.'

Salka the Cossack had returned to this world. And that's how my mother came back to life. My father and I were kissing and hugging her and embracing her and she just didn't know what the fuss was all about.

As Mama recovered over the next week and finally came home, the survivors of our town came out of their hiding places in the barns and the cellars; from living without shelter in the woods; from the pigsties, where my friends who owned the bus company had spent weeks and weeks in frozen slush, their hands and feet frostbitten. Papa was sitting on the front steps and a girl walked past him, also dressed in rags and as thin as we all were. She turned and walked by him again. Then again. Papa had a big nose which she started at, and then she asked if he was really Jewish too. She was a jumper who had hidden in the woods with another child, a boy. Mr Taffet, my Hebrew teacher, emerged from the woods in rags with his feet blackened from frostbite. I was amazed he was able to walk at all. In the bunker, Papa had a day shirt and a night shirt. They were the only clothes he now had. Mama gave Mr Taffet Papa's night shirt and we took him to the hospital, which the Russians had taken over. Dudio, who had joined the partisans, emerged from the woods with a machine gun and a bandolier filled with cartridges around his chest. We embraced him like a brother. Zygush and Zosia were so happy to see their uncle.

I was asleep when I heard Mama screaming in the kitchen. I thought it had to be Ukrainian marauders. I ran to the kitchen and I saw Mama wasn't screaming from fear. She had thrown open the back door and standing on the steps, like two ghosts risen from a grave, were Giza Landau and her mother. I ran down the stairs and embraced her. Klara Letzer, Genya Astman and so many others were all gone. To find a friend, alive, flesh and blood with smiles and tears at the sight of me, was a miracle. We brought them inside and Giza told us a Russian soldier had given them a ride to Zolkiew to see what remained of their lives. When they walked by our house, Giza wanted to knock, but her mother said not to. It was too much to think that we were alive. But Giza insisted and they went around to the back because they were afraid to knock on our front door.

She told me their story. One night in March 1943, her father, a member of the Judenrat with special privileges, took her to the train station and handed her to a stranger. He told her that this man would take care of her. The man, whom she later found out was a partisan arms dealer, took her to his flat in Lvov. Giza's two aunts were there. Two days later her mother joined them. Her father never made it. He died in the March *akcja* when the SS murdered the entire Judenrat.

From the stories the survivors told us, I realized we had it better than most. I learned of friends hiding in the homes of peasants where they were betrayed in the last days of the war. One woman lost her daughter, the week before the liberation. She went out to forage for food while the Nazis were preparing to run for their lives. With Zolkiew surrounded by Russian troops, they were still killing Jews. And that's how we found out who was alive. Over the first days of the liberation, they wandered into town, in ones and twos, amazed to see that anyone else survived.

Out of 5,000 Jews in Zolkiew, there were only 50 left. Klarunia, Igo and I were the only children who still had both their parents left. Our house became a gathering place for all the survivors. The 50 of us clung together as if we were in a life raft in the middle of the ocean. Artek was a constant visitor at Lola's. The three families, the Becks and Lola ate every meal at our house and only went to the Patrontasches to sleep at night.

We hadn't been out of the bunker more than a couple of days, when there was a knock on the door. It was Pavluk. In one hand he was holding our pillows and the featherbed, freshly laundered, we had given him for safekeeping. In the other he carried a chicken, which he brought as a gift. He stood as straight as a pine and proud as a new father. He looked even more like a giant to me than he did before we went into the bunker, and the tears he was holding back told me he was grateful we were alive. For months and months before we went into the bunker, when I went out, I was used to being looked at like I was dirt; like I was nothing; like I was an affliction. And to see this one man with so much gratitude for our survival was more important than food. He knew Papa, but I was a stranger to him. And I knew his tears were not only for Papa. I saw the way he looked at us. He told Papa that anything he could do for us, he would do. And I knew he would. He shook Papa's hand and said goodbye. Mama made us some soup from the chicken.

Over the next several days, we didn't wander more than a few metres from our house. I was still afraid. The Nazis were gone, but the area was still filled with Ukrainians, marauders and bandits. Beck still kept us informed and told us of several pogroms where surviving Jews were brutally murdered. I didn't want to be far from Papa and the children. I didn't want to be far from the Russian soldiers who passed up and down the street in front of our house. Zosia asked about Uchka all the time. 'Where's Mama? When am I going to see Mama? When's she coming back?' She'd sit on the steps and watch the street waiting for her return. But nobody knew how to tell her and we kept up the ruse that she would be reunited with her at some point. Poor Zygush knew and was silent during all these conversations. He never mentioned his mother to us or asked about her.

When Mama started to feel better, she decided we should have a gathering of the 50 survivors at our house. I was over-joyed to see anyone who survived, but in that same moment was filled with grief and loss for their family members who perished. It was a party of ghosts. I couldn't help being reminded of all the other parties at our house, which seemed to bloom like new flowers over the course of the summer. With all our family and friends, dozens of them, laughing, eating and talking like there was no tomorrow. Everybody brought whatever food they could find. We had the rations from the Russian soldiers, and the Poles when they fled had left their vegetable gardens, which had been taken over by weeds. But there were still potatoes, carrots, onions and other vegetables to be dug up and picked. Mama was able to make a good soup.

And despite the fact that we were 50 out of 5000, we still felt like we were a community. We were still the Jews of Zolkiew. We were eating in our backyard, sitting on the steps and under the fruit trees like in the old days.

I don't know when I noticed, but I sensed Zygush was missing. Mama was panicked and furious. It was my responsibility to look after the children. I didn't know when Zygush slipped off, where he went or why he went. He knew as well as any of us there were still pogroms and marauding bands of Ukrainians. He was a survivor and knew what he could do and what he wasn't allowed to do. All 50 of us went to find him. To lose him now would have been more than any of us could bear. We searched everywhere. The town. The Melmans'. The factory. Zygush's pre-war friend Helen's house down the street from us. He might have looked for her since he didn't know that Helen and her family had been deported. But he wasn't there. I thought he might be at the park and I started running there, praying that nothing happened to him. Not after all he went through. Halfway there, running past the bombed-out buildings and the streets littered with the burnt-out shells of German artillery and tanks and the earthworks and barricades that guarded the plaza, I thought, *Oh my God. He ran home.* I didn't know how I knew, but I ran there with the certainty I would find him.

The orchard at the back of the house was ripening with apples as if they already had no memory of the war. But I had no time to waste gazing at their beauty. When I got to Zygush's house, there was an old *babushka* tending her garden. I asked for Zygush and she told me he had a job watching some cows for a local farmer. She pointed to the far fields at the back of their house. A job? He was eight. And he didn't tell any of us. Not me, not Mama, not Papa. I ran through the field and saw Zygush about 400 metres away. He had his shirt off and already his tiny body was walnut brown. He had a switch in his hands, with which he made figure eights in the air. When he heard me screaming his name, he turned and waved, happy to see me. He wore a proud smile. When I got to him, before he ever said a word, my arm and hand jerked away from my body and I slapped him across the face. I was as stunned as he was. But I couldn't stop hitting him. I was crying with relief and rage and it took several minutes for me to realize what I was doing. I had never struck anyone before and I couldn't stop hitting him. And Zygush, the boy who never cried, was crying now. Zygush didn't fight back and his weeping stopped me. I couldn't stop crying and I embraced him. I was forgiven as soon as his brown arms moved round my neck.

'Are you out of your mind? Do you want to get yourself killed? We were worried sick! Never. Never, do you understand me, leave the house without me!' I was horrified at what I had done and held him. 'I'm sorry. I'm sorry. We couldn't find you. We were so scared.'

'I thought you'd be proud of me. We'll have milk. And butter and cheese,' was all he said. I was proud of him. Here in this field, there was no sign there ever was a war. The cows were content and the fields and hillsides had their usual high summer carpet of ripening rye, wheat and corn. These were the fields I'd look out upon from Paradise Hill, which from here, lost in the haze of a summer sky, looked like less of a hill than usual. Zygush didn't have to say it, but he was now the man in his family and he was doing what a man does. Taking care of his loved ones. I wanted to tell him that he was just a child and I wanted him to stay a child. But after losing Uchka and Hersch and enduring the bunker, at eight years old he was not a child any more. I stayed with him in the field until the end of the day and we drove the cows home to their barn.

Zygush collected his pail of milk and proudly carried it back to our house.

The next weeks were spent, as with all the other survivors, engaged in two tasks. Regaining our strength. And trying to locate family members. We never went anywhere alone, so all three families made a pilgrimage to the cemetery to see if we could locate where Mania and our other relatives were buried. We passed the synagogue and looked in. There was nothing but fire-scarred and blackened brick, broken windows, old hay and garbage. At the cemetery, even though there was nothing there but a few cows grazing, just knowing Mania was buried somewhere made it hallowed ground. We also kept asking after Tilzer and Schitling, the boys who betrayed her. We asked dozens and dozens of people, but they had probably fled with the Germans and the other *Volksdeutsche*. We knew it was futile, but we kept asking.

We gained our strength just from the process of living, doing the small things that we had come to miss. Walking around the house. Speaking in a normal voice. Cooking our food. We wrote several letters to Rosa, but hadn't heard back yet. Dudio. Rosa. Manek. Babcia. They were all we had left.

And Mama was becoming Salka the Cossack again. She was sending me with soup to the hospital for Mr Taffet and the other survivors. Eastern Europe in those days was filled with exiles, wandering from town to town looking for loved ones, hoping to find even one family member who had survived, or just trying to go home to see if there was anything left of their lives. Chances are there would be nothing and no one there. But I understood why they came. It was all they had left and the only place they had to go. They came through Zolkiew exhausted and starving. And, somehow, Mama had gained a reputation. If you came to Zolkiew, go to the Schwarzes where there would be a meal and a bed. We kept a mattress in the front room for the travellers, who were all afflicted with lice. She renamed our front room the louse suite. And she was also mother now to Zygush and Zosia, which was formidable because Zygush was something of his old self and you still needed a whip and a chair to take care of him. Zosia, still as silent as a memory, turned brown in the sun and clung to me and Mama, hardly ever letting us out of her sight and, more often than not, holding a hand or a bunch of skirt.

The Russian authorities came to my father and the other men and asked them to take over their factories again. It was a godsend for my father. But even though he was busy with a thriving business, the spark that had come to Mama's eyes never returned to Papa's.

It was summer and even though there was a war, the fields were filled with ripening grain that the farmers brought in on their carts. Papa offered Beck a job, but Beck declined. He was exhausted and was happy to be taken care of, as he had taken care of us. Now that Papa, Mr Melman and Mr Patrontasch were making money, they made sure the Becks didn't have to lift a finger. But they didn't know where Ala was. They didn't know if she was alive or dead. The war was still being fought in western Poland and there was no mail or any way to find Ala. There were close calls we relived that had become almost legend, but in Beck's retelling there was a light missing from his eyes. The person he wanted to share these war stories with was lost. Whenever we made a little money we always gave some to Beck and he always said the same thing, 'This is for Ala. This is for Ala.'

Since the very first day of our liberation, convoy after convoy had been going through Zolkiew to the front. Every night they bivouacked in the town plaza. Sometimes there would be several thousand soldiers setting up their tents and their cooking fires. The Russians were always crazy for music.

Of course, we and everybody else in town had to inspect the troops, who looked more like boy scouts than soldiers. Most nights, the different battalions organized singing competitions around huge bonfires. Each company had their own group and on a summer evening they were all practising ballads, folk songs, love songs, dirges, work songs, army songs, songs from Borodin and Shostakovich, and as chaotic as this might sound, the songs and voices wrapped themselves around each other in one harmonic choir. This was our entertainment. Around dusk, we'd walk down to the plaza and wander through the troops. I knew some of the songs and sang along from time to time, which brought us large smiles from these boys who were far away from home, many for the first time. I had never sung in front of strangers before and this was the first time I realized I had a pretty voice. In the evenings, the damage from the war faded into shadows and the castle, the colonnades and the church spires were as beautiful and consoling as ever.

The fountain of the Virgin Mary had been repaired and the children of the Ukrainians splashed and played, laughing and screaming with delight. There were no Jewish children left to play and all the Polish children had fled with their families. I was singing along with some of the soldiers and I noticed a girl from my classroom. Nina was a little older than me, sweet and very serious. Everybody knew that her father was a colonel and the ranking officer in Zolkiew. Consequently she was fawned over like a Russian princess by any adult who knew who her father was. But she didn't care. We never said much to each other at gymnasium, but I considered her a schoolfriend, although I never saw her outside the classroom. I didn't know what moved her, but she came up to me and we started talking to each other and became real friends that day.

The Russian army was running the town in a laissez-faire way. There was no central authority. Just troops coming and going. But they were all so kind to us. I never gave a thought to the NKVD, the Russian secret police. We were free to reconstruct our lives.

I was looking forward to starting school in just a week's time at the beginning of September. I learned the NKVD had returned when Comrade Dupak stopped by to see if we were still alive. He, too, looked happy to see us. I didn't know his title, but from the look of his car and the way he was dressed, he had done well in the war and was very high up in the NKVD. He greeted us warmly and gave my father a present. A bicycle.

The next day, in the quiet early morning hours, a car drove up to the house where the Becks were living, just up the street from ours. I was still asleep. We all were. It was the NKVD, and before any of us had awoken on that summer morning, they had been arrested and taken to the jail in town, to be held until they were transported to Lvov for questioning. The news of their arrest swept up and down the street as fast as the fire. The NKVD had found several rifles in the house. Beck and Julia, who everyone in town by now knew were the heroes who had saved 18 of us, were German spies. They were left behind by the Nazis to commit acts of sabotage. They were starting an underground *Volksdeutsche* partisan group. All these ideas were insane. Except for the guns that Beck insisted he keep after our liberation.

Papa had begged Beck to get rid of them. The authorities were clear. Anyone caught with a gun was guilty of treason. The idea that the Becks were going to be shot as traitors or sent to

Siberia, after all they had sacrificed for us, was the final, most bitter irony of the war. We were determined to get the Becks out, no matter what it cost. Papa and Mr Melman went to Lvov almost every day, telling our story to the army, to the NKVD, to the civilian administration. They spent all their money on bribes. But it was hopeless. The Becks were *Volksdeutsche*. They were criminals. And they were sent to a concentration camp to await their trial. We woke up every morning worrying about the Becks, looking for answers, looking for anyone who might help. We went to bed every night having failed them. I prayed for them as I had prayed in the bunker for Mania, Uchka and the children. Even after we had been liberated I felt safer, happier, more secure, more trusting, more optimistic with Beck and his wily, laughing blue eyes and unrepentant confidence just a few doors up the street. Week after week went by and we still hadn't any hope of success. I started school, which I had been looking forward to with so much enthusiasm. But it meant nothing if the Becks weren't free.

Chapter 18

THE DIARY

September 1944

I was sitting on a bench in the park by the river. Behind me the castle walls were intact and I could see the windows of my classroom. The grass was overgrown and the park littered. Up ahead, above the train station and the orchard, Paradise Hill still looked down upon the town, unchanged and uncaring. I didn't think I could ever go up there again without Mania and Uchka. I was across the street from Nina's house. It was the largest house on Railroad Street and it was always taken by the ranking officer of the last three occupations. It had a large garden filled with pink peonies behind a wrought-iron fence. Now that it was autumn, the peonies and other flowers had died, and the garden, filled with dried brown stalks, needed to be cleaned out and prepared for winter. This is the house from which the German officer's wife had foreseen Jewish revenge as our family and friends were led to the train station. I couldn't stop weeping about the Becks. They had been taken to the Brigitka jail in Lvov before being shipped off to a nearby concentration camp.

Papa learned that the Becks were scheduled to be tried for treason and sent to Siberia. Once they were in Siberia, there would be no hope for them. Even if they survived the journey, all they would receive as a reward for their years of courage and generosity would be a short hard life in a labour camp.

Nina must have seen me weeping from her balcony and had come down to where I was sitting in the park. She asked why I was crying. I didn't know where to begin. I had never talked about the Becks and the bunker to anyone but my family, who knew and felt everything I did. When we talked about the bunker, there was no need for tears because so many had already been spent inside. I didn't want to reveal what we had gone through to a stranger, I couldn't possibly. It would be too painful.

But as I spoke to Nina, the words poured out in spasms, choked out between sobs and halted breath. Mania. Uchka. The children. And the countless times, like the fallen leaves at my feet, that the Becks had saved us and almost lost their own lives. And how Papa and Mr Melman had made trip after trip to Lvov, sometimes almost every day, begging, bribing and pleading for the Becks' lives with anyone they hoped might help them. They had no success and we were free and safe.

Nina sat next to me without speaking. She was sensitive enough to know that there were no words of consolation that would serve as a balm. After a long time, she broke the silence.

'Clara, please, what I'm about to tell you, you cannot tell anybody. My father would kill me and they might kill him.'

'Of course.'

'You know that the trial will mean nothing. Last night, the new party secretary had dinner at our house. He seemed like a very nice man. You should take your diaries to him. You have to hand them over personally. You have to do exactly as I tell you. He likes pretty girls. Wear your best dress. Maybe, he'll read your diary.'

I ran home to tell Mama and Papa what Nina had said. I decided to take Lola with me, because even though her hair was

white, she was still quite beautiful. And I also decided to bring
Zygush and Zosia. I knew they could make the hardest heart
cry. Lola made new dresses for me, Zosia and herself overnight.
When we got up in the morning, I washed my hair and Mama
combed and brushed it as she hadn't done since before we went
into the bunker. She did the same with Zosia. Once I was
dressed, I looked at myself in the mirror. I looked as if I had
never been in the bunker. I had gained back all the weight I had
lost and my skin was still brown from being outside for hours
and hours almost every day since we were liberated. Zosia's hair
shone and her face had the rosy complexion of the porcelain
figurines in Mrs Melman's china closet.

Lola walked in carrying flowers and smiled. 'How do I
look?' She had found some lipstick and rouge. Any man would
have been proud to have her on his arm. I tied up the four
copybooks of my diary in brown paper and twine, kissed my
parents and off we went, hand in hand, to the party secretary's
office. It was across the street from the opera house and had
been built in the construction spree of Emperor Franz Josef in
the optimistic style he adored. The building, like the train
station and the colonnaded plaza, almost smiled, they were so
inviting. There were soldiers, young, some only a year or two
older than me, guarding the walkway and they stopped us as
soon as we went in the gate. It was clear they had their orders.
No one was to be allowed in.

I told them the papers were only for the party secretary's
eyes and that he needed to see them right away. One of the
soldiers volunteered to take them in.

'You can shoot me if you want to. But I have to see him!'

They looked at me and then at the four of us, deciding what
to do. I knew they weren't going to shoot us.

'Please, a man and his wife are about to be killed. They

saved our lives' – I gestured to the four of us – 'and 14 other people's as well. They're heroes.' The tears had already started and the soldiers, I could see, were looking at Lola and the children.

'I'll take you in.'

Nina had been right so far and I prayed that the secretary would be as kind as the soldiers. I felt that this was the most important moment in my life. And somehow I had to find the words to convince this man to override the massive bureaucracy of Soviet justice. When I was led into the secretary's office, I was frightened, frightened not so much of the secretary and what he might do to me, but of failing Beck and Julia. The room was a study panelled in dark wood and the secretary sat behind a massive desk, nursing a cigar. Nina was right. He did seem like a nice man and, to my surprise, I didn't feel intimidated by the most powerful man I had probably ever met in my life.

'So what's so important it's worth getting shot for?'

I told him about the Becks and the bunker and how many times he had saved us and how he had risked his life for us. I also told him that the Becks had many opportunities to leave, but stayed because they had promised never to abandon us. I showed him the package and told him it was all documented in the diary. I offered it to him and he put it down on his desk.

'You know the Becks are spies. He was caught with a gun.'

'Please, don't believe me. Just read the diary. It's all in there. Everything.'

I was in tears now. So were Lola and Zosia. Zygush was stoic as always, but he had the grave expression of an old man.

'When we went into the bunker, my mother told me I had to write, to keep a record of what happened to us in case we were killed. What the Becks did to save us, I couldn't have made up. He knew what would happen if the Germans arrested him. He knew it and still he stayed. Please. Don't believe me. Please read the diary.'

The secretary looked at the twine-covered package on his desk.

'I'll read your diary,' he said. 'I promise.'

He thanked us for coming and asked his adjutant to make sure the children were given a cookie on the way out.

There was hope. The secretary didn't tell us if or when he would make up his mind. There was nothing to do now but wait. Papa and Melman still went to Lvov every day to try and find someone who could help the Becks. They knew it was futile. They knew their money was being stolen. But they had to do something. We could not lose the Becks. A few days later one of the young soldiers who guarded the secretary's office returned the diary. The books had been rewrapped in brown paper and twine. There was no accompanying letter or message of any kind. He told us he was simply ordered to deliver the package.

If the secretary was going to help the Becks, he would have written. I couldn't comprehend how he could not be moved by the Becks' courage or how he could believe that Beck was a spy. But that was the only conclusion left. After all that we had gone through, what right did I have to expect a happy ending with the Becks? Why should the world make any sense? Why should courage and generosity, loyalty and selflessness be rewarded? The world had changed and those qualities were so rare, it seemed, that anyone exhibiting them could not be trusted. The joy I had felt at our liberation slipped away like a lost memory. I knew I had to live because that was what Mania would have wanted. But how to live in a world that would destroy the Becks, who were living saints, as noble and courageous as any, was something I could not face or understand. All I wanted was for the Becks to come home.

A few evenings later, I was reading when there was a knock. I looked out the window. Beck and Julia were standing on our steps, waiting to be let in, smiling, looking like hell. Exhausted. Thin. Pale.

'Mama, it's them!' Everyone knew who 'them' meant. There was only one them. I ran to the door and opened it. I couldn't believe it. Beck's look said: 'What's the fuss all about?' I hugged him and Julia and Mama was screaming for me to get the men. She led the Becks inside as I ran across the street to the factory, screaming, 'They're here. They're here!' By the time I got there, Papa, Melman and Patrontasch had heard our cries of joy and were already running home from the factory. Within minutes, the news of their arrival had spread up and down the street and our house filled with the 16 of us, the few of Becks' friends who hadn't left town and many of the other survivors he had helped. Food and vodka appeared out of nowhere and the first true celebration since the day we walked out of that bunker began. The Becks were overwhelmed and wanted to kiss and hug and touch every one of us.

As I watched the outpouring of love and gratitude, I knew that we would be bound to the Becks forever. The Becks, the Schwarzes, the Melmans, the Patrontasches had been united by a marriage under God that no man could ever put asunder. Whatever future awaited our families, we would be as intertwined as any vines that clung to the tree that supported them. Our tree had been the Becks. Julia was smiling now without any embarrassment over her teeth. Beck found me a few minutes later and took me aside. 'Clarutchka, they told me about the diary. I guess you said some nice things about me after all.'

Epilogue

LIFE GOES ON

September 1944 to present

Today, I'm an 81-year-old woman, living in quiet, leafy, suburban New Jersey. I have a wonderful husband, Sol, and two great adult boys, Philip and Eli and five grandchildren, Micki, Tracy, Brian, Jamie and Mindy. How I wish Mania could have met them. I still miss my sister so much. Not a day goes by that I don't think of her. I wonder what kind of person she would have become, had she only had the chance.

I often look at the photographs, the only thing of value left from the war. The school pictures of my sister and me in our sailorsuit uniforms. Mama and Mania in the Carpathians with tall pines and brisk clouds moving in the background. Mania, Zygush, Zosia and me, little twigs of children trying not to squint in the sun. Aunt Giza in full stage make-up and bright lighting with raccoon eyes from too much kohl. The engagement portraits of Uchka and Hersch Leib, looking like twins. My grandparents looking so severe in their black clothes, so unlike the boisterous couple I remember, laughing often and always talking.

And my few pictures of the Becks. Julia with a smile trying to emerge from her lips. Mr Beck just a few years after the war with his hair turned grey and looking a generation older. Lola swaggering down a street in a Parisian hat. And Ala at 16, just before the war, a smile on the face that charmed dozens of Nazis and saved our life countless times. It was easy to see why they all fell in love with her. Anyone looking at these pictures who had no knowledge of the Holocaust and the fate of most of them could only draw one conclusion. What a lovely, happy family. There are over 30 of us in the pictures.

There were over 50 of us in the immediate Schwarz/ Reizfeld clan. After the war, including Rosa and Manek, who survived in Aktyubinsk, there were eight of us. At a recent wedding in Tel Aviv, the eight had multiplied to over 60. When I think of the Holocaust, I don't think of 6 million lost, I think of the 50 million who never had a chance to be born.

In retrospect, and in rereading my diary, the fact that the eight of my family survived at all seems like a miracle, much more even than it had while I was living through it. There was no logical reason for our survival. It wasn't will alone that had saved us. How many who had had the same had perished? We had been lucky, of course, but it was more than that. How many had been saved time and again by luck, only to perish in the end? You only need to be unlucky one time. When I think of the one thing that we had, and the others didn't, it was the Becks. Everything I have learned about love, honour and courage, I learned from them. After all that they did for us in the bunker, I know that nothing in life is impossible. When I left that bunker over 60 years ago, I felt that my life was no longer mine alone. I knew I would have to lead a life worthy of having been saved.

The war ended on 8 May 1945. The Becks had left for southern Poland a month earlier. The Ukrainians had made sure that the Poles would have no future in Zolkiew, and the Russians were doing nothing to defend them. The Becks had to leave before they were murdered. As soon as the travel ban was lifted, they left on the first train out of town. We all went to the train station to say goodbye. For more than 28 months we had seen each other every day. They had been our lifeline and had become our family. It felt like a part of ourselves was leaving with them, but we knew they had to go. The Polish government had promised them a beautiful farm, which had belonged to one of the six million who had died in the war. We prayed that they would be safe there. How do you say goodbye to someone to whom you owe absolutely everything? I told them how very much I loved them. How much they meant to me. That whatever I would accomplish in my life would be in their honour and in their name. But it would never be enough to repay them.

Over the course of the winter, we knew there was nothing left for us in Zolkiew. The town we loved existed now only as a communal memory. There was no Jewish community left. The Ukrainians were still as anti-Semitic as before. We couldn't practise our religion and were barely making a living. We decided to leave Zolkiew and join Beck. The Patrontasches and the Melmans were already there. As we left Zolkiew by train, in the same cattle cars that had once gone to Belzec and Auschwitz, the hairs on my neck stood on end. Nobody talked about it, but I knew we all were feeling the same thing. None of us looked back as the train left the station.

A letter had finally arrived from Ala. She was alive and living in Krakow. The first thing we did was to give Beck the letter. We hadn't dared send it by the unreliable post lest it get lost. Beck broke down in gratitude, as if we had saved his daughter.

We were all together, but the local economy was still in chaos. There were no opportunities for my father. We had to move on after only a few months. We went to Liegnitz in Silesia, which bordered Germany. As a result of the Potsdam conference the town had been given back to Poland and 95 per cent of the town's population had been repatriated to Germany. My father was able to take over an oil-press business. The children and I were able to go back to school. After school, the other children would run and greet their mothers calling out, 'Mama, Mama.' On the first day, Zosia ran out too, calling 'Mama, Mama' to my mother. She had always called her auntie. But from that day onwards, it was official: my mother was hers too. There are certain moments that stay with a person for ever, and the first time that Zosia called my mother Mama is one of them.

The business was doing well and I was doing well in my studies. Life seemed normal, but we knew it wasn't. With the communist government and the pogroms, we knew there was no future for Jews in Poland. In the winter of early 1946, young men, boys really, from the Brichah, the organization of Warsaw ghetto survivors, Jewish partisans and the Jewish Brigade, which had fought alongside the British Army, came to Liegnitz. They circulated through Eastern Europe encouraging immigration to Palestine. If there had been a Jewish State in 1939, the international community couldn't have turned its back on the extermination of six million Jews. The idea of our own country was intoxicating. They were blunt and told us that it might take years; that we would have to smuggle ourselves across borders; that if we were caught, we might be sent to concentration camps. There was no guarantee that we would reach Palestine. Despite the setbacks, it wasn't hard to convince us to take part. We settled our affairs and in the summer of 1946 found ourselves in the back of an old canvas-topped army truck, singing Zionist songs to keep up our spirits. Zygush was more than excited. He was on the adventure of his life. When I think back, I was excited as he was. The only one of us who didn't share this spirit was my father. I worried about him. He was no longer the man he had been before the war. I worried that he would never find peace again. Mania's death had robbed him of his joy.

We were dropped off in the middle of a forest on the Polish/Czech border. There was a quota on immigrants from Eastern Europe, so we were told to destroy all our identity papers and anything else that would give us away. We were supposed to be Turkish workers en route for Germany. As I took my diary out of the suitcase, ready to throw it away, my mother stopped me. 'You'll throw away that diary over my dead body.' She led me into the train station bathroom and we hid half under her clothing and half under mine. We boarded another cattle car and were taken to a displaced-persons camp in Austria near the German border. The saga of the Jews in the displaced-persons camps, where we lingered for years, often behind barbed wire, deserves its own telling, and I hope some author undertakes the task. The world simply didn't know where to put us.

Most of the camps were old factories with large floors that served as our barracks. In every camp we were kept under guard by US or British troops. Each camp was filled with bulletin boards with thousands and thousands of notes requesting information about lost relatives and family. We read every note hoping we might find just one survivor. We met Mr Melman's beautiful distant cousin Inka, who had survived the war in a nunnery. Most of the floors of the camps were made of stone, but there was one wooden floor. We were all longing for normal lives; for everything that had been taken from us. The young men got down on their hands and knees and waxed the floor using candles, if you can imagine such an effort, just so we would have a proper dance floor.

Sol Kramer asked Inka to dance. He was tall, handsome and charming in the most blunt way. After a couple of dances, Sol whispered to his brother, with whom I had been partnered, 'Can the fat one dance?' Sol and I danced together and we've never left each other since.

The beginning of our relationship was uncertain. My father asked if I was serious about Sol. I said it didn't make any difference because he was going to America and my mind was made up about Palestine. We hadn't gone through everything to survive the war to be separated from our parents and siblings now.

We had leave to go to another displaced-persons camp near Munich, which was the staging camp for illegal immigration to Palestine. I said goodbye to Sol and we were then smuggled across the Austrian border by the Jewish Brigade... The Bricha devised a clever system to account for all the trafficking. If 20 Jews left the camp for Palestine, the Jewish Brigade would smuggle 20 new Jews into the camps to take the papers of the émigrés who had just left. My mother, father, Zygush, Zosia and I all had identity papers of three different families. I was a Weiss. My mother a Rosenberg and I can't remember my father's name.

Sol, however, was determined to make me his wife. He paid professional smugglers to smuggle him from Austria to Germany to see me. We were in love, but I felt I was lucky still to have parents. I wasn't going to leave them and move to a country 6,000 miles away. Neither Sol nor I would consider not respecting our parents' deepest hopes for us.

His father and my father started corresponding. His father finally said that since he had most of his family with him, Sol had his blessing to go to Palestine with me. My father asked if I wanted Sol, and we became officially engaged... via mail by our fathers.

The displaced-persons camps were more than a hotbed of romance. There were marriages almost every day. And there was no such thing as linen. There might be one pair of sheets in the entire camp. For their honeymoon, new couples were given the sheets and a private room for the night. This was our honeymoon. I can tell you this, we didn't need the linen. Being alive was honeymoon enough.

After Israel was declared a state, we were able to emigrate just a few months later. We had been writing to the Melmans and the Patrontasches and they emigrated to Israel about the same time as we did. After living in tents for months, all three families found apartments on the same street. It was little Zolkiew and we were back and forth between apartments all the time. We prospered. You could not be a Jew in Israel at that time and not feel you were part of building a nation. It was the perfect antidote to the tragedy of the Holocaust. Every *shtetl* and town formed associations to memorialize their towns. Ours was no exception and we spent years gathering stories and tracking down the fates of all 5,000 of us. My son Philip was born in 1950 and Eli was born in 1954.

Throughout the early 1950s, we kept in touch with the Becks with frequent letters. We included money because we knew how hard it was to make anything in postwar Poland. Beck couldn't tell us how he felt, but I know how much this man, who loved freedom more than he could say, would hate every moment of living under the communists. He had become his true self during the war and his personal rebellion had saved 18 lives. I know he would love the sunshine of Israel and the bright blue Mediterranean. Most of all he would have enjoyed the cafés where there was always a good argument to be had, as much in his native Polish as in Hebrew. I hated that the Becks were suffering in the grey winter of communism and wished they could have come with us. When we received a kind letter asking us not to send them any more money, we knew it was because it put them in danger, and so for the next 20 years our communication was brief and sporadic. When Julia wrote that Beck had died, we felt that the world had lost one of the 36 righteous. We were devastated.

Manek, Rosa and her family and all my surviving relatives had settled in Israel. We had lived before the war as a pack and had become one again in Israel. When Zygush was grown he joined the air force, and Zosia married when she was a young woman. Sol became a supply officer for the Israeli police force. We were happy in Israel, but there came a time when Sol started to miss his family. We had saved a little money and he went to visit his parents in Brooklyn. When he came back, nothing felt right in Israel any more. He longed for his family. Sol was not a complainer and he had sacrificed ten years of his life, separated from his own family, so that I and my loved ones could heal and start a new life. His selfless love compelled my decision to move to America... It was very hard to leave my family, especially Zygush and Zosia, who had become more than brother and sister. I had helped raise them. They were my own children.

In 1957, we arrived in Brooklyn, New York. Sol went to work, managing one of the grocery stores owned by two generous brothers named Sam and Arie Halpern, both survivors. They hired him even though Sol didn't speak a word of English at the time. Sam married my friend and cousin Giza Landau, who is now called Gladys. I don't know why, but so many of the Gizas and Genias are now 'Gladys'. No one could ever replace Mania, but Gladys has tried every day of her life to be the sister I lost. She's the first call I make every day. I love her like a sister.

In 1959, we received a letter from Ala telling us that Julia had died. We mourned her passing and the fact that we weren't able to go to the funeral.

In 1960, when Sol and I saved enough money from working for Sam, we opened a small luncheonette in Brooklyn, five booths and a counter. Sol had been terribly spoiled by his mother and when we were married couldn't even butter his own bread. I asked him, 'How are we going to run a luncheonette?' He said, 'I learned the grocery business. You don't think I can learn to run a luncheonette?' Of course he named the lunch-eonette after himself. I wish I had pictures of him trying to flip the fried eggs. I cooked the food Mama made. I cooked the food my customers loved from before the war. My speciality was *petcha*, jellied calves' feet. My clientele raved about it. It was very hard work to make, but I didn't care. Because the ingredients were so cheap, the profit margin was high. It was the same with pirogis. Flour and potatoes. I loved the luncheonette with its chalkboard menu and the customers who ate their breakfast and lunch and answered the phone for the 'to go' orders when I was too busy to do so.

When the Halpern brothers started their construction busi-ness in New Jersey in the early 60s, they took Sol with them and made him a partner. They have been in business together for the past 42 years. We have been very lucky in our adopted home-land and are grateful, especially to the Halperns, who have become family.

Finally, in 1990, the communist regime fell. The first thing we did was contact Ala and arrange for her to come for a visit. She had two sons, and I had two sons and five grandchildren. Zygush and Zosia had children. Our families were reunited. The first time our children met each other, they wept as much as we did. The recognition that they owed their very lives to the Becks overwhelmed their senses as much as ours. We were closer than blood. Our families had been brought together in a crucible and had become one. At every important event, wedding, celebration or bar mitzvah, we were together.

In 1995, the Becks were honoured at Yad Vashem in Israel. Ala came from Poland and we and the rest of our family came from the United States. Lola, who had married Artek, came from Montreal with her two sons. Ala planted a tree in the Garden of the Righteous. More than the tree itself and the honour it represents, the generations they protected by their heroism is their true memorial. We had a dinner in their honour with over 200 people, the survivors of Zolkiew and their families.

Looking back at my life, I can be proud that I have tried to live a life worthy of the Becks and my sister. I have devoted my life to Holocaust education. In 1982, I helped found the Holocaust Resource Center, which in association with Kean University educates 1,200 teachers a year in Holocaust history and prejudice reduction. In recent years, we have struggled to combat genocide wherever it occurs. I still speak between 50 and 100 times a year about my life and diary. Unless there is a family event, I never say no. I donated my original diary to the US Holocaust Memorial Museum in Washington, DC, where it is kept in the archives. I am still amazed that the entire document was written with one blue pencil that Beck gave me in December of 1942.

In the past 15 years, I have taken three groups of family members back to Zolkiew, which is now called Zhukova, its Ukrainian name. The Becks' grandchildren always join us on these expeditions. The last trip we made was in the summer of 2005. We had a bus filled with 30 survivors and their children and grandchildren, all wanting to know and see their legacy first-hand. The bus was stuck at the Ukrainian border for over six hours. During the delay, someone asked if I remembered any of the songs we heard in the bunker above us. I was sitting next to Rosa's daughter, Mania. We started singing. Sixty-five years later and I still remembered the words and the music. The songs I had sung along to silently in duets with Norbert were imprinted into my mind. I realized it was the first time I had ever sung these songs aloud.

After 65 years, my house is still there. The factory has been rebuilt, but is still there. My school. The orphanage. The town walls. The churches. The castle. The church where Mania was caught. All there. The synagogue begs to be restored. The Lvivsky road still goes by the house, but now it's been repaved and widened. The garden is still behind the house, but there are new fruit trees. The Jewish cemetery where Mania lay had been used as a market during Soviet years, but is now empty except for tyres half buried in the ground (it is used for a soccer field) and a half-built house. The owner stopped building. He said the field was haunted and built somewhere else. Out in the marsh, by the mass graves, the survivors had a memorial built. Nothing has changed there. The willows. The tall marsh grass and the blue-birds. To say *Kaddish* there, with the breeze catching the ancient words before they retreat into the silence, is a blessing. There is not one Jew left in Zolkiew to say a prayer even once a year.

Diagonally across the street from my house, and across the street from the 800-year-old wooden church whose gardens are still tended by the great-great-grand-daughters of the women who tended the garden when I was a girl, is the Melmans' house. The scars and holes have been covered with new wood, plaster and mortar. The house is the true reason for the visit. It's owned now by a Ukrainian couple, who let us in. They greeted us warmly. They'd been expecting us. Through the living room to the left is a bedroom. On the other side of the bed, he bends down and lifts up a wooden hatch built in the parquet floor. The bunker is still there.

ACKNOWLEDGEMENTS

There are many many people without whose help and inspiration this book would never have been written. *Clara's War* came to life as part of a film project based on children's diaries, the Holocaust and contemporary genocide with Artur Brauner, who at the age of 90 is still memorializing the Jewish experience in World War II. Working on his 23rd film has been an inspiration. I am very grateful to have worked with him on our Holocaust film projects. Dee Dee Witman's appetite for challenges led her to undertaking the enormous task of creating the apparatus that supported my work for the past several years as well as the infrastructure of the Children's Diaries project. I am also very grateful to her husband, Dr Gary Witman, and their children, Samantha, Zachary and Amanda Rose, for their tolerance and affection. Alan Hassenfeld was the first to see the project's possibilities and his sweeping generosity and leadership was our bedrock. I would also like to thank the Rhode Island Holocaust Education and Resource Center and in particular Selma Stanzler, Ellie Frank and Arthur Fixler. Our work would not have been possible without the ecumenical generosity of the community in my home state of Rhode Island as well as the generosity of so many others across the country.

Agnieszka Holland's insight in the early drafts of *Clara's War* helped ground the story in the reality of her native Poland. And without the partnership and friendship of Zlata Filipovic and

Melanie Challenger and their eloquent book of children's diaries, *Stolen Voices*, I would never have found my way to our wonderful agents and colleagues at Susanna Lea Associates. In particular, Mark Kessler, Jon Broadbridge and Susanna Lea, who is the wisest, most far thinking and committed of shepherds who has always brought her sheep to the greenest pastures. And especially Katrin Hodapp, muse with a capital M and friend who has guided the writing of this book with relentless dedication, talent and integrity and who was compelled to reach deep into the briar patch upon many occasion to pull this writer to safety. At Ebury Press, I would like to thank our editor Charlotte Cole whose belief has given *Clara's War* life itself and whose gentle hand shaped the book with so much grace. And also to Mari Roberts, our copy-editor, who made so many saves she could be in the goal for Manchester United.

To Michlean Amir, Vincent Slatt, Caroline Wadell, Nancy Hartman and Andy Hellinger at the United States Holocaust Memorial Museum in Washington, DC. To Shimon Samet, the editor of the *Sefer Zolkiew* and all the survivors, especially Joseph Rosenberg, who wrote of their experiences in this book which is a moving and factual memorial to the town and its inhabitants before and during the Holocaust. To Gershon Taffet, Clara's Hebrew teacher during the Nazi occupation, author of *The Annihilation of the Jews of Zolkiew*, his account of the history of Zolkiew prior to and during the war. To Andrew Maximov, my guide in Lvov and Zolkiew who made history come alive. To Konbay Mykhajlo, director of the Zolkiew Historical Society and his prodigious knowledge of the town's history and architecture. To Zygush and Zosia for their remembrances. To Lola Patrontasch for the generous use of her diary which allowed us to better remember crucial conversations and events in Zolkiew. To her son Solly Patrontasch for his many photographs. To the

Dobriks, the couple that presently resides in the Melmans' house and who proudly make their home available to anyone who wants to look at the bunker. To Dr Bruce and Reba Evenchik, Margo and Eric Egan, the Tooles, John and Dawn, for their friendship and safe haven. To Ryan, Jena, Johnny, Justin, Nathan and Garret at Lenox Coffee, where much of this book was written, for their good natures and the over 1,000 cups of perfectly brewed coffee it took to get the job done. And to Charisse Charbonneau, owner of Lenox Coffee, who graciously allowed me to monopolize my lucky table for such a long time. To Clara's husband, Sol, for allowing me to interrupt his dinner almost every night for the last two years without a word of protest. To my brother and sister, Morton Glantz and Freyda Winick-Zeiff, and their spouses, Mary Ann and Norton, for their cheerful support over many years. And to my children, Jack and Harper, who have kept a sense of wonder alive in such an old dog.

And Clara. Words fail me. You've been more than an inspiration. It's been one of the great honours of my life to be able to help tell your story. Thank you.

Stephen Glantz

Clara Kramer has dedicated her life to speaking about the Holocaust. Still today, at 81 years old, hardly a week goes by without her speaking publicly about her experiences. Her audience has included university presidents and politicians, but Clara's passion is speaking to children. She is one of the founders of the Holocaust Resource Center at Kean University, New Jersey, which trains 1,200 teachers each year. She lives in New Jersey.

Clara's diary, which she kept while in hiding, is in the US Holocaust Memorial Museum in Washington, DC.

Stephen Glantz is a writer and screenwriter with a special interest in World War II and the Holocaust. He is a scholar in residence at the Hadassah-Brandeis Institute at Brandeis University.